Cruising the Inland Waterways of France and Belgium

edited by

Brenda Davison, Roger Edgar & Margaret Harwood

CRUISING INFORMATION Series

CRUISING INFORMATION

Published by the Cruising Association
CA House
1 Northey Street
Limehouse Basin
London
E14 8BT
Tel 020 7537 2828
Fax 020 7537 2266
email
library@cruising.org.uk
www.cruising.org.uk

First published 1975
Sixteenth edition 2013
Details to December 2012

Cruising the Inland Waterways of France and Belgium
© Cruising Association 2012 All rights reserved

All rights reserved. No part of this publication may be reproduced, stored in
a retrieval system, or transmitted in any form or by any means, electronic,
mechanical, photocopy, recording, or otherwise, without prior written permission
of the copyright owner and the Cruising Association.

Front cover photograph: Homps, Canal du Midi (Brian Blackmore)
Back cover photograph: Rochers du Saussois, near Merry-sur-Yonne, Canal du Nivernais (Brenda Davison)

Contents

Disclaimer	4
Preface	4
About the authors	4
Introduction	5
Preparations before you go	7
Cruising Routes	9
Making Your Choice of Route	11
Your Boat	11
Maximum dimensions	12
Equipment (France & Belgium)	13
Cruising Details	15
Supplies	19
Communications	20
The Seine and Upper Seine	22
Yonne and Nivernais	29
Bourbonnais	34
Burgundy	41
Marne	46
Saône and Rhône	51
The Midi – Biscay to the Med	63
Brittany	72
North East France	78
North France	93
South West France	104
Future developments	105
Belgium	105
France to Belgium	105
West Belgium	115
North East Belgium	124
Other waterways in Belgium	129
Appendix	
i Signals	130
ii Bibliography	130
iii Addresses	133
iv Web sites	134
Index to place names	136
Join the Cruising Association	149
CA Application form	150
Report changes form	151

CRUISING INFORMATION

Cruising Association Disclaimer
The Cruising Association, its officers, members, the editor and individual authors make no warranty as to the accuracy or reliability of any information contained in this publication and accept no liability for any loss, injury or damage occasioned to any person acting or refraining from action as a result of the use of such information or any decision made or action taken in reliance or partial reliance on it save that nothing contained in this publication in any way limits or excludes liability for negligence causing death or personal injury or for anything which may not legally be excluded or limited.

Preface
This publication aims to assist members considering cruising in inland waterways of France and Belgium (and Luxembourg). It has been compiled by people who have cruised there and gives an idea of what the area is like, what challenges have to be overcome, what equipment is needed and many items of interest to the cruising sailor. Members can be put in touch with other members who have cruised in and/or have a special knowledge of European Inland Waterways. They are listed in the CA Regional File and/or known to the authors, HLRs and/or the editor. The Authors gratefully acknowledge the advice, comments, additions and corrections contributed by the many members who submitted Cruising Information Reports, and co-editors of previous editions.

The publications in this Series are revised regularly and we welcome comments and contributions from our readers. Any corrections, amendments or new information can be sent to the authors by way of CA House in writing or by email.

ABOUT THE AUTHORS

Brenda Davison is a former university lecturer in business studies who also had her own business as a training consultant. She came late to sailing after meeting her second husband, John, in 1987. John was already a keen sailor and Brenda developed a great enthusiasm for the sailing life. Since retiring they spent some years sailing in the Mediterranean and now spend their summers on the French canals in their boat, *La Vie en Rose*. Brenda is the author of two books about the European inland waterways (see bibliography). She now does freelance work and gives talks on the French canals. She has also developed a website for French canal users; www.davisons-afloat.com.

Dr Roger Edgar worked in Maldon as a physicist and engineer designing optical measuring instruments. His boating activities began over 30 years ago with dinghy sailing in the Blackwater Estuary. He has cruised both the coasts and the inland waterways of France, Belgium and Holland in various boats, both sail and power. Over the last fifteen years Roger and his wife Sandra have concentrated on cruising the canals and rivers of Europe in their Dutch 12m steel-hulled motor yacht *Alceon of Maldon*.

Margaret Harwood worked for many years in the property industry, dealing with corporate communication and marketing. She took up sailing in the early 1970s when she met husband John and they cruised the coasts of southern England, Normandy and Brittany in their yacht based in Portsmouth. Now retired, they have moved inland and since 2001, have cruised waterways in Holland, Belgium and France in a 12m Dutch steel motor boat, *Adelante*, currently based in France.

CRUISING THE INLAND WATERWAYS OF FRANCE & BELGIUM

Introduction

The rivers and canals of France and Belgium are a very fine cruising area. Many people use them as a way through to the Mediterranean. But don't forget their possibilities for a purely inland cruise Here are just a few of their attractions.

Calm waters – little need to worry about weather forecasts and gale warnings.
Varied scenery – often very beautiful.
Fascinating little villages.
Fine towns, where you can frequently moor your boat near the centre more easily than you could park your car.
In larger cities easy access to theatres, concert halls and other places of cultural interest.
Modest costs, even after licence fees and mooring charges.
Incomparable food and drink.

Notes on French Inland Waterways was first published in 1975, and significant changes have occurred during the intervening 40 odd years, not least a change of title.

Whilst the re-opening of long abandoned but attractive waterways, especially in Brittany and the South West is very welcome, much of this is a result of local initiatives rather than being driven by the VNF (*Voies Navigables de France*), the national navigation authority.

Lock opening hours reflect the maximum 35 hour working week which means that in many parts of the country there is no service to locks and moving bridges before 9 am, or during lunch hours. In addition, maintenance of the network in recent years has simply not kept pace with deterioration, and there are too many entries in this current edition where we now report a depth at moorings of only 1.4 or even 1.2m, when it would have been 1.8m a decade ago.

In recent years the VNF have indicated that on waterways where the freight traffic is light, they may not undertake further major repair or renovation work without a financial contribution from the local and regional authorities. For example the Sambre route between France and Belgium was closed in February 2006 as a result of problems with a single bridge and the associated aqueduct. In spite of local efforts to agree a payment package involving local authorities and a 'Canal Set' a local voluntary organization, it remains closed and no date has been set for its re-opening. Recently the VNF decided to concentrate its resources on the routes with significant commercial traffic, such as the Rhône, and is now actively working to devolve responsibility for the predominantly recreational waterways to the local regions. An example is the recently re-opened Canal de Roubaix, which crosses from France into Belgium, north of Lille which has now been handed over to the Metropolitan Borough of Lille, who have only committed to running it for a few years. If such trends continue then, especially for the deeper draughted craft, the choice of cruising routes will become progressively more limited. Advice therefore for anyone thinking of taking the inland route to or from the Channel to the Med is to do it soon!

The situation in Belgium is rather better: almost all the waterways handle some quantity of freight, and tend to be well maintained, but there is also a far more positive attitude to small waterways.

Except for the shipments of grain from central France to the Belgian breweries, (and limited amounts of aggregates and other bulk minerals) commercial traffic on most of the *péniche* size (300 tonnes or less) canals has steadily declined. Whilst this means fewer queues or delays at French locks, it also means that there is less pressure for a good water depth to be maintained. There is also an inevitable loss of canalside infrastructure, such as shops, restaurants and fuelling points. This has exacerbated the general decline in small shops and restaurants which have steadily lost ground to supermarkets and to ready prepared foods. A well stocked store-cupboard is recommended.

CRUISING INFORMATION

These cautionary notes aside, it is still possible to eat well and at fairly modest cost in France, even given the fluctuating exchange rate. That is why, in revising these notes, we have tried to offer more information about restaurants and shops, especially in rural areas. Cooked dishes from the local *charcuterie* or supermarket can ease the ship's cook's burden. Canned or bottled prepared dishes such as *Cassoulet* and *Coq au Vin* are usually of good quality and a better flavour than might be expected. Many shops and restaurants close on Mondays. The number of small bakers has not declined as fast as that of general food shops and they often open amazingly early. Sunday opening is still fairly rare in France.

Mooring charges remain modest with just a few exceptions, such as Paris and ports close to the Mediterranean. Many small towns and villages provide free moorings as a way of encouraging travellers to stop and spend and even where charges are made, they are usually less than one half of what one might pay when cruising the south coast of England. (Changes may be expected where the VNF has devolved responsibility for moorings to the local communes.)
Yachtsmen in many parts of Europe envy their British counterparts for being able to pursue their sailing interests relatively free of cumbersome and expensive bureaucracy. The main requirement for European Inland Waterways is to hold an International Certificate of Competence (ICC) with the CEVNI endorsement. This can hardly be regarded as onerous and familiarisation with the CEVNI rules which govern navigation on European Inland Waterways is obviously sensible. **(See also Permits, Certificates)**.

Indeed, with the rigours of the UK Boat Safety Scheme in place, it is now probably simpler to cruise a seagoing craft through Europe than through Britain. These notes now include detailed information about Belgian Waterways. As well as providing interesting cruising in their own right, the Belgian routes provide convenient links into both the Netherlands and France. We have also extended our notes about the Moselle, to cover the about 40km downstream of France where it is bordered on the L bank by Luxembourg, and the right bank by Germany.

Cruising the Inland Waterways of France and Belgium is an entirely voluntary publication, intended to supplement, rather than replace, the established chart/guides such as the Breil Fluviacarte/Navicarte and Vagnon series, and has the advantage that it can be kept very much more up to date, and can tell what the moorings are like (albeit subjectively), not just that they are there.
However, there are areas, such as the Brittany canals, where the number of reports is very small, and so our coverage is less helpful than for the well-used routes to the Mediterranean.
It is continuing surveillance by our members that makes these Notes so useful, and we ask you to continue to tell us (by mail or email) where our information may be out of date, inaccurate or incomplete and the editors would like to offer their grateful thanks to all who have sent in reports. We have many more new moorings to add as a result.
Navigating on canals can be hard work if you are in a hurry. Relax if you can, allow plenty of time. Things can go wrong in many ways, involving locks, navigational hazards, other boats, etc. Careful watermanship and constant vigilance are necessary at all times.

"R bank' and 'L bank' Following the normal convention in these notes mean respectively right bank and left bank when going downstream.

Distance markings on canals and inland navigation charts often appear confusing. Frequently river navigations have been shortened by bypass canals, but the original km posts remain, as do distance signs at locks. Often the numbering starts again from zero when the name of the canal changes or when two waterways meet. There is no consistency about whether numbers increase travelling upstream or downstream. The 'official distances' which the navigation authorities define, are also used by the chart makers, who use the abbreviation 'pk' for *point kilometrique*. The same abbreviation is used here, so that the positions in these notes will correspond with what you see on the map and on the canal bank. Only when referring to actual distances is 'km' used.

Weather patterns and when to go
French weather patterns are similar to the UK but rather warmer, particularly in the south. Weather apart, the main considerations of when to go are:
- The time of year, conditions vary greatly according to season.
- The main routes to the Med rise to over 1000 feet.
- Navigation in the winter can be interrupted by seasonal canal closures or by ice.
- In spring, floods can make some rivers difficult and even dangerous.
- Very occasionally some stretches of canals may be closed due to high water levels, particularly where a river crosses a canal.
- In a dry summer, water levels may be reduced, occasionally leading to canal closures, or boats may be asked to wait until two or more boats can lock through together.

Preparations Before You Go

- Permits and certificates
- Passports - for everyone on board.
- Ship's Certificate of British Registry - the Small Ships Register is acceptable.
- Proof of VAT payment - EU residents can only use a boat in the Community if it is VAT paid or treated as VAT paid. For further information, especially on the meaning of the words 'treated as VAT paid', HM Customs should be consulted. Note that the former rules, which allowed temporary importation into France without payment of VAT, no longer apply to EU residents.
- Certificate of Competence and CEVNI Rules. Any helmsman who does not hold the relevant French or Belgian qualification should hold an International Certificate of Competence (ICC) with CEVNI rules endorsement. Any unqualified helmsman may only navigate under the supervision of one who is qualified and the helmsman must not be less than 16 years old.
    - The RYA now offers a CEVNI test (which can be taken online) and an endorsement to the ICC, and this is strongly recommended. An ICC so endorsed is accepted as equivalent to the French Permit C, for moderately powered boats of up to 15m length or the equivalent Belgian Boatmaster's Certificate. For longer craft in France, there is currently no alternative to the French permit PP.
- If your craft exceeds 15m, it is suggested that you contact the Barge Association, (formerly the UK based DBA - Dutch Barge Association,) who will be aware of the latest position and run courses for the PP licence.
- A copy of the CEVNI Rules must be carried on board.
    - The CEVNI (**C**ode **E**uropéen des **V**oies de la **N**avigation **I**ntérieure) Rules are available in English in the Adlard Coles Book of EuroRegs by Marian Martin (3rd Edition 2008), and in French as **Vagnon Carte de Plaisance** or in a fuller well-illustrated version as **Code Vagnon Fluvial** by Henri Vagnon.
- Ship Radio Licence and Operator's Certificate of Competence - the normal UK documents.
- Boat's insurance policy - not an official requirement but occasionally is demanded by yacht harbours or boatyards. Proof of 3rd party insurance is required in some marinas. A relevant translation if available would be helpful.

Licences - France
Inland Waterways Licence (*Péage or Vignette*) a charge to contribute to the cost of maintaining and developing the waterways. It is payable by all boats (except those less than 5m overall with a motor of less than 9.9 hp) navigating on most inland waterways. It is only required on the VNF controlled waterways, so not on the Seine below Rouen, the Somme or on the Brittany canals and there are a few other exceptions.

CRUISING INFORMATION

From 2013 the method of calculating the tariff will be based on the length of the boat only, and not the product of the length and the beam of the craft as previously, and are modest in comparison with their British equivalents. VNF (see Chap. 1) issue a new tariff and any variation in licence periods each January. As an example the 2013 fee for a 8m – 11m boat is estimated to be €264.75 for a full year. Licences are also available for a specific single day; 3 days; a *vacance vignette* for 16 or 30 consecutive days; or for 3 months, i.e Winter – Jan 1st to Mar 20th, Spring – Mar 21st to Jun 20th, Summer – Jun 21st to 30th Sept, and Autumn – 31st Sept to 31st Dec (but under the new considerations these might be done away with). A 10% discount is offered on the full year licence if it is purchased before 31st March.

The licence can now be purchased online from the VNF website www.vnf.fr. Alternatively a list of addresses in France that issue licences may be obtained from the website, from French Government Tourist Office in London and a copy is kept in the Regional File in the Library at CA House. There are over 30 offices including Rouen, Le Havre, Calais and Dunkirk. If planning a personal, rather than a postal application, note that most of these offices are closed at weekends, and may not offer full office hours on all weekdays, so it is a good idea to check by phone first.

VNF Offices Rouen Tel:02 32 08 31 70　　　Calais Tel: 03 21 34 25 58
Le Havre Tel: 02 35 22 99 34　　　　　　　Dunkirk Tel: 03 28 24 90 70

Credit Card payments are now accepted by most VNF Offices and by the website, www.vnf.fr. which has an English translation (click on Français in blue box in top right hand corner and it changes to Anglais). Licence dodgers may be heavily fined. This licence fee does not cover the special charges that are still made at certain tunnels and inclined planes and for the opening of some locks outside normal hours. It does not, of course, cover mooring charges which are payable at many quays and yacht harbours.

Licences - Belgium
Flanders: All pleasure craft using the navigable waterways in Flanders must have a ***vaarvergunning*** which consists of a certificate of identity and a disc. The disc must be displayed on the boat. The fee for the disc depends on the period and the boat's length and/or whether or not 'high speed' - maximum speed greater than 20km/hr (about 10.7 knots).

In Belgium the fees have not changed for years. In 2012 the fees were:
For boats of not more than 12m LOA or high speed boats of not more than 6m LOA:
€50 15 months from 1 January to 31 March in the following year.
€25 6 months from 1 January to 30 June; or 3 months from 16 June to 15 September, or 6 months from 1 September to 31 March in the following year.

For boats of more than 12m LOA or high speed boats of more than 6m LOA double these figures.

Wallonia In an attempt to improve the competitiveness of water transport, fees for both commercial and pleasure craft were abolished in 2006. Unfortunately, the issuing of a rather pointless *'permis de circulation et document statistique'* does not seem to have been abolished, and this may still be inspected and stamped at many locks. However, there is some amelioration, in that when you first register a journey at a lock that has an office described as a 'Bureau de Perception' you will be issued with a 'MET Number' and from then on, you can quote this no. at any lock that expresses any interest. They can retrieve your details on their computer system, so for this and subsequent journeys, there is no need to take the actual document up to the lock keeper, except at the end of your voyage.

Official Authorities
Voies Navigables de France (VNF) is responsible for the administration of most of the French Inland Waterways except certain estuarial waters, the Brittany canals, the River Rhône, and a few others which are run by regional authorities, usually to promote tourism.

In Belgium, responsibility for the waterways is divided among several authorities. The federal government (notably *Ministère des Communication et de l'Infrastructure Administration des Affaires maritimes et de la Navigation*) has responsibility for certain aspects, while port authorities have considerable autonomy for their ports and surrounding areas, particularly in Antwerpen, and Brussels.

The other main authorities are: Flanders - Ministerie van de Vlaamse Gemeenschap.
Wallonia Ministère Wallon de l'Equipement et des Transport - Direction Générale des Voies Hydrauliques.

Navigation Broadcasts

Belgium Radio Oostende broadcasts waterway information on the hour on VHF 10. RTBF. The French language television network, transmits inland waterway news on its teletext service, page 519, and these pages can also be viewed on www.rtbf.be.

CRUISING ROUTES

From the North Sea, the principal points of access to the main waterways of France and Belgium are via sea-locks at Terneuzen and thence to Gent, various points on the River Schelde (notably at Antwerpen) and the entrance to the Sea Canal to Brussels, Zeebrugge, Oostende, Nieuwpoort , Gravelines, Calais, the Somme and the Seine. Those arriving by sea can find details of the ports mentioned above in the Cruising Association Almanac. Another useful reference for those entering inland waterways from the sea, by way of the French and Belgian ports between Calais and Oostende is The European Waterways – A Manual for First Time Users by Marian Martin.

There are several rivers and canals which provide routes between France and Belgium: River Meuse, River Sambre, L'Escaut and la Scarpe which merge into Haut Escaut (also known as the Bovenschelde) and then the Canal Nimy-Blaton- Péronnes, La Lys (also known as the Leie), Canal de Furnes and Kanaal Nieuwpoort-Dunkerken. The main routes to and from the Netherlands are by way of the Rhine-Schelde Canal and through the port of Antwerpen. or the River Maas (Meuse) via Maastricht and the Canal de Lanaye; the Zuid-Willemsvaart and the Zeekanaal Gent-Terneuzen.
Many routes, including round trips, can be worked out from the maps. Some of the finest canal scenery is in eastern France, especially on the Canal du Rhône au Rhin, and on the eastern section of the Canal de la Marne au Rhin.

Routes to the Mediterranean

The French inland waterways are often used to travel between the UK and the Mediterranean. The alternative routes from Paris to Lyon (after which the route continues down the Rhône), are:

The Burgundy Route

This is a slow route because of the large number of locks. It goes from Paris up the Seine to Montereau and then up the Yonne to Laroche-Migennes. From there the Canal de Bourgogne runs to St-Jean-de-Losne on the Saône. The northern end of this route is popular with hotel barges, which tend to travel more slowly even than *péniches,* particularly when entering and leaving locks for fear of damaging their paintwork.

Route	Paris to Lyon	625km 219 locks 1.4m depth 3.1 air draught
River Seine	Paris to Montereau	97km 8 locks 2.8m depth 5.5 air draught
River Yonne	Montereau to Laroche-Migennes	86km 17 locks 1.8 depth 4.4 air draught
Canal de Bourgogne	Laroche-Migennes to St-Jean-de-Losne	242km 189 locks 1.4m depth 3.1m air draught
River Saône	St-Jean-de-Losne to Lyon	200km 5 locks 3m depth 3.7m air draught

The Bourbonnais Route

This route runs up the Seine from Paris to St-Mammès. It crosses to the valley of the Loire via the Canal du Loing and the Canal de Briare. The Canal Latéral à la Loire then follows the Loire valley from Briare to Digoin. From there the Canal du Centre climbs over the watershed to join the Saône at Chalon. Some commercial barges operate as well as numbers of hire cruisers.

Note that in years with below average rainfall, the highest (Canal du Centre) part of this route has been impassable during late summer as a result of water shortages. However, engineering works are planned to improve the reliability of the supply in the future.

Route	Paris to Lyon	641km 158 locks 1.8 depth 3.5m air draught
River Seine	Paris to St. Mammès	87km 7 locks 2.8m depth 5.5m air draught
Canals du Loing and de Briare	St. Mammès to Briare	103km 50 locks 1.8 depth 3.5m air draught
Canal Latéral à la Loire	Briare to Digoin	196km 37 locks 1.8m depth 3.5m air draught
Canal du Centre	Digoin to Chalon-sur-Saône	112km 61 locks 1.8m depth 3.45m air draught
River Saône	Chalon sur Saône to Lyon	43km 3 locks 3m depth 3.7m air draught

The Marne Route

This route follows the river Marne that joins the Seine at Charenton, about 7km upstream from the centre of Paris. The Canal Latéral à la Marne leaves the river at Dizy near Epernay, and this runs to Vitry-le-François. From here the Canal entre Champagne et Bourgogne, (formerly the Canal de la Marne à la Saône), runs to the Saône at Heuilley. Conditions are generally easy although there is some freight traffic that can cause delays.

Route	Paris to Lyon	708km 155 locks 1.8m depth 3.5 air draught
River Marne	Paris to Epernay	178km 18 locks 1.8m depth 4.4m air draught
Canal entre Champagne et Bourgogne (formerly Canal Latéral à la Marne)	Epernay to Vitry	68km 15 locks 1.8m depth 3.5m air draught
Canal entre Champagne et Bourgogne (Canal de la Marne à la Saône)	Vitry to Heuilley	224km 114 locks 1.8m depth 3.5m air draught
River Saône	Heuilley to Lyon	238km 8 locks 1.8m depth 3.5m air draught

All these routes take the river Rhône south from Lyon

River Rhône	Lyon to Port-St-Louis-du-Rhône	310km 13 locks 3m depth 6m air draught

The Midi Route

This route runs from the Atlantic up the Gironde and Garonne rivers to Castets, about 53km above Bordeaux. From there the Canal Latéral à la Garonne runs to Toulouse where it joins the Canal du Midi to the Mediterranean. The canals pass through a remote and picturesque part of France. Much of the Canal du Midi runs round the contours of the hills and is set between tree-lined banks.

From Bordeaux to Agde may be expected to take about 100 cruising hours. A very few barges, largely hotel barges, may be encountered, but the traffic is mainly of hire cruisers and other pleasure boats. In recent years the hire boats have increased in number and in size and, coupled with reduced lock operating hours, this has led to queues and delays, especially in the peak season from June to August. Mooring is generally easy but beware of disused quays where the canal has silted up. Conditions can be nasty in the Gironde estuary and up to the river Garonne to where the canal starts 53km above Bordeaux. The Canal du Midi has sometimes been closed for long periods because of drought or maintenance problems. Check with the list of chômages and preferably also with the waterways authority in Toulouse. Note the bridge restrictions on this route given under Cruising Details.

| Route | Bordeaux to Sète | 503km 139 locks 1.4m depth 3.3 air draught |

Making your choice

This will depend to some extent on the starting point:

South Coast of England   The most direct way starts up the Seine from Le Havre to Paris. From Paris there are three possible routes to the river Saône and so to the Rhône. The quickest and easiest is the Bourbonnais route which is generally in better condition than the others. A reasonable journey time by this route is five or six weeks from the Channel to the Med. It is possible to do it in less but the effort is likely to damage the canal banks and exhaust the yachtsman.

East Coast of England   Enter at Calais (or Dunkirk (Dunkerque)) and go south by the Canal du Nord or, more agreeably, the Canal de St-Quentin. From there go down the Oise to the Seine and Paris and then follow any of the routes to the Med. Alternatively go through the Aisne and Marne canals which connect with the Marne route. Members report that the canal at Gravelines is now open and this is an alternative and attractive entry point.

The Somme Estuary   An alternative to Calais or Dunkirk is to enter France at St-Valéry sur Somme and use the canalised R. Somme to its junction with the Canal du Nord at Péronne.
Entrance to St-Valéry through the Baie de Somme is via a buoyed channel which changes frequently. Also in recent years this route has silted up, and in places the depth is little more than 1.2m. Further, since summer 2004 the stretch linking the Canal du Nord to the Canal de St-Quentin at St-Simon has been closed whilst awaiting dredging.

West Coast of England   The Midi route may be attractive. It involves a sea passage round Brittany then to Bordeaux, but available depth only 1.4m.

Your Boat

Engines should be fairly powerful, especially if you are going in spring or early summer when rivers may be flowing fast. Must be reliable and capable of running for long periods at slow speeds without trouble.

Twin screws   If you have twin screws remember that some locks and quays and most canal banks, have sloping sides. Great care is necessary to avoid damage unless the screws are well protected by skegs.

Bilge keels can cause difficulty when wishing to moor to the bank. They can also be very tricky when you have to pull over to meet a barge. If the bankside keel grounds, the stern of your boat may be swung round into the barge. This may also happen with a catamaran.

Masts (with a few exceptions) must come down for any waterway. A yacht can carry her mast on deck but if it is much longer than the overall hull length it may be a source of anxiety in locks. It must be well secured; you may experience heavy wash from other boats. Remove or protect vulnerable furling gear, lights or antennae.

Cooling water intake may easily get blocked by debris or weed. Watch out for engine overheating and clean raw water filters frequently.

Toilet Unlike British rivers and canals, there are relatively few facilities for emptying holding tanks. In practice, 'discreet overboard discharging is tolerated' and most craft on French and Belgian inland waterways currently use marine toilets. French legislation prohibiting this came into force in January 2006, but the necessary network of pump-out stations is only now appearing, and the boat hire companies have been installing (and temporarily bypassing) the necessary holding tanks in their new craft for several years, in anticipation of the change. It seems likely that both enforcement and facilities will vary between regions. Common sense suggests use of shore facilities where convenient, and short term, for craft with holding tanks, discharge on the move and downstream of urban areas seems sensible. In the Flemish part of Belgium, pump out stations are being installed. It is to be expected that there will be increasing enforcement of the prohibition in both Belgium and France from now on, following the example of the Netherlands.

Water draught Do not place too much reliance on published depths. Actual depths can vary appreciably according to the season and, where locks are closely spaced, on the amount of boat traffic. The full depth may only exist in the centre of the channel. A loaded barge will be constrained and may be unable to make room for you in the deep channel.

Some UK yachtsmen report that displaying a sign on their bows, based on the 'official' CEVNI reduced depth sign, and indicating their draught, is helpful to them and to approaching traffic.

On the whole, it is better not to attempt the canals in a yacht whose draught is right on the maximum limit, especially with bilge keels. If working in depths close to the draught of your yacht, it is prudent to seek advice from lock keepers or the nearest office or depot of the Navigation Authority.

Maximum dimensions:
France: On main rivers and canals between the English Channel and the Mediterranean locks can accommodate boats not exceeding:
Length 38.5m (124.7 ft) Beam 5m (16.4 ft)
Draught 1.8m (5.9 ft) Height (Air draught) 3.5m (11.4 ft)

These are the '*Freycinet*' dimensions, named after a Minister of Public Works who did much to upgrade the network circa 1880. A barge of these dimensions is known as a *péniche*.

Exceptions include:
Seine as far as Paris is navigable by boats drawing up to 3m with a maximum height of 6m .

Canal du Nivernais The maximum draught is officially 1.2m but there has been silting and boats drawing more than 1m should anticipate occasional difficulties. The maximum height published is 2.71m. but it appears that this applies over a 5m width. Most pleasure craft will have their maximum height over a much narrower width, and we have a report of a craft 3m high over a 3m width being able to cruise the full length of the canal. Lowest bridge appears to be near Châtillon-en-Bazois.

Canal de Bourgogne Since 1997 the official height of the tunnel at Pouilly-en-Auxois is 3.1m. Canal draught is 1.4m.

Canal du Centre Although nominally a Freycinet canal with 3.5m height, there are several bridges fractionally lower, and 3.45m is a more prudent figure.

Canal du Midi Atlantic to the Mediterranean:
Length 30m Beam 5.5m
Draught 1.4m Height 3.3m
The height is to the centre of the bridge arches; at the sides it may be as low as 2m (6.5 ft).

River Baïse beam restricted to 4.3m and shallow.

Brittany between the Channel and the Atlantic:
Length 25.8m Beam 4.5m
Draught 1.2m Height 2.5m
(See also table in **The Brittany Canals**).

Belgium in general, all the canals and rivers mentioned can accommodate vessels of up to 38.5m in length, a beam of 5.0m, a draught of 2.2m and an air draught of 3.55m. However, certain rivers and canals have a draught of less than 2.2m - where known, details are given in the text.

Equipment
France and Belgium

- Engine: have it serviced. Make up a set of spares. Silty canal water can wear raw water impellers – carry an extra spare. Obtain Handbook and list of local agents. Check water filter daily as weed in the canals can quickly choke it.
- Safety equipment: regulations require fire blanket, one or more fire extinguishers according to size of boat, a lifering, and lifejackets (at least one per person on board).
- Mooring lines: two of 5m minimum, and one the length of the boat are mandatory. But longer lines will be found to be necessary – 15 – 20m for some locks. Lock use is hard on ropes. Soft polypropylene is reasonably comfortable to handle and it floats, making it a good choice.
- Boathooks: one long, one shorter. Mark the long one with a band of paint or adhesive tape, indicating the draught of the boat, so that it can be used to probe the depth when approaching the bank. If the short one is fairly light, it can also be very useful for getting lines round bollards, when locking up, especially if it has a reverse hook. A strong boathook (bargepole) can also be used for fending off in sloping sided locks and holding the boat off from the bank where it shallows.
- Fenders: Note that fenders that are used in locks must float, so that if lost, they will not pose the risk of sinking and obstructing the movement of the lock gates. If you use tyres as fenders in locks, then they should have an inflated inner tube so as to ensure that they will float. If you lose sinking fenders in a lock, you run the risk of having to meet the costs of their removal, possibly involving significant delays and the use of a diver. Select fenders to suit hull shape: you will need rather more than you would in a well equipped marina. Larger ones are useful for mooring against corrugated steel piles.
- In addition, when mooring alongside a sloping quay, or a bank with low or shallow edges, scrap Mini or similar tyres are useful as underwater protection (Normal fenders are useless as they float.) They should be secured by two ropes from different positions on the tyre to two different points on the boat. Apart from providing greater security, the use of two lines allows greater adjustment as to where the tyre protects.
- Mooring stakes: or rond hooks, preferably 4. Must be strong. Drive stakes in at least a foot and use reasonably long lines so that stretch reduces shock loading .
- Large hammer for hammering in the stakes.
- Knives: Have readily accessible one or two sharp knives, preferably saw-edged, to cut warps in an emergency such as being 'hung up' in a lock. Some prefer an axe.

- Hose: take at least 30m of water hose with different fittings. A squashy end fitting tightened by jubilee clip is useful with non standard taps.
- Electricity cable: mains power (220/230 volts) is widely available, often free of charge. Take 30/40m cable with international 16 amp 3 pin plug as commonly used for caravans, which has a plug diameter of about 45mm. In France you may also need an adaptor lead for the "2-pin and 1 socket" type of 10 amp plug (with a diameter of about 36mm) widely used in Europe and obtainable from UK chandlers/camping shops as well as any French DIY shop (bricolage). In Flemish parts of Belgium, you may also encounter electricity supplies that take a rather larger 32 amp 3 pin (56mm diameter) plug, which you will probably need to buy locally. (DELVA DIY stores in Veurne, Ypres and Diksmuide sell them.)
- Binoculars: for approaching locks, reading signs, etc.
- Mobile Phone: increasingly useful as waterway manning levels decline, especially to be able to contact itinerant lock-keepers, and in Belgium, the volunteer harbour masters who supervise the smaller but welcoming yacht clubs.
- Coverage of the waterway network is generally good and few places are now out of operating range. Provided that your phone is not 'locked' to operate only with one operator, it can be economical to buy a local pre-paid SIM card to make your local calls rather than have your UK service provider bill you for them.
- Gangplank (passerelle): essential for shallower canals and the Med and useful for fendering. The deeper the draught the longer the gangplank needed: 3m is suggested for 1.6m draught.
- Mosquito screens: if you are sensitive to flying insects.
- A loud horn: necessary when approaching ferries, outlets from sand and gravel quarries, locks and blind corners.
- Bicycles: can be useful if you have room to stow them.
- Wooden planks to use outside fenders can be useful in tunnels, but these should be attached sufficiently loosely so as to break rather than causing damage if obstructed.

Belgium

A really useful web site is www.jachthaven-antwerpen.be. There is a section in English with an 'Information leaflet for foreigners who would like to use a pleasure boat on the Belgian waterways'. There are links to a map, and a 'Guide on the water' which can be downloaded and lists compulsory and recommended equipment, and documentation required.

Every pleasure craft, including those that are foreign registered, must carry certain items of equipment. None will come as any surprise to the prudent skipper:-
- one or more paddles or oars for each person on board
- within easy reach, a lifebelt, flotation device or life-jacket
- a rope of at least 30m in length
- one or more lines of at least 10m in length
- an anchor or grapnel
- a bailer or manually operated pump
- a (fog)horn
- an approved dry-chemical extinguisher (if the boat is fitted with an engine)

Boats proceeding along the Belgian coast and in tidal waters and certain canals must carry other items of equipment, which are set out in the relevant regulations for that particular area. Again, there should be no surprises for a prudent skipper. Until 2007, every vessel underway and intending to pass through locks, was required to display a red rectangular flag with a white rectangle in the middle, preferably in the bows. This is no longer necessary, but some Belgian vessels still display one.

Entry and Exit Documents and Formalities
Foreign pleasure craft must carry the shipping documents that would be required in their country of origin. That is as listed under Permits, Certificates. You will need to carry original documents - photocopies are usually not acceptable.

France There is no need to stop and report to the authorities or fly the 'Q' flag, provided that you arrive direct from another EU country, that the purpose of the journey is a legitimate non-immigrant one and all relevant Customs regulations are observed.

Belgium When a foreign pleasure craft arrives in Belgium, whether through a sea-port or via one of the waterways, the arrival must be reported at the first tax collector's office encountered on her route – usually this will be at one of the locks. A licence or registration fee may be payable as described in Permits, certificates. On leaving Belgium, an exit report (verbal) must be made at the last lock encountered.

Cruising Details
Other boat users
Save for the Seine, the Rhône and the Saône, there are now very few commercial barges on the through routes to the Med. However, do not assume that there will be none since even on canals where there are few freight-carrying *péniches*, you may come round a blind corner and meet a large hotel barge. The big rivers, especially the Seine, still carry a good deal of traffic and many of the canals of northern France and almost all of those in Belgium continue to be busy.

- When you meet commercial traffic it is important to observe the normal rules and conventions. Remember that they are being hard pressed to earn a livelihood while you are boating for pleasure. Never try to overtake a barge in a narrow waterway without making sure he has seen you and agrees with what you intend to do.
- Ask permission before mooring alongside an occupied barge and moor clear of the accommodation. Check his departure time – it will probably be early!
- It can be noisy and irritating to be moored close to the stern of a hotel barge with continuous running generator.
- Fast flowing rivers. In fast-flowing rivers keep the anchor functional and ready for instant use in case of engine failure or propeller damage. Note the warnings given in the section on the Rhône.

Speed limits
- Do observe the speed limits. Much damage has been caused to some of the canal banks by boats making excessive wash. The canal authorities do not have the resources to do all the dredging and repairs that are needed. On most canals the limit is 6km/hour. On rivers limits vary from 10 to 25km/hour but are 35km/hour on the lower Saône and Rhône. Details are given in the Fluviacarte/Navicarte and Vagnon Carte-Guides.

Mooring
- Conditions vary a lot. On canals it may be possible to moor to the bank almost anywhere, but watch out for broken piling, rocks or shallows and sometimes sloping concrete edges. Be careful if there is any commercial traffic because of the powerful suction caused when a barge passes. Moor as securely as possible with springs in both directions. On major rivers such as the Seine and Rhône bank mooring is rarely safe or possible except at proper quays. When mooring in shallow water, especially in the south, be aware that local farmers extract canal or river water for irrigation and levels can drop overnight.
- There have been occasional cases of vandalism and theft, so choose moorings with care, especially in urban areas. Graffiti and nearby large municipal housing blocks are negatives. Where possible take rope ends back on board, so that they cannot be casually untied by passers by.
- Many waterways now have mooring places with accommodation for visiting yachts. A port de plaisance (yacht harbour) will have most facilities, though often not fuel. A visitor should check

in at the capitainerie (harbour office) and pay the mooring fee. Smaller mooring places may be called relais nautique, halte nautique, or halte fluviale. Most of these have a water tap and rubbish bins. Some also have electricity, toilets and showers. There may be a charge but some are free for a stay of 1 or 2 nights.
- Towpaths are often used by mopeds and bicycles. Do not moor to trees across a towpath, even for a short period.
- Do not moor to pontoons provided for the use of boats at lifting bridges.

Tunnels
- Except for a few tunnels where towing persists, boats usually proceed through tunnels under their own power. The longer tunnels, where the traffic at the other end cannot easily be seen, are controlled by traffic lights which must be obeyed. Usually one end of the tunnel will be manned, and the other monitored by television. The unmanned end will also have an intercom, which can be useful if you believe that you have not been seen, or if delays seem excessive.
- Never enter a tunnel unless you are sure you have been seen and have permission.
- Barges, especially laden, may barely be able to maintain 1 knot (2km per hour) through a tunnel. Smaller craft can go faster, but should not exceed 2 knots.
- Wash generated in a tunnel takes a long time to subside. This makes steering difficult for following craft. If following another boat, leave at least a 100m gap, this will help you steer a straight course and give time for exhaust fumes to dissipate.
- Tunnel lighting is never adequate and you should use navigation lights and a broad spot, or even better, a flood-light. Since you will wish to hold a course parallel to the tunnel wall, it is helpful to illuminate on at least one side of the boat as well as ahead. If being towed, a tow line of at least 30m is advised to help keep the tow straight and provides space in event of the tug slowing.
- Where electrical wires on the tunnel roof are within reach, resist the temptation to touch them!

Lock Keepers and Bargees
- All are generally very helpful, but remember most of them have a tough job. Lock keepers usually work single-handed. Bargees either work long hours or else have to hang about for weeks without any work at all. Lock keepers are under no obligation to take your lines or to help you with mooring. If they do it will be a friendly gesture. Do not complain if you are kept waiting for another boat to arrive; the lock keeper may well be under instructions not to pass boats through singly in order to conserve water supplies. In the high season the professional lock keepers are often supplemented by students who make up in energy for what they may lack in skill. A lock keeper who gesticulates from afar by drawing a square in mid air is indicating that he/she wishes to inspect your papers.
- Whatever the aggravation, avoid disputes with lock keepers or bargees. The waterways grapevine operates with remarkable efficiency and things can become unpleasant for anyone who falls out with them. On the other hand a friendly and reasonable approach will usually find a response of tolerance and helpfulness. Some people tip the lock keepers but this is not normally necessary except for any special service. The offer of food and drink may be appreciated by travelling lock operators who sometimes accompany boats for a considerable distance.

Locks
Locks and sections of waterways are periodically closed for repairs and maintenance. Planned closures are announced in advance. Details can be had from end of February/March each year from the VNF website, from the VNF offices that sell the Vignette, or from the French Government Tourist Office in High Holborn, London. Ask for the list of *chômages*. Unscheduled closures are also possible in the event of damage or serious drought.
- The French Carte-Guides classify locks as 'Manuelle/ Mechanisée', and 'Automatisée/Automatique'. In the first category, if you have a crew member who can assist the lock operator, this will be appreciated and the process speeded up. 'Mechanisée' indicates that a lock operator is still in control, but he or she has electrical or hydraulic power assistance. 'Automatisée', hereafter

'Automatique', means that in some way your boat is detected and the lock is prepared. Your contribution is to start the lock cycle once your boat is safely moored inside and to leave when you are instructed.

- If yours is the only boat in the lock, you will have an easier ride at the end farthest from the ingress or egress of water. Stay close to the bottom gates if going up. Stay close to the top gates if descending; though not so close as to risk grounding on the sill below the top gates when the water level drops.
- If a boat is adequately fendered and moored at bows and stern, it should be possible to switch the engine off, making locking cleaner and quieter and minimizing problems to other boat users.
- On a few routes, such as the Moselle, some busy locks are paired, with 2 chambers side by side. Sometimes on approach, as an alternative to red/green traffic lights, you may be faced with a horizontal pair of white lights, one fixed and one flashing between the chambers. If the left hand one is flashing you will use the left hand chamber and so on.
- In some Carte-Guides the instruction is to put a crew member onto the ladder on the lock gates. This is rarely necessary and should only be attempted when there is no other means available to put a crew member ashore.

Freycinet-sized Locks and Smaller

Sizes as given under boat Maximum Dimensions. When going up, it is sometimes possible to put a crew member ashore before entering the lock, but frequently shallows or unsuitable banks prevent this. With practice it is possible to throw lines over bollards or position them with the aid of a short boathook.

- On entering the lock, loosely fastening the stern line first will provide better control until the bows are secured. Despatching crew up slimy ladders is the least favourite option, though it is sometimes necessary. Going down is easier, since crew can usually get off to deal with lines as the boat enters the lock. Make sure that lines can run freely without jamming as the boat descends.

Large Locks

- Generally the larger and more intimidating the lock, the easier it is, the filling or emptying being carefully controlled. The deepest locks usually have floating bollards, which rise or fall with you, or alternatively, vertical sets of recessed fixed bollards to which you secure in turn as the water level changes. Occasionally you will encounter a lock with no bollards, recessed or floating, and the lock-keeper will lower a large fishing line onto which you loop your line, preferably whilst keeping hold of the free end. He/she will pass it round the bollard and back to you.
- In large locks shared with other craft, the lock keeper will usually wish you to enter after the larger commercial craft. Be particularly careful not to go too close to the stern of a barge, which may keep its screw turning in order to maintain position by motoring against a single spring. When the gates open, do not release your lines until the barges ahead of you are well clear, since the power that they apply on leaving produces severe stern wash and leaves the water so turbulent that steering is very difficult.
- Some large locks on the Grand Gabarit from Dunkirk, on the Rhône and the larger Belgian canals, are operable in 2 halves with gates part way down their length. If traffic is light you will need to moor in the 'in use' part, usually the forward half. Commercial craft, including hotel barges, usually have priority at locks. If you come to an open lock and the lights are green, look behind you before entering. If there is a barge in sight, let it go in first.
- In a small boat never enter a large lock unless the lock keeper knows you are there, he may give permission for commercial traffic to enter when gates are open, before your exit.
- Life jackets must be worn in large locks.

Automatic Locks

- Many locks operate automatically. The approach of your boat is signalled and the lock is prepared for your entry. Your entry is detected and when you are moored and ready, you start the locking sequence. After the exit gates open, your departure is detected and the gates close behind you.

- Your approach is detected several hundred metres before the lock. Detection may be by radar, by your boat breaking a light beam or by you working a small radio 'télécommande' similar to a TV remote controller, which will be loaned to you. A lower technology method requires you to twist a semi flexible pole, which hangs down above the water. In the case of a linked chain of locks, notice of your approach will be a signal caused by your exit from the preceding lock.
- Sometimes a flashing white or yellow light indicates that your approach has been detected. The light panel outside each end of the lock usually carries 2 red and one green lights. Two Reds lit means that the lock is not operational. One Red that it is operational but closed against you. Red and Green together shows that it is being prepared for you, and Green, that you may enter. (No lights, showing during normal working hours, may indicate that the system is out of order or it may indicate that the lock is being controlled by an operator rather than automatically).
- Your entry into, and exit from, the lock are usually detected by photoelectric beams mounted on the masonry just outside the ends of the lock. In parts of northern and eastern France, a swinging arm projecting from the side of the lock entrance is used. This arm must be pushed aside and held back for upwards of 10 seconds, which is easy for a barge but quite difficult for a small craft. It can be done, with some difficulty, with a boathook or a stout, forked stick. The boat should stop and it may help if the end of the boathook is covered with an old cloth to prevent it slipping on the arm. (Most of these swinging arms have now been replaced by easier to use technology.)
- There are usually red and blue rods, mounted in front of a pillar on the lockside, and continuing downwards in a recess in the lock wall. When the boat is secure, lifting the blue rod starts the lock cycle. Red is an emergency stop, normally worked by pulling downwards and the intervention of a VNF engineer is needed to resume. As the lock is unattended, there is usually an intercom (called an Interphone) on the lock side, to call the controlling office.
- Swinging arms excepted, most of this technology is easy to use and reliable but the radar and photoelectric detectors were set up for big slow barges, not small, speedy pleasure craft and must be approached slowly, so that your presence is registered for at least 10 seconds.
- Automatic locks are often grouped as a chain, and this is usually indicated in the Carte-Guide. If you want to stop between locks in a chain, it is essential to warn the controller, who will usually be based at one end of the chain. Failing to do this may make it impossible to operate the next lock when you want to go on and may hold up other users. The lights at the entrance to an automatic lock may turn to red as soon as one boat has entered.
- However, the gates will not close until the blue rod is lifted, so it is safe to follow another boat in. Leaving is a different matter. If there is more than one boat, they must keep close together, otherwise the gates may start to close soon after the first boat has left. Do not try to enter or leave a lock if the alarm bell rings.
- During 2006, the VNF trialled its new generation of radio 'télécommandes' on which all the operations needed to work the lock can be carried out. Even if these prove to be highly effective, it will no doubt be many years before the instructions given above become totally redundant.
- Note that if you experience a lock breakdown, you may find that sometimes you get no reply from the intercom. However, the origin and time of your call will have been logged, and someone will usually turn up reasonably quickly.
- Slope sided locks: These are met with on the Yonne, the Upper Marne and occasionally elsewhere. The obvious risk is grounding whilst locking down. If possible moor to the knuckle close to the top or bottom gates where the side is vertical. Do not moor alongside another craft unless you can be sure that the lock will continue to be wide enough for both of you as the water level falls.

Hours of navigation and operation
- With the exception of the Seine upstream of Honfleur, navigation is normally permitted at any time in tidal rivers, although it would be ill advised on those that are not well lit. The hours during

Lock operating times
- As a broad guideline, on canals where pleasure craft heavily out-number commercial craft, the high season (April to October inclusive) operating hours are 08h30 to 19h00 with an hour lunchtime closure, usually 12h00 to 13h00. As a rule one hour less is available on Sundays. In the low season, (November to March inclusive) the evening closure is one or two hours earlier and sometimes there is no operation on Sundays. Commercial barges can make special arrangements for a limited extension of these hours, but still cannot operate for as long as they were able pre-2002. This remains a significant source of annoyance for barge skippers, most of whom are self-employed. On waterways where there is still significant péniche-sized traffic, especially in the north, 07h00 or 08h00 starting times are the norm, without lunchtime closure, and with a few exceptions the same hours are offered to pleasure craft.
- On routes taking larger craft, the hours are significantly longer. On the Seine downstream of Conflans Ste-Honorine, 07h00 to 19h00 applies every day and from Conflans to about 70km upstream of Paris 07h00 to 19h00 applies except on Sundays, when there are 3 hours less.
- On the lower Saône (south of St-Jean-de-Losne) there are at least 14 operating hours daily in summer, and 12 in winter. On the Rhône, locks operate all year round from 05h00 to 21h00. (not that winter navigation in the dark on an unlit river would be sensible, even if it is permitted.)
- Almost all locks are closed on Christmas Day, Easter Sunday, 1 May, 14 July and 11 November. In some sections they also close on 1 January, 8 May, Whit Sunday, 15 August and 1 November. The 2002 reduction in hours was the first major change in schedules for some 50 years. The new hours were negotiated with staff at a very local level and there are lots of local variations. You are advised to consult the VNF website www.vnf.fr. then select the page Horaires.
- Note that the new season's information is usually posted in the last two weeks of February/March. These 'Horaires' pages also indicate those waterways where you need to advise of your cruising plans the day in advance, so that an itinerant lock keeper can be allocated.
- Be aware that communication between VNF staff working on different waterways and even different sections of the same waterway, is often poor, and, especially in the low season, you may not be made aware of temporary closures or problems until you arrive at them. If on a tight schedule, make telephone enquiries ahead, especially at 'critical' junctions. In Belgium, operating times on Sundays are frequently restricted. (Fluviacarte/Navicarte 23 lists the Belgian hours but is not up to date.)The Dutch ANWB Wateralmanak vol.2 is a generally more accurate source of Belgian information.
- Further details can be found in a number of publications, notably La Plaisance sur les voies navigable de Wallonie and De pleziervaart op de bevaarbare waterwegen in Vlaanderen.
- Lock keepers will often phone the next lock ahead to warn of your arrival. Tell them if you plan to stop before the next lock.

Supplies

Water
Usually easy to get at haltes, quays and some locks, but there are a few long gaps between taps. The Canal entre Champagne et Bourgogne (formerly the Canal de la Marne à la Saône) has relatively few water points and the Rhône can be awkward in this respect too. More taps are being provided but top up whenever you get the chance.

Fuel
In France petrol (essence or carburant) and diesel (gas-oil or gazole) are obtainable, but there are some long gaps between convenient bankside filling stations so it is wise to fill up whenever possible. Not all suppliers accept Credit Cards, so be prepared to pay cash. In some places it is possible to get a garage to deliver by tanker lorry provided a reasonably large quantity is required. For smaller quantities the only

possibility may be to transport it in jerricans. Delivery by tanker or in cans usually involves a delivery charge.

It is now illegal to use commercial (red) diesel in pleasure boats, except as fuel for heating stoves.

In Belgium, as the ban on red diesel for pleasure craft has been enforced, waterside refuelling points for pleasure craft have become few and far between because operators do not consider the small and seasonal demand from pleasure craft justifies the additional expense and complexity of maintaining 2 sets of tanks and pumps. As at November 2009, we are only aware of inland refuelling possibilities in Antoing, Antwerp, Brussels, Bocholt, Comines, Diksmuide, Givet, Liège and Namur.

On French waterways charts the word 'fuel' often refers only to fuel for commercial craft, not pleasure boats. On the other hand fuel for pleasure boats is usually obtainable (if not particularly cheap) at hire boat bases but avoid the busy changeover times, which are usually Friday pm, Saturday and often Sunday am. The mention of 'fuel' in these notes generally means that both petrol and diesel are available.

Gas
It is not normally possible to get Calor Gas in France or Belgium. Several other kinds of bottled gas are available and some may fit the Calor regulator but bottles cannot be exchanged outside the country of origin. The only brand whose cylinders can be exchanged internationally is Camping Gaz.
Camping to Calor adaptors are available at UK camping shops or chandleries.

Members have reported occasional difficulties in buying Camping Gaz in remote parts of France. Many areas of France do not have mains gas supplies and supermarkets often sell the larger containers from racks at their filling stations. Usually the smaller ones such as the Camping Gaz R907 that many yachts use, are on sale inside the supermarket. Sometimes the local dealer is an unexpected shop, such as the radio and TV shop, or the one selling sports gear. Try the *bricolage*. Ask someone!

Services, Spares & Repairs
There is no difficulty if you want to leave your boat in France for a short or long period. For preference choose a yacht harbour or boatyard where it can be left under supervision (*gardiennage*).

Away from the coast, chandlers are few and far between, although there are excellent ones at Compiègne, St-Jean-de-Losne and Port Napoléon, Port St- Louis-du-Rhône, Le Grau-d'Agde, Bordeaux Bassin à Flot. Do not overlook the local '*bricolage*' a French hybrid of the DIY store and the old-fashioned ironmongers, especially in rural areas.

For a useful France-wide spares service, see the note about Marine Diesel, at Chitry-les-Mines on the Canal du Nivernais.

In this edition of the Notes we have tried to note where hire boat bases are located. Most have on-site service engineers, and if not, they will know where to find one. But avoid their rather frantic changeover days when they will be entirely preoccupied with their own boats and clients.

Communications

Language
In France language can be a problem. It is not essential to be able to speak French but it will help a lot if someone on board knows at least a little. In Belgium language is both less and more of a problem than in France. Belgium is a tri-lingual country. French is the language of Wallonia and Flemish is the language of Flanders. There is also a small German-speaking area in eastern Belgium. Many Belgians speak excellent English and are eager to use it. However, some Walloons prefer not to speak Flemish; likewise, some

Flemings prefer not to speak French. Unless you are reasonably fluent in the relevant language for the area, it is probably best to try in English first.

Radio
In both France and Belgium many larger locks, including those on the rivers Seine, Yonne, Saône, Rhône and Belgian Meuse use VHF radio, commonly on channels 18, 20 or 22. So do the offices supervising some lengths of little-used canals, or sets of automated locks, in which case the channel number will be displayed at the locks. Often useful information can be gained just by listening, but if you have adequate knowledge of French, calling locks in advance of your arrival can be helpful.

Channel 10 is used as an intership channel, and when visibility is limited, by topology or weather, barges may use it to broadcast their position, their direction of travel (*montant* – upstream, *avalant* – downstream) and possibly whether or not they are empty (*vide*) or loaded (*chargée*). Locks and canal offices use quite efficient aerials directed along the line of the waterway, so transmissions should be made on low power.

In Belgium a requirement to use VHF equipped with an Automatic Transmission Identification System (ATIS) applies to recreational craft greater in length than 7m. For craft over 20m the requirement is to be able to monitor and talk on two channels simultaneously (not simply dual watch) and therefore two radios may be required, one or both of which may be a portable unit (with ATIS). Craft between 7m and 20m need only use a single radio, but in future (at a so far unspecified date) the 2 radio rule will be extended to them.

The use of portable VHF transceivers has been permitted in both Holland and Belgium from the beginning of 2007. For UK registered vessels, the Radiocommunications Agency will issue an MMSI and advise the BIPT (their Belgian equivalent) of this.

To date the French have taken no steps to implement the use of ATIS and except possibly on the large rivers, seem unlikely to do so.

Signals
You are advised to study the CEVNI Rules (see Permits, Certificates), See also Appendix i.

THE SEINE
Tancarville Canal

| Le Havre to Tancarville | 5km 2 locks | 5m water 7m air | Fluviacarte/Navicarte 1 |

Runs from the docks so avoiding the lower part of the estuary. Useful if weather conditions are nasty. There may be delays at the locks and 7 swing bridges.

The River Seine

| Coast to Paris | 338km 6 locks | 3.5m water 6m air | Fluviacarte/Navicarte 1 |

A fine river with some magnificent scenery. Sea-going ships go up to Rouen. Above Rouen there is barge traffic but most stop at night except for some pusher convoys which run all night. It is possible to reach Rouen with mast stepped.

There can be a considerable current in the early Spring following heavy winter rain or snow. Enquiries to 01 40 58 29 99 (Paris) or 02 32 48 71 40 (Amfreville lock).

Yachts travelling between Rouen and Honfleur, in either direction, must log in and out to the Port Autonome de Rouen using VHF 73. Upstream of the Pont de Tancarville, navigation by pleasure craft is not permitted between 30 minutes after sunset and 30 minutes before sunrise, east of buoys 27 and 28 (about 6km east of Honfleur).

Ascending The fastest passage will be made by leaving Le Havre in time to be in the main Seine channel as the flood begins. Since the time of high water is progressively later ascending the river, a yacht of moderate speed can reach Rouen on one tide.

The lock and new lock gates on to the Seine at Honfleur means that craft can leave at most states of the tide and Honfleur to Rouen is some two hours shorter than starting from Le Havre. A good strategy is to leave Honfleur so as to be at the Pont de Tancarville close to low water. To achieve this it may be necessary to wait between the bridge to the Vieux Bassin and the lock. Inner harbour dirty but charges €68 for 14m boat per night. http://www.cnh-honfleur.net/Advice,1,11,107.html This is a useful link showing pictures of harbour with information for boat crews.

Descending from Rouen to the sea will involve some time opposing the tide and it is better to face this upstream, where the current is less. Stategies and timing are discussed in Paris by Boat, by David Jefferson, and tidal and current curves are given both by Jefferson and in **Fluviacarte/***Navicarte 1*. Whether bound upstream or downstream, there are no good places to moor en route. Caudebec or Duclair are the least poor.

Masts Best facilities for unstepping masts are in the yacht harbour at **Le Havre**. They can be left there by arrangement with the club (Société des Régates du Havre). At **Honfleur**, Honfleur Nautic can also unstep masts. Tel: 02 31 89 55 89). At **Rouen**, Lozai Maintenance at **pk 251** (Tel 02 35 69 42 86) do not have their own crane, but the Port Authority will step/unstep masts in the Bassin Gervais at **pk 245** where there is a 25m pontoon reserved for pleasure craft awaiting mast stepping or unstepping. (Port Autonome de Rouen Tel 02 35 52 54 30).

Recent report of good service given by Lamanage, located next to the marina at Rouen, www.lamanage-rouen.fr. Employee Christophe Dobos speaks good English, contact at: activiteplaisance@lamanage-rouen.fr.

Transport of masts between Channel and Mediterranean is offered by:-
- Atlantitrans Transport Multitrier of La Rochelle (Tel 05 46 44 33 33)
- Chantier Naval de la Baie de la Seine, 126 Quai Frissard, Le Havre. Tel: 02 35 25 30 5.
- SOMALOIR of Montoir de Bretagne (Tel 02 40 90 05 75)
- Marine-Plus, Hangar 31, Quai Frissard, 76600 Le Havre. Tel: 02 35 24 21 14.
- MMarine, Chantier Naval, Port Napoléon, 13230 Port Saint-Louis-du-Rhône. Based at end of Rhône on Mediterranean coast. Do not have own transport but are happy to help with arrangements.
- Yachtservice Wolfgang Graf, Seiner Weg 8A 24236, Laboe, Germany. info@masttransporte.de www.masttransporte.de Tel: +49 4343 499045 Fax: +49 4343 499047. €900 for 2 masts in 2010.

These are companies that regularly deliver new boats by road from the builders' yards to the Mediterranean and your mast will be added to a scheduled delivery trip. There have been occasional reports of slow delivery, so make sure your requirements are clearly understood, and take responsibility for checking the labelling – own name, name of destination and name of boat. Ensure rigging is secured and that bottle screws are taped up or removed, together with other small items. Do not leave it to the delivery company to tell the destination marina that the mast is arriving. Do this yourself, even if it means they get two phone calls. Two is better than none.

Le Mascaret The Seine bore, which formerly caused a dangerous tidal wave on lower part of river between Quilleboeuf (pk 332) and La Mailleraye (pk 302) officially no longer exists. But, it may be encountered around LW Springs and should be considered if anchoring or mooring.

Navigation Below Rouen ocean-going ships travelling at high speed may be encountered at any time, even when visibility is bad. Keep to the right and remember Rule 9(b) of the Collision Regulations. 'A vessel of less than 20m in length or a sailing vessel shall not impede the passage of a vessel which can safely navigate only within a narrow channel or fairway'. Radio watch essential. The channel buoys have an official minimum depth of 1.7m so it is usually possible for a yacht to navigate outside the marked channel. But take care - there are shallows. It is worth checking the tide curve at the capitainerie in Honfleur.

Above Rouen it is important to follow the deep-water channel. There are usually arrows indicating the direction to take at the end of islands but some are dilapidated and some have vanished altogether. Maps of the river are desirable. Watch out for enormous barges and other commercial traffic. (See note on **blue flagging** in section on Signals.)

In the lower non-tidal Seine it is possible to navigate for many kilometres behind the islands in quiet backwaters off the main channel. This is pleasanter, less stressful and more interesting. Opportunities for anchoring here too, but look out for local tourist boat which also uses these channels.

Repairs and chandlery (see individual entries for details)
Honfleur (pk 356), Rouen (pk 242), Port-St-Louis (pk 81), Méricourt (pk 121), Limay (pk 110)

Moorings The few moorings below Rouen are likely to be uncomfortable and possibly dangerous. Above the first lock at Amfreville mooring is easier at quays or at haltes nautiques. Anchoring is often possible out of the main channel, e.g. in backwaters, but watch depth carefully when navigating out of the dredged channel.

Honfleur (pk 356) Outer harbour pontoon has space for 3 boats. Water & electricity. Small boatyard facility at far end of east Carnot basin, not shown on harbour plans. Accessed via 2 swing bridges (lock keeper knows times). Under new management and small pontoon has been installed. Step and unstep masts. €200 for stepping plus €50 for lifting masts off truck onto storage rack. €60 month for storage of masts (2009). Pretty town and impressive church. Worth a short stay.

Tancarville (pk 338) Mooring inside the dolphins may be possible but not recommended owing to the strong current, tidal range and possible dangerous wash from ships.

Quilleboeuf (pk 333) Possible anchorage between L bank and ship mooring buoys. Not recommended at spring tides.

Caudebec-en-Caux (pk 310) Large floating landing stage available if not required by hotel or tour ships. Check at Tourist Office 100m upstream. (or in advance by Tel: 02 32 70 46 32). Be prepared for wash from shipping and remember that at Springs the tide turns very suddenly and strongly, about 2 hrs. after indicated high water at neaps.

Duclair (pk 278) Halte nautique on R bank used by commercial vessels. Check at Tourist Office in Hotel de Ville.

Darse des Docks (pk 251) See previous note under **'Masts'**

Rouen (pk 246) Bassin St-Gervais on R bank below the bridge is last possible stop for boats with masts stepped. New port de plaisance (La Crea) in north arm of the Bassin St Gervais. Email: plaisance@la-crea.fr, www.port-de-plaisance@la-crea.fr. €15 per night 12m yacht in 2012. Free showers, toilet, washing machine, drier, ice-machine, WiFi, communal room and kitchen. Over-wintering possible. Good security with card key entry.
Boat yard next door (Lamanage) has travel lift with crane and will remove masts and store prior to collection, also boat storage and repairs. www.lamanage-rouen.fr. Email: service.rouen@lamanage-rouen.fr. Busy commercial area. Boats with masts down - see next entry.

Rouen (pk 242) Villetards boatyard is on the N side of the Ile Lacroix upstream of the fourth bridge. Chandler and repair facilities. Closed on Sundays and Mondays. Halte de plaisance for visiting yachts also on N side of the Ile Lacroix and should always be approached against the tide (2 knots at Springs). Port Tel: 02 35 07 33 94. €16.50 for 11m. Phone ahead to book berth. Shops close. Excellent for visiting Rouen. Access may be restricted temporarily by racing on odd dates in May and September. http://www.youtube.com/watch?v=Ell7JfPJ18s YouTube post of halte nautique at Rouen.

Members advise leaving for Amfreville at the head of the tideway early on the tide in order to stay ahead of commercial traffic and avoid queueing for the lock (could be hours!).

There is a fuel barge R bank upstream of the city at about **pk 238.8** where one can lay alongside. Cards accepted but expensive. Fuel cheaper at garage in Rouen.

Oissel (pk 229.5) New halte fluvial in form of 40m floating pontoon, L bank. No facilities visible.

Elbeuf (pk 219) Good L bank quay with ladder steps & bollards, well away from wash from barges. Convenient for shops.
Club Nautique (pk 218) in approach to old lock on R bank. Entrance has over 2m, between HW-2 and HW+2, marked with 1 red and 2 green buoys. Marina has electricity, water, showers, diesel but is remote from town.

Amfreville (pk 202) The first lock. The river is tidal up to this point. Deep water mooring at quay above lock.

Poses (pk 199) L bank above lock in quiet backwater. Turn into starboard at first opportunity between Iles du Tait and Vadeney. Pontoons and several quays in same area. Water & electricity available by pre-pay jetons (try tourist office – only open at week-ends), plus toilets and showers, but varying depths.
Also free mooring on stone quay with rings and 2.5m depth directly ahead and slightly to port behind Isle du Tait. Le Mesnil de Poses slightly upstream has a good quay with 1.5m depth.
Small shop and 2 auberges here. Supermarket 4km cycle ride at Val de Reuil. It is possible to walk or cycle over passerelle above the barrage and lock to large restaurant on Amfreville side.

Islands above Amfreville. If you do not need to go ashore, it is possible to anchor or moor in the backwaters south of the channel with care. Fluviacarte/Navicarte 1 shows depths.

Val St. Martin (pk 176) YC de Paris/Normandy and port de plaisance Nautikhome, a private port open all year round with space for 40 boats up to 12m and draught 1. 40m only in entrance, then shallows. Tel 02 32 21 00 67.

Les Andelys (pk 174) Port de plaisance des Andelys closed. Prone to silting up but may be dredged again in the future. Ruins of Château Gaillard, built by Richard Coeur de Lion, provide a magnificent view and are well worth a visit. Green coloured pontoon by village green with water if have long hose but now reserved for hotel boats. Limited small boat berths off main waterway on both banks, one below the chateau which is worth a visit.

Vernon (pk 150) Halte nautique on L bank just upstream of the bridge is for large tourist ships - avoid. Yacht Club de Vernon (R bank below bridge) has Visitor berths near the Race Box, with depth about 1.4m, in soft mud at the upstream end of the Visitors' pontoon. Tel 02 32 21 51 26. Beware of shallows in the approach. From downstream, follow a course of 100°T with the L bank silos astern in line with the club's race box ahead. Approach from upstream not advised. Attractive surroundings. Water, electricity, showers, and toilets in summer. Giverny, former home of the painter Claude Monet, is about 5km from Vernon. Visit house and wonderful garden by bike or taxi. It gets very crowded – best to go early, and avoid summer weekends. Cycle route along old railway line that is continuation of Rue Andre Touflet.

Méricourt (pk 121) Port de plaisance de l'Ilon at pk 120 on R bank at upstream end of Isle de Sablonnière has gone into receivership. (Aug 2012) but is rumoured to become part of the H2O group. Showers, water & electricity still available. No capitainerie, fuel or chandlery. Quiet country stop with no shops nearby. Enter just upstream of barrage, then take NE exit from first lake and find bridge entrance to port de plaisance on NW side of lake. Depth over 2m. Tel 01 30 92 23 23.. €24 for 11m in high season incl. water & electricity. Better value for longer stays.

Mooring is also possible at upstream end of barge quay above lock, but check with lock keeper.

Rolleboise (pk 119) Fuel from BP garage, L bank quay.

Limay (pk 110)
- Marines de Limay, small port that may be crowded.
- At pk 109 free small halte in northern branch, but unfortunately in area with bad reputation for vandalism and crime, so do not leave boat unattended. Shipyard, Marines de Limay downstream of official halte nautique in N. branch, 01 30 98 43 71).

Mantes-la-Jolie (pk 109.2) Pontoon next to yacht club pontoons, L bank behind Ile l'Aumone. 400m of L bank quay in southern arm, with *péniche* spaced bollards, dominated by live-aboards. Shops and restaurants close, and railway station with frequent service to Paris about 1km. R bank channel navigable right through – stone bridge has had central span removed.

Meulan (pk 93) Small halte in northern arm which is now reserved for motor boat training school. Mooring possible. Depth 1.8m at pontoon and 1.4m at quay 50m upstream.

Pk 90.3 New pontoon downstream of bridge. R bank.

Verneuil-sur-Seine (pk 89.5) New port in old L bank sand quarry, opened Spring 2005. Should offer all facilities including pump-out and food shop at adjacent camp site, Du Val de Seine VHF Ch 78..

Detroit Marine (pk 87.5) R bank dilapidated and crowded pontoon. Capacity of crane stated as 15 tonnes in Navicarte, but it is marked 30,000lbs, so only 13.4 Imperial or 13.6 Metric tons.

Port St-Louis (pk 81) Yacht harbour R bank. Depth 2m. Volvo agents. All repairs. Tel 01 30 74 38 46. Looks a bit forlorn but better pontoons are further in. Sand barges use quay just inside basin. €13 for 11m.

Poissy (pk 78) Pontoons on bank side of landing stage for passenger boats. Also Port des Migneaux, about 1km down southern arm (Bras de Migneaux) all facilities, but may be crowded.

Andresy (pk 72) Halte in R bank arm about 1km downstream of junction with R Oise. No facilities and depth about 1.5m at quayside, but over 2m off small pontoon (which has water & electricity.) Good food market on quay Wed & Sat.

Conflans-Ste-Honorine (pk 69) Ambiance Yachting (pk 69) R bank port de plaisance, crowded with small boats.

La Frette (pk 63) Small halte R bank. Wash may be uncomfortable.

Bougival (pk 48) Small quay for yachts in west arm above Bougival lock, R bank just upstream of the road bridge. Shops and restaurants over the bridge. There is also a sailing school pontoon further south which is good.

Rueil-Malmaison (pk 45) in the Bras de Marly. Small halte on R Bank close to Pont de Chatou lacks security. Halte on L Bank about 200m upstream of bridge. No water or electricity but good for shops, restaurants and fast RER rail service to Paris. Maison Fournaise on opposite bank was setting for Renoir paintings.

Port Sisley (pk 28) On L bank of L Bank arm is a crowded port de plaisance with shops nearby. In a one way stretch, and approach must be from down stream and departure upstream.

Asnières (pk 24 Port de Van Gogh. L bank pontoons with limited spare space. Water & electricity but suffers from wash.

Suresnes/St-Cloud (pk 15) Clubs mentioned on Fluviacarte/Navicarte have limited space

Canals de l'Ourcq, St-Denis and St-Martin
Backwaters of Paris. Short cut but 16 locks and small fees. Entrance from R bank of R bank arm at pk 29 and ends some 10km on, in the Paris Arsenal marina. During high season, last few km down to the Arsenal very busy with passenger boats with priority at locks. Free guide from Arsenal Marina (Mairie de Paris guide **Le Reseau Fluvial de la Ville de Paris: Guide du Plaisancier**).

Paris Old Port de Plaisance R bank downstream of the Pont de la Concorde reportedly no longer has space for visiting boats. Better to continue upstream to the **Port de Plaisance de Paris-Arsenal**, (pk 168) a large yacht harbour in a former commercial basin with pontoon moorings for yachts up to 25m length, 1.9m draught. €48.50 incl. water & electricity in 2011 for 13m. WiFi available. Look out for small yellow floating bollards in lock, to port when entering. http://www.fayollemarine.fr/en/

From the Seine, entrance is through a lock on the R bank about 1km upstream of Notre Dame. There is not longer a waiting pontoon at the entrance. The lock has more useful bollards on its port side (when ascending) but is often crowded, so fender well. Harbour Master keeps watch by TV and VHF 9. Reception pontoon and capitainerie just inside the basin on the right. All facilities except fuel which is only available occasionally from a visiting barge. Restaurants, shops, metro stations, opera house, etc. within few minutes walk. Charges are higher than elsewhere in France but not unreasonable considering the facilities and situation. Advance booking recommended during holiday season, especially July. capitainerie, Port de Plaisance, 11 Boulevard de la Bastille, 75012 Paris Tel 01 43 41 39 32.

An 'overflow' marina for Paris was opened in 2008 in the Bassin de la Villette, which is reached by the 4.5km long Canal St-Martin that runs north out of the Arsenal Basin. Room for up to 15 boats of up to 15m length.

Fuel in Paris No longer available at the old port de plaisance on the R bank downstream of the Pont de la Concorde, and the diesel barge about 4km upstream of the entrance to the Arsenal Port de plaisance, is no longer prepared to service pleasure boats. You can check by phoning 06 72 16 89 41. A fuel barge has usually been sent into the Arsenal once a month but that service appears to have stopped too.

Navigation through Paris It is important to note the one-way system round the Ile de la Cité and Ile St. Louis. The Bras de la Monnaie (the channel on the L bank round the islands) is one-way upstream. The Bras de la Cité and Bras St. Louis are upstream from the hour to 20 minutes past the hour, and downstream from 35 minutes to 50 minutes past the hour. There are traffic lights on the upstream side of the Pont Sully and on the downstream side of the Pont au Change. Look out for these lights; it is easy to miss them. It is obligatory to have your radio tuned to Channel 10 when crossing the city.

Beware vandals on bridges who delight in throwing things onto passing boats.

Upper Seine

Paris to Montereau	100km 8 locks	2.8m water 5.5m air	Fluviacarte/Navicarte 2

The Seine above Paris is a beautiful river once the industrial sprawl of eastern Paris has been left behind. There is a considerable amount of barge traffic, but navigation is easy and the only problem is the shortage of good mooring places. Best places are Port-aux-Cerises, Melun and Chartrettes, other mooring places exposed, and crowded. Distances on the upper Seine are measured from the upper limit of navigation at Marcilly.

Repairs and chandlery (see individual entries for details)
St Mammès (pk 81) – in Canal du Loing.

Villeneuve St. Georges. (pk 153) Harbour on R bank. Permanent barges, may find space.

Pk 155 High quay on L bank.

Vigneux (pk 148) Port de plaisance on R Bank. Water & electricity, but visitors are discouraged.

Port-aux-Cerises (pk 147) Entrance on R bank just downstream of Pont de Juvisy. Part of an outdoor leisure complex. Re-opened in 2010 with new facilities. Members note the entrance is still narrow and little depth, but there is now more space. Facilities include water, electricity, toilets and laundrette. A possible place to overwinter if no space available in Paris. Good rail service from Juvisy (10 mins. across bridge) to Paris.). Bakery, but otherwise few shops close. €27 for 10m boat in 2011, 2nd night ½ price. www.portauxcerises.fr. Tel 01 69 40 33 10. WiFi available but very new and did not work in 2011.

Evry (pk 139) Long stone quay just above lock. No facilities except rubbish disposal.

Coudray-sur-Seine (pk 129.5) Lock has rough piled walls – fender well. About 1km downstream the small R bank port of Saintry was reported as closed and near derelict in 2006, but there is a substantial R bank quay above the lock without facilities, and a restaurant L bank across the bridge.

Melun (pk 112) Tiny Port de plaisance R bank 2km downstream from town. Mooring quays on both sides of island..

Chartrettes (pk 100.8) R bank port de plaisance just above La Cave lock. Tel 06 72 83 38 47. Water & electricity. €7 in 2011. If heading downstream call lock before leaving.

Samois (pk 93) Halte behind island on L bank, with coin-in-slot water & electricity points. The town commemorates its most famous resident, guitarist Django Reinhardt with an annual jazz festival at the end of June.

Valvins (pk 90) Port du Pays de Fontainbleu (formerly Port Stephane Mallarmé), L bank. Good facilities, including water, electricity & showers. Visitors' berths on last pontoon upstream. Occasional smells from upstream sewage outlet. Nearest mooring to Fontainebleau (€10 - €12 taxi ride). Go to main road, turn L up steep hill for the superb castle. Supermarket on R on the way back, and another about 2.5km away on other side of river. Station L bank about 1km. Access difficult because of strong current. Tel 01 64 22 51 34.

Champagne-sur-Seine (pk 83) Good deep-water quay just above lock on R bank. Fuel from builders' merchants on R bank by jerrycan only. Water. Closed Saturday pm and all day Sunday and fêtes.

Pk 85 (approx) L bank quay by park

St-Mammès (pk 81) The Canal du Loing enters on the L bank. Filling station R bank below the bridge has fuelling quay for pleasure craft, but access sometimes difficult as busy barge centre. Good L bank port de plaisance, although the short unstable pontoons projecting into river can be difficult if current running, in which case pontoons approached from downstream are easier. €10 incl. water & electricity, 3rd night free (2009). Open May–Sep. Tel 01 60 74 44 00. Much movement due to passage of fast barges. Free WiFi.

Moorings in Canal du Loing may be possible if room amongst barges, or otherwise, 2km up, just before first lock are L bank halte nautique with access to Moret-sur-Loing. Small boat moorings at Club de Voile (pk 80).

La Celle (pk 79.5) Jetty on R Bank seems to be for public use, but often occupied by static *péniches*.

Pk 71 Mooring quay with water at lock gates on downstream side, R bank.

Montereau (pk 68) The R Yonne enters on the L bank. On L bank of Seine, just upstream of the road bridge is a quay with a grassy bank. Depth variable between about 1.1m and 1.6m. Halte with water & electricity just upstream of Pont de Moneteau on Yonne.

La Petite Seine

| Montereau to Marcilly | 68km 12 locks | 1.2m water 3.4m air | Fluviacarte/Navicarte 2 |

Quiet and well worth a visit. Minimum depth 1.8m as far as Nogent; reducing above that. Note that it is necessary to advise lock keepers of plans the day before to pass through lock 10 (La Grand Bosse) and those upstream.

Marolles (pk 62) moorings with water point in arm upstream of old lock.

Bray (pk 46.5) Halte nautique which sometimes has working water & electricity, with shops and large supermarket close. Also an uncrowded commercial quay downstream.

Nogent-sur-Seine (pk 19) Quay with water & electricity in closed arm above mill and lock. Take care to avoid submerged training wall between canal and mill race. Deeper draught craft can use L bank quayside a few hundred metres downstream of the mill with no facililties, but close to good covered food market.

Conflans-sur-Seine (pk 3) Quay.

YONNE AND NIVERNAIS

River Yonne

| Montereau to Auxerre | 108km 26 locks | 1.8m water 4.4m air | Fluviacarte 20 – Bourgogne Ouest |

The Yonne, one of the most beautiful of French rivers, enters the Seine 101km above Paris. Some barge traffic and hire boats. Locks mechanised, some with sloping sides, but some with sliding pontoons (boats up to 15m). Slow in operation (½ hour) so forewarn lock keepers. Lock opening times 09h00 – 12h30, 13h30 – 19h00. Between Villeneuve and Armeau 08h00 – 12h30, 13h00 – 18h00. (Downstream of **Barbey** no lunch break during the week). At weekends lock-keepers may tend 3 locks each, there will be delays and radio may not be answered. Temporary moorings included for lunch stops.
- **VHF 8** Cannes (No 17) to Rosoy (No 8) inclusive.
- **VHF 12** Étigny (No 7) to Épineau (No 1) and Gravière (No 9) to La Chaînette (No 1) inclusive
- **VHF 69** at week-ends.

Repairs and chandlery (see individual entries for details)
Laroche Migennes (pk 22.5), Auxerrre (pk1)
Hire base at Joigny (pk 31)

Montereau (pk 108) See Upper Seine.

Cannes (pk 104) Just above lock 17 it is possible to moor in deep water under the road bridge. Port de Plaisance du Pharle (pk 94.5) has closed but reopened as 'Oasis Beach'. Unsure of depth.
Pk 100. Dolphins on R bank.

Port Renard (pk 92) Mooring possible to outside of lock wall in river, with permission of lock keeper. Depth 2m for up to two-thirds length of lock, then shoals. Note that about 3km of the old river above this lock is navigable and regularly used by large sand barges. Sloping sided lock but floating pontoon just inside downstream gate on L bank. Also mooring below lock R bank.

Pk 89 Disused silo quay R bank, good for lunchtime mooring.

Pk 87 L bank above port de garde, mooring posts at which commercial boats have priority.

Pk 84 Small quay R bank by tennis courts and swimming baths, no bollards.

Pont-sur-Yonne (pk 79) New pontoon L bank downstream of the bridge. No facilities Some alongside moorings. Quay upstream of bridge has sloping wall and is shallow.

Pk 68.5 Industrial quay. Suitable for lunch stop.

Sens (pk 67) Town quay, 2m. Town centre mooring now has water on the quay, & limited electricity, but questionable security and wash. Long lead needed for electricity. WiFi at Bar L'Etoile at end of bridge.

Evans Marine, All service and repair work moved to Laroche Migennes in 2012 (pk 22.5).

Pk 57 Small mooring quay. R bank.

Villeneuve-sur-Yonne (pk 50) Good R bank quayside mooring with no facilities in 2010, best depth near red "Welcome" sign. Water at lock. Municipal Base Nautique on L Bank in backwater just downstream of road bridge run by couple who live on campsite upriver. Showers by arrangement, water, electricity and good security. www.villeneuve-yonne.fr. Email: lesaucil@orange.fr.

Pk 44. Quay, R bank. No facilities.

Pk 45. Dolphins R bank above lock (Armeau).

Pk 41.5 Mooring quay. R bank above bridge.

Cézy (pk 35.5) Small halte in backwater just below suspension bridge. Depth 1.5m. Bollards. No water or electricity. Approach nearer to L (Cezy) bank than to centre of channel.

Joigny (pk 31) Picturesque little town. Hire base on L bank offers facilities for visiting yachts except on Friday and Saturday. Diesel, water, electricity, maintenance and repairs. In 2008 €5 for first night, €10 thereafter including water & electricity. Gardiennage service. Tel 03 86 62 06 14. Various possibilities for mooring downstream of base, L bank, and although town quay downstream of bridge, R bank, looks as though it must be noisy there are reports that it is OK. Small quay upstream of bridge L bank.

Pk 25. Small metal quay L bank.

Laroche-Saint-Cydroine (pk 24) Halte R bank – 50m quay with free water & electricity, depth 1.5m. Shop and boulangerie close.

Pk 23 Widely spaced bollards on R bank after junction.

Laroche-Migennes (pk 22.5) Chantier Fluvial de Migennes Gare d'Eau 89400 Migennes, a substantial boatyard which is now run by Simon Evans of Sens. Tel 03 86 92 93 13 or 06 80 30 11 53. Upstream of junction with the Canal de Bourgogne on R bank. Gardiennage. Chandlery. All repairs including woodwork. Services. Crane (40 tonne). Surveys. Mobile repair van. www.fluvial-migennes.com . Mooring €5 per night (2012). 15 mins walk to town. Close to railway station.

La Gravière (pk 21) Free halte L bank above lock. Shallow only 0.7m.

Bassou (pk 18) 30m pontoon R bank. No water and no electricity.

Pk 15.4 Mooring dolphins, R bank below Raveuse lock gates.

Pk 12.7 L bank, little used commercial quay with good depth but no facilities close.

Gurgy (pk 10.8) Low quay, R bank with water & electricity which need €4 jeton (from local hostelry). I jeton for 1 hr. electricity or 100 lts. water. Shallow.

Monéteau (pk 7) Halte on R bank under trees, but depth only about 1m. Supermarket and fuel close. L bank quay at pizzeria has 1.3m depth at upstream end.

Auxerre
- Town quay on L bank free but on noisy road and no facilities.
- Port de plaisance on R bank, Société Aquarelle, has over 420m of quay and offer repairs, WiFi, winter storage, good chandlery, and all facilities including washing machine, €6.30, dryer, €6.30, and diesel €1.39. Rafting up often required in summer months. In 2012 cost for 10m boat was €12.15 plus water & electricity (€5.35 per day, or with meter €0.21 kw.hr). Pump out facilities. Car parking. Under the new management of France Afloat from April 2012. Address is Port de Plaisance, Rue St. Martin, 89000 Auxerre, Tel 03 86 46 96 77. contact@aquarelle-france.fr. www.aquarelle-france.fr. Beautiful situation in popular city with excellent shops and restaurants. Supermarket close and laundrette charging €5 machine and €1 dryer, near fuel pumps. In the winter of 2011/2012 there were break-ins to boats on hard standing, but new owners plan security cameras.

Upstream of Auxerre the navigation becomes The Canal du Nivernais.

Canal du Nivernais

Auxerre to Decize	174km 108 locks	1.2m water 2.7m air	Fluviacarte/Navicarte 7 or 18 Breil 11 or Vagnon 3

Distances start from the southern end, the Loire junction. Locks are numbered in both directions starting from the summit level. Lock opening hours 09h00 – 12h00, 13h00 – 18h00.

This canal is **open Summer only**, usually 1 April to 31 October. Tyre fenders not allowed. Scenery beautiful and varied. Many good moorings. Numerous hire boats. Little commercial traffic. The depth in a dry summer may be barely 1m. There is now a local society, Les Amis du Canal du Nivernais, to increase awareness. Substantial improvements have been carried out in recent years, and there is some prospect that available depth may be increased to 1.3m in the future. Be careful to follow the correct channel in places where the canal branches off from the River Yonne.

From Auxerre to Clamecy, there is usually 1.3m depth, but upstream of Clamecy several pounds need dredging, and in Spring 2004 craft with 1.1m draught were experiencing difficulties. Whilst the official figure for water draught is therefore optimistic, that for air draught is cautious, being based on the available height across a full 5m beam. It was reported in Spring 2004 that a craft with a height of 3.0m across a 3m beam had passed the full length of the canal. Low bridge, 3.25m at pk 146.

From Chitry to Auxerre there are several lift bridges. Each has pontoons for mooring whilst bridge is lifted. Do not moor to these pontoons unless using them for this purpose.

Repairs and chandlery (see individual entries for details)
Vermenton (pk 154), Chitry-les-Mines (pk 82), Baye (pk 66). See also Auxerre on R. Yonne.

Bailly (pk 162.5) 80m stone quay. Water & electricity have been cut off. Depth only 0.8m. Wooden pontoons just below 'Caves de Bailly' – excellent sparkling wine – Crémant de Bourgogne

Vincelottes (pk 160.7) R bank moorings in cut to lock, close to road bridge, with good restaurant (*Les Tilleuls*) in village.

Vincelles (pk 160) No longer hire base. Long quay on L bank, shallow at downstream end and low sloping quay in centre. Toilets. Water. Electricity €3 night payable at Le Lavoir crêperie – closed Wed & Thur.. WfFi, launderette and shop at nearby campsite.

Cravant (pk 156.5) Attractive basin/restaurant. No electricity in 2011. Town with shops, 5 mins walk.

Pk 154 Side arm up to **Vermenton**, 4km and 2 locks.

Pk 153 Bollards in basin, L bank above lock. Depth uncertain.

Accolay 2.7km up side arm has 40m sloping stone quay. Upstream end used to be and may still be reserved for hotel barge. Water and limited electricity. Good restaurant, Hostellerie de la Fontaine close. Booking advisable at week-ends. 03 86 81 54 02. www.hostelleriedelafontaine.fr.

Pk 155.5 Mooring in basin, bollards, R bank, check depth.

Vermenton (pk 154) 4km up side arm. Small town - worth visit. Good canal basin expanded in 2011 to make more room for visiting boats. In 2004 overnight mooring charge €8 including electricity. CA member and HLR Leigh Wootton lives near. Hire base for **France Afloat**, English owned (Mike and Lesley Gardener-Roberts, Stephen and Zoe Adams) with all facilities including washing machine, repairs, diesel, overwintering and WiFi. Also offers RYA approved training and testing for ICC with CEVNI rules endorsement. Tel 03 86 81 67 87.

Pk 151 Bollards R bank below bridge.

Mailly-la-Ville (pk 145) Halte nautique (2 pontoons) with water & electricity. Limited shops & restaurants. Swimming place in arm of river across lock. Mooring in basin downstream of town. Free WiFi at post office.

Pk 141.5 Bollards in basin, L bank.

Merry-sur-Yonne (pk 137.7) Small pontoon R bank. No facilities but restaurant close.

Pk 136.5 Bollards R bank above and below lock.

Châtel-Censoir (pk 133) Halte nautique and hire base. May be crowded at changeover times.

Lucy-sur-Yonne (pk 126) Bollards on L bank above and below bridge. L bank bollards 10m apart. Small village. No facilities.

Coulanges (pk 122.5) R bank basin above lock. Depth about 1.1m. No facilities. Supermarket in village.

Pousseaux (pk 121) Mooring in basin possible, but only 1m depth.

Clamecy (pk 114) Good port de plaisance above lock, with water, electricity, pump-out station and basic shower/toilet block. If full, moor to quay downstream of lock. €5 per night collected by municipal police. Small supermarket in town, larger one on outskirts. Launderette near cathedral.

Pk 111.5 Civil engineering works to create a new marina started several years ago but progress seemss to have stalled.

Chevroches (pk 110) Halte with water & electricity. In 2010, €10 barges, €5 for boats. *Auberge du Port* reportedly offers laundry service for yachts..

Pk 108 Bollards R bank before turning basin.

Villiers-sur-Yonne (pk 105.1) Slightly curving R bank quay with limited water & electricity.

Tannay (pk 96) Le Boat hire base. Diesel. Cost €11 per night in 2010 inclusive of water & electricity. Showers. Diesel. Restaurants in town (1 with WiFi) but no shops.

Pk 90.5 Mooring in basin. Water. Shops close by. Woodyard with water spray for timber which may encroach on boats.

Marigny-sur-Yonne (pk 84.4) Hire boat base now closed.

Chitry-les-Mines/Chaumot (pk 82) Port de plaisance. €3.50 for all size of boats, €3.50 electric, €2.00 for water. Summer guardiennage. Secure car park €3.30 per vehicle. Snack bar open Jul – Aug every day, May – Sept (closed Wed). Bread can be ordered from campsite over bridge. Trains to Paris and shops at Corbigny, 3km. Plans to lay new pontoons in 2012.
Marine Diesel Technical information and shop 200m from the port. Diesel no longer available but Ted Johnson & John Johnson offer a very comprehensive spares service. Parts carried include BMC, Leyland, Morse, Jabsco,Vetus, Whale, ZF, and many others, which can be shipped anywhere in France, or sent *Poste Restante* to a nominated post office for collection, and paid for by credit card. Tel 03 86 20 14 80 & Fax 03 86 20 14 84. Email: contact@marine-diesel.fr

Les Granges (pk 77.7) Recently built facility for hire base on R bank. All facilities. Temporarily closed in 2012 due to depth fluctuations, but due to re-open in 2013.

Sardy (pk 74) Flight of 16 locks, then 3 short unlit tunnels to the summit. Excellent scenery.

Pk 73.5 Office de Tourisme and WiFi in old lock cottage. Bollards in basin L bank. No facilities.

Baye (pk 66) Port de plaisance with all facilities. Can be very crowded. Alternative is 250m of concrete dyke with bollards and rings, a depth of over 1.5m, but no other facilities.
Aqua Fluvial (03 86 38 90 70) offers mobile breakdown and repair service.
The bridge at pk 62 is reported to be the lowest on this canal with 2.70m air draft.

Pk 62 Lowest bridge on this canal, 2m 50.

Châtillon-en-Bazois (pk 51) Halte nautique and hire base, with water & electricity. R bank in basin.

Pk 47.5 Two bollards L bank below bridge.

Fleury (pk 38.1) R bank above lock, bankside bollards almost opposite a *Crêperie*. Water, electricity & showers. Bar/restaurant at lock cottage.

Panneçot (Limanton)(pk 30) Poorly signposted port de plaisance in basin. Electricity, water, showers and pump-out station. Depth 1.2m. €8per night in 2010. No shops or restaurants shops in village.

Cercy-la-Tour (pk 16) Small basin R bank above lock is shallow. R bank 200m below lock are 50m of pontoons with 3 water & electricity points and over 1m depth.

Champvert (pk 4.9) Below lock R bank. Small quay. No bollards. Water. Toilet.

St-Léger-des-Vignes (pk 1.5) R bank wood faced concrete quay near supermarket and other shops.

Decize (pk 0) The Canal du Nivernais joins the Canal Latéral à la Loire by way of about 2km of the R Loire.
There are several mooring possibilities. (See also Canal Lateral à la Loire.)
- There is a buoyed channel running about 1km eastwards from the end of the Canal to a quay close to the centre of the town by the tourist office. Depth is about 1.2m at upstream end, and 1.5m at downstream end. Water & electricity.
- On the Loire R bank immediately upstream of the entrance to this channel is a 20m long quay with 1.8m depth, and about 800m upstream is a 75m quay with about 1.5m depth. There are also bollards both sides of the canal, set well back. No facilities.
- In the basin between the two locks at the end of the Canal Lateral à la Loire is a Hire base. Water, electricity, diesel, and 10 tonne crane. €11 for 10m boat in 2010.
- **Le Port de la Jonction** is a new marina also in this basin, which opened in July 2011. Secure access to pontoons, all facilities, launderette, WiFi, guardiennage, gîtes, hotel, restaurant, water gardens, etc. Boats up to 15m only. Tel: 03 86 25 27 23. email: portdecize@ccsn.fr.

Loire - The (unbuoyed) channel is close to the R bank (and these quays), until upstream of the road bridge, where it crosses to the L bank for the lock entrance. May close at times of flood.

BOURBONNAIS
Canal du Loing and Canal de Briare

St-Mammès to Briare	103km 50 locks	1.8m water 3.5m air	Fluviacarte/Navicarte 6 or 20 Vagnon 4 or Breil 2

There may be significant barge traffic in the length from St-Mammès to Souppes-sur-Loing. Several places where quays are reserved for hotel barges, e.g. Montargis, Rogny and Briare. Mooring is usually permitted when no hotel barges are scheduled. They have an agreed programme with the lock keepers. In some places their schedules are posted, and in others the halte staff or the local Bureau de Tourisme will have the schedule.
Canal de Briare, locks 1-18, 27-30 & 34 are automatic, remainder are manual. Scarcity of ladders and very deep. Lock keeper will have hook on line for ropes. Lock hours 09h00 – 12h00, 13h00 – 19h00. VNF Tel: 02 38 95 09 25
Canal du Loing lock hours 08h00 - 12h00, 13h00 – 18h00. All locks have waiting quays. Canal du Loing, emergency phone no. 01 64 28 02 36.

Repairs and chandlery (see individual entries for details)
St Mammès (pk 49.2), Rogny (pk 19), Briare.

St-Mammès (pk 49.2) See Upper Seine for moorings etc. beyond junction. Reported depth barely 1.8m, though mud bottom. R bank quay if space. Boat yard between St-Mammès and Moret-sur-Loing (M Rousseaux).

Moret-sur-Loing (pk 47) Picturesque small town where impressionist painter Alfred Sisley lived and worked, with Son et Lumière beside the river in summer. Small halte fluviale, L bank. below lock No. 19. 3 wooden jetties (20m) with 1.6 to 2.0m depth (downstream deepest). Water, electricity and.WiFi €10.60 1st night, less for subsequent nights. Showers in capitainerie. (2008) Bankside mooring is not easy but may be possible R bank above the second lock (no. 18) with 1.8m depth and cycle museum and supermarket close.

Pk 41 Stone quay with bollards above lock L bank.

Nemours (pk 30) Old halte nautique **CLOSED – ignore sign on bridge**, now on L bank above Lock 12, 1.8m depth. Notify Tourist Office of arrival, 01 64 28 03 95 and employee will arrive to connect electricity and give information about town (see notice on electricity post). Supermarket and launderette nearby.

Pk 25 Bollards L & R bank each side of Lock 10.

Pk 21 Small quay with bollards L bank above lock.

Sully (pk 18) Quay modernised and improved.

Souppes-sur-Loing (pk 18.6) Old quay of *sucrerie* now halte with water & electricity, depth 1.8m. In 2008 €7 per night, but not always collected outside high season. Very near factory, between bridge and conduit. Shops and restaurants in town 20 min walk over bridge. Internet at computer shop in square, WiFi at Hotel La Vielle Halle opposite.

Néronville (pk 15.7) Rural L bank mooring upstream of lock 7, depth 1.8m.

Dordives (pk 14.3). Mooring possible L bank upstream of bridge with good depth. Over bridge and into town for good restaurant at cross roads.

Pk 14 Long quay with rings on L bank.

Pk 10.3 Quay with bollards on L bank below Lock 5.

Pk 9 Long quay with bollards on L bank below Lock 4.

Pk 8 Bollards above lock, R bank.

Pk 7.9 Bollards above lock, R bank.

Pk 5 Bollards above lock, R bank.

Cépoy (pk 3) In 2011 mooring not available because of major bridge works. Normally long quay – difficult to spot - with electricity. Look out for light control on R bank for upstream traffic, not obvious.

Montargis (pk 52.3) Port de plaisance above lock 33 (La Marolle) which is close to picturesque town centre and has all facilities and 1.8m depth. The length between here and Briare is popular with hotel barges. In 2010 charges were €10 per night for 10m boat plus tax of €0.10 per person per night. SNCF station 25 mins. walk from Port. Laundrette nearby.
Also quayside mooring at upstream end of the commercial port at about pk 53.

Pk 45.8 At lock 31 (Sablonniere) lockside building houses small fairground organ which is sometimes played whilst boats lock through.

Pk 42.5 L bank mooring, No facilities.

Montcresson (pk 40.5) 40m concrete quay on R bank above bridge. No facilities.

Montbouy (pk 35) Attractive quay, depth about 1.7m, just N of lock 26. Water, electricity by jeton from Mairie or local shops. No longer toilets, showers. New mooring between bridge & lock but no facilities.

Pk 33.5 Pleasant mooring below lock 25.(Lépinoy) R bank.

Châtillon-Coligny (pk 29) Good halte with pump out, water, electricity showers and WiFi, but rather short wobbly pontoons. Small shop with local produce. Laundrette at campsite. Free in 2010 except for laundry and showers, but plans to charge in 2012. Depth 1.6-1.8. Room for 14 boats and 1 barge. Deeper draught boats can also use high quay just short of halte. Supermarket and all shops in town. Internet access at Tourist Offices at halte and in town.

Pk 23 R bank mooring with electricity above lock.

Rogny (pk 19) Halte on Quai Sully below lock 18. Water & electricity and shower/toilet block. €15 in 2011 inc. water & electricity by jeton from capitainerie. Toilet block appeared vandalised in 2011. Hotel boats have reservations at upstream end of quay. Depth 1.8m. Shops and restaurants near. See the disused flight of 7 locks built in the late 17th century. Also a paying halte/hire base in inlet just downstream of locks with diesel available. (End-on mooring may be necessary.) **Boat Engineering Services here.**

Rogny to Briare, locks automated, sometimes necessary to use intercom to call keeper.

Ouzouer-sur-Trézée (pk 8) Halte on L Bank downstream of lock 7. Water & electricity. Limited shops. Depth 1.5m. In chain of locks. Warn lock controller if stopping between locks.

Canal Latéral à la Loire

Briare to Digoin	196km, 37 locks	1.8m water 3.5m air	Fluviacarte/Navicarte 6 Breil 2 Vagnon 3

Occasional commercial or hotel *péniches*, but mostly hire boats. Some haltes & ports shown on charts were never built when money ran out! Most of locks operated manually.
Lock hours 09h00 – 12h00, 13h00 – 19h00 but in 2011 restricted opening hours to save water and boats were grouped together for passage through locks.

Repairs and chandlery (see individual entries for details)
Marseilles-lès-Aubigny (pk 124.5), Gannay-sur-Loire (pk 52.5), Briare.

Briare Very popular port de plaisance in the old canal which goes down (3 locks-electrified and manned) to the R Loire (no access). Recommend ringing ahead to book place. VHF 12, or 02 38 31 24 65. Mobile 06 08 95 03 20. Depth 1.2m in lower basin. Under new management but Bruno Chanal remains as capitaine. New quay alongside Socio-cultural centre open in 2011. All facilities including diesel and free WiFi. Several hire boat companies operate. Pleasant surroundings. Capitaine will take orders for bread and deliver next day. Supermarket in town will deliver to boats. Laundrette by bridge. Blue Flag. Alternative deeper mooring with water & electricity at pk 197.7 in the Bassin de Commerce just before the spectacular aqueduct over the Loire partly built by Gustave Eiffel. Hire boat base and hotel boats have priority on part of the quay, and their schedules are posted on a noticeboard.

Châtillon-sur-Loire (pk 192) Hire base and halte. Water, electricity, showers and good depth. Attractive town up hill with supermarket. Also sloping quay. €9 including water & electricity.

Pk 187 Prior to the opening of the Briare Aqueduct, the canal locked down to the west side of the Loire at Châtillon. A 4km section of this route has been restored, and is navigable by craft with a draught not exceeding 1.2m. Lock keepers should be given advance warning (Tel: 03 38 31 26 20 or 06 21 78 61 25 as at July 2004).

Beaulieu (pk 185) Good landscaped quay R bank. Water, electricity & showers shared with campsite over hedge. Depth about 1.5m. 400m of quay reserved for hotel boat on Tuesdays. Mooring points obscured by greenery.

Belleville (pk 179.5) Pleasant welcoming halte with water & electricity downstream of lock 37, depth 0.6m at upstream end increasing to 1.6m at downstream end. Also moorings above lock 37 with water & electricity – key from Information Office.

Sury-près-Léré (pk 177) L bank quay with water & electricity, and bakery near.

Léré (pk 175) Halte downstream of bridge on L bank at end of silo quay. Water & electricity. Depth 1.7m. Favourable reports of hotel/restaurant *Lion d'Or*. Shops in village.

Pk 169 Mooring basin with bollards, L bank. No facilities. Looked shallow.

Pk 165 Overgrown quay with posts L bank above lock. No facilities.

St-Thibault (pk 158) Port de plaisance de **St-Satur**. Don't be put off by narrow-looking entrance. Moorings in large basin. Depth about 1.4m. At the far end is a small dry dock for boats up to 1.2m draught. Water, limited electricity, laundrette and **fuel**. €12 in 2010 for 10m boat. Looking run down in 2011 and harbour master not available. Pleasant village on the edge of the Loire with several restaurants. '*Au Bord de la Loire*' recommended for both setting and food. The harbourmaster offers a shuttle mini bus to visit the spectacular hill top town of Sancerre - €7 per person (return).
Also quay further upstream L bank outside supermarket with **fuel**. No bollards and protruding reinforcing rod.

Ménétréol-sous-Sancerre (pk 157) Alternative mooring for Sancerre. Sloping quay at street level. Halte with water, showers & electricity. Depth at quay 1.5m. Electricity and water €6 (2011) key from La Florine. Bakery, bar and restaurant. Mooring noisy as close to main road, but attractive ancient village.
Pk 153 Mooring bollards in small basin L bank. No facilities.

Champlay (pk 148) Quay – L bank below lock. Water available.

Herry (pk 143) Quay for hotel barge, but room for other boats. Depth about 1.6m with 1.8m at north end. Water at south end. Tokens from boulangerie needed for water €0.50 for 50 litres.

From Herry to Marseilles les Aubigny some bridges have projections below the nominal 3.5m air draught.

La Chapelle-Montlinard (pk 137) Sloping quay alongside silo with electricity & water (by Carte Bleu only) €1 per hour. Depth 1.8m. Café de Port alongside – basic fare. Commune employee keeps port tidy and can be approached for help. La Charité-sur-Loire worth visiting (Taxi or cycle ride or ½ hr. walk).. Numbers of taxi firms and commerces posted in office windows. In 2011 this rather unwelcoming quay looked as though it was being improved.

Pk 134 Quay below lock R bank opposite hotel sign.

Ecluse 27 - Beffes (pk 128) report that sill depth upstream of lock barely 1.8m after water level had fallen due to heavy traffic during day. No mooring facilities here but 2 bollards above lock, R bank. Shops in town.

Marseilles-lès-Aubigny (pk 125.5) Boatyard just below lock 26 with water, electricity, showers & diesel. Tel 02 48 76 14 40.
(pk 125) Municipal halte with water & electricity in basin above lock 25 (€4.50 per night in 2009 payable at Mairie, or Alimentation opposite). WiFi signal. Supermarket and 2 small shops 3km. away. Bread from Mairie in mornings. Limited space.
(pk 124.5) Small boatyard.
(pk 123.5) Bankside moorings that seem to be run by English residents and taken up by barges.

Cours-les-Barres (pk 120) Attractive quay with water, electricity (long lead with 2 pin plug connector), basic showers & toilets. Pretty town with boulangerie, restaurant and Tourist Office (open 09h00 – 10h00, 15h00-18h00). Reported depth 1.5m.

Le Guétin (pk 111) Very deep double lock (no 21-22) and aqueduct over the R Allier.
Good deep-water quay on L bank just below locks with good auberge, close to le Bec d'Allier, and Apremont-sur-Allier – worth visiting for gardens and restored village. Also mooring at grassy bank under the bridge in disused canal L bank downstream of locks, but enter slowly, checking depth.

Plagny (pk 103) Hire boat base, 2 pontoons & bankside mooring. Depth 1.5m but 1.8m outside pontoons. Large supermarket 2km. Taxi to Nevers €10, or use regular bus service

Nevers (pk 100.5) Port with good facilities in large basin 1.7km and 2 locks down branch from pk 100.5. If approaching from upstream cord to pull for lock is past the entrance. Attractive town centred on the opposite bank of the Loire - film buffs will recall it from *Hiroshima Mon Amour*. Swimming pools closed.

Fleury-sur-Loire (pk 81) A pleasant quiet halte with water, electricity, showers and snack bar. Depth 1.2m. In 2008 no charge for mooring, but €2 for water & electricity.

Avril-sur-Loire (pk 76). Halte. Water tap behind hedge.

Decize (pk 68.5) Junction with the Canal du Nivernais. Just before the junction on the R bank is a good quay with water and a halte convenient for supermarket and laundrette. Deep draught craft may be able to moor to barge on VNF quay outside. VNF suggest donation. For other mooring possibilities see earlier notes about Decize under Canal du Nivernais.

Gannay-sur-Loire (pk 52.5) Hire base & halte, with water, electricity, showers and launderette on L bank just above lock 12 (Vanneaux). Depth 1.5m. Tel 04 70 43 49 27. The Chef de Base is English and offers limited repair service. Book swap, or buy for €1..

Pk 41.5 Quay with 2 bollards.

Garnat-sur-Engièvre (pk 40.5) Halte just below lock 9. Water. Depth about 1.8m. Small village with shops. 2 bollards at restaurant, La Grenouille, above bridge.

Beaulon (pk 37) Halte with water, 1km from shops and restaurants. Electricity points are shared with an adjacent site for camper vans.

Dompierre-sur-Besbre (pk 29) Halte at end of lock free 3km branch. Depth 1.2m. Free. Also hire base with occasional space for visitors. Water at both.

Diou (pk 25) R bank 40m quay with water point. Depth 1.5m but shallows rapidly at ends. Small supermarket close.

Pierrefitte-sur-Loire (pk 19) L bank halte with water (no screw thread on tap). Depth 1.1m.

Coulanges (pk 14.5) R bank halte close to village, water. Depth 1.6m.

Molinet (pk 8) Small quay with water, and depth 1.1m but shallower patches close by. Near to busy road.

Digoin (pk 4) Junction with the Canal de Roanne à Digoin is at pk 6. Over the aqueduct, at pk 3.6, the port de plaisance & hire base, with all facilities including diesel and showers. Priority for hire boats on L bank. Traffic noise from busy road bridge. Depth 1.8m on pontoons. €5 per night + electricity €2.7 (2009). Tel 03 85 88 97 26. Camping Gaz from Intermarché 100m north on bridge road. Also several quays/bankside moorings.with less depth. The aqueduct over the Loire and its approaches need dredging, with depth barely 1.8m. 'ObservaLoire' exhibition centre close to aqueduct worth visiting. Good reports of the *Hotel de la Gare*.

Canal de Roanne à Digoin

Digoin to Roanne	56km 10 locks	1.8m water 3.45m air	*Fluviacarte/Navicarte 6 or 19 Breil 2*

Not part of route but has little traffic. Worth a detour.

La Croix-Rouge (pk 49) Rural halte with depth 1.4m and basic restaurant close.

Bonnand (pk 43.2) Halte but very shallow (0.7m).

Avrilly (pk 38.6) L bank quay just upstream of bridge has 1.8m depth.

Arlaix (pk 30) Halte with showers, toilets & picnic table.

Melay (pk 26) Halte with water.

Le Dépôt (pk 31) Quay with derelict water & electricity.points.

Briennon (pk 15) Port de plaisance - water, electricity and diesel. 1st night free.Tel 04 77 69 92 92.

Roanne (pk 0) Large port de plaisance. All facilities. Popular wintering place with very low mooring charges; usually fully booked by preceeding August. Tel 04 77 23 02 13.

Canal du Centre

Digoin to Chalon	112km 61 locks	1.8m water, 3.45 air	Fluviacarte/Navicarte 6 or 19 Breil 2

The canal meanders through pleasant rolling countryside, with vineyards rarely far from sight. There is still a small amount of commercial traffic, about which lock keepers will usually warn you. Some of the locks are automatic. It is essential to enter and leave slowly. Some locks are full to overflowing, so low fendering is needed. In 2011 lock hours were 09h00 to 19h00 with no lunch break. (See also Locks in Cruising Details).

Two types of lock a) 2.5m rise and b) approx 5m rise. Latter have floating bollards but these don't keep pace with water and lines go slack at times of greatest turbulence. Mooring to central bollard not satisfactory, best to moor to 2 bollards if space. Starting mechanism contains 2 ropes – blue to start and red to stop but colours difficult to discern because of weed. Ladder not always by mechanism. If crew member can be spared to go ahead, this may be best arrangement. Automation of locks in process 2009.

Lift bridges upstream of Montceau-les-Mines controlled by bridge keeper and camera with no pull ropes.

Repairs and chandlery (see individual entries for details)
Montchanin (pk 51.8)

Paray-le-Monial 2 haltes, the first at pk 103.5 shallow, with bollards only. Second at pk 101.5 alongside parkland below lock 23. Water & electricity on quay, shower block down bank on edge of park. Depth 1.8m. €12 per night including water & electricity (2011). Shops. Good rail links. In July & August town hosts pilgrimage. Pilgrim activity in park with tents and singing.

Pont de Bord (pk 98) possible R bank mooring with stakes. Bins and picnic tables.

Palinges (pk 85) L bank quay with bollards and no other facilities.

Génélard (pk 82) Basin below lock 16, both banks have quays with electricity & water, free in 2009. Bollards very widely spaced. Depths R bank 1.5 to 1.8m and L bank 1.8m. SNCF railway station. "Centre d'Interpretation de la Ligne de Démarcation" beside basin (museum of the wartime division of France). Château de Digoine at pk 88 worth a 7km cycle ride.

Montceau-les-Mines (pk 64) Formerly a heavy industrial area, now being extensively redeveloped and has good shops in town centre. Port de plaisance with water, electricity, toilets and showers. €7.55 per night for 15m boat + €2.55 for water & electricity (2006) No charge made in 2011. Tel 03 85 69 00 00. Good depth, 1.8m off outer pontoons, shallowing to about 1m close to quayside. Market on quay on Tuesdays & Saturdays. Be aware of Disco opposite the moorings open Thurs – Sun evenings until 06h00. Complaints of minor vandalism.

Blanzy (pk 61) R bank upstream of road bridge. Pleasant 50m quay with water, electricity.

Montchanin (pk 51.8) Montchanin Marine just above écluse Ocean 1 on summit level. Appeared closed and abandoned in 2011. Bollards on opposite bank outside VNF offices, but no facilities. Supermarket near and 2km from nearest TGV station with fast service to Paris or Lyon. English speaking marine engineer, **Jeffrey Rénèl,** offers spares procurement, repairs & gardiennage. Tel 06 33 43 20 42.

There are no other satisfactory mooring places on the summit level.

Ecluse 6 Motte (pk 45.8) Quay above lock, good depth, opposite canal museum, no facilities.

St-Julien-sur-Dheune (pk 44) R bank halte with 30m quay, 4 bollards and picnic table. Depth 1.1m. Restaurant & pleasant walk up to lake that feeds the canal.

St-Bérain-sur-Dheune (pk 36) halte with bollards and picnic tables. Good depth.

St-Léger-sur-Dheune (pk 33) Hire boat base plus quay for 3-4 boats. Water, electricity and a pump-out facility. €12 per night for 12m in on bankside moorings includes water, electricity and shower (digicode) Depth from 1.8m – 1m. by entrance to small basin.

The St-Léger bridge and the next two downstream are several cm lower than the nominal 3.5m of the standard *péniche* canals, which is why we indicate that this route is limited to 3.45m air draught. The L bank a few hundred metres downstream of the bridge permits mooring with about 1.4m depth.

Cheilly (pk 26.2) Basic halte .

Santenay (pk 24) Basic but peaceful halte between locks 23 and 24, with 30m quay, good depth, picnic table and attractive views. Popular with hotel barges.

Some local wine *caves* will deliver to boat.

Chagny (pk 19) Good quay in old canal basin with good depth. Water & limited electricity. Base for several hotel barges. Shops and restaurants 5 min walk. An important commercial centre of the Burgundy wine trade. Large market on Sundays.

Rully (pk 16.5) Basic halte between locks 26 and 27.

Fragnes (pk 8) L bank 300m downstream of lock 34. Halte with water & electricity. 1.8m depth over 80m of gravelled quay, and for about 12m farther at each end. Cost €6.20 per night in 2011 for 12m boat, inclusive of water & electricity. Good showers for €1.20. Boulangerie and restaurant, closed in early season. Small market on Saturday.

Chalon-sur-Saône Junction with the R Saône, 2km north of Chalon. For Port see R Saône.

BURGUNDY
Canal de Bourgogne

Laroche to St-Jean-de-Losne	242km 189 locks	1.4m water 3.1m air	*Fluviacarte/Navicarte 18 Breil 3 Vagnon 3*

Evidence of improved maintenance in this canal in 2012 - renewed locks and strengthened banks. The canal used to have a depth of 1.8m, but it is currently reduced to 1.4m to reduce leakage on the summit level and in addition the length south east of Dijon is in need of dredging, so there seems little prospect of 1.8m being restored in the near future. Weed cutting is in operation frequently. Check canal conditions with the VNF Office in Dijon, Tel 03 80 29 44 44.

Emergency phone numbers for the canal – Dijon 03 80 53 16 30, Tonnerre 03 86 54 82 70, Montbard (Côte d'Or) 03 80 92 54 50. Lock hours 09h00-12h00, 13h00-19h00 including Sundays. See also www.burgundy-canal.com

Locks numbered in both directions from the summit level. A few locks on the Yonne side of the summit converted to automatic operation with keeper. Locks 100 & 101 near Flogny are operated by one keeper and there can be long delays at peak periods.
Hotel barges are frequently found between Dijon and Vandenesse (pk 163) and between Pouillenay (pk 120) and the junction with the Yonne. They travel slowly and take priority at locks and on quays. They leave port on Monday mornings with stops at Fleury, Gissey, La Bussière and Pont d'Ouche, arriving in final port for Friday, Saturday and Sunday. Most pilots and crews are English speaking.
There are many hire boats during the holiday season. A few commercial barges operate between the Yonne and Tonnerre, and between Dijon and the Saône.

Quayside moorings with water and rubbish bins are reasonably frequent but check the depth when approaching quays as they are often silted up.

Tyre fenders – Discouraged when passing through locks. Risk of a big bill if a tyre falls off and a diver has to remove or recover it.

Repairs and chandlery (see individual entries for details)
Laroche-Migennes (pk 0), St-Jean-de-Losne (pk 242)

Good rail links (TGV) at Laroche-Migennes and Dijon for crew changes.

Laroche-Migennes (pk 0) Mooring in basin above the first (deep) lock, close to busy railway junction. Hire boat base. All facilities including showers, fuel, washing machine. €4.50 water and €4.50 electricity in 2011. Supermarkets in town with fuel. (See also in section on R Yonne for boatyard, repairs & chandlery). Internet café – 400m upstream at Auberge de la Poste – cost €4 per hour in 2008, and free WiFi in computer shop.

Pk 6 Bas d'Esnon. Pretty quay with bollards by restaurant. R bank. No facilities. Wine cave.

Pk 8 Bollards above lock.

Brienon-sur-Armançon (pk9)
- Hire boat base alongside port, downstream of bridge. Depth over 1.3m.
- New port de plaisance, €10 including water & electricity (2012). Showers €2. Washing machine €6. Dryer €6. WiFi. Supermarket and butcher across road. Other shops and restaurant close. Attractive town.
- Free moorings on L bank.

St-Florentin (pk 19) Port de plaisance and hire base with 10 tonne crane. France Afloat are meant to be taking over in August 2012. €6 incl. water & electricity. (Showers etc. available when changeover takes place.)
Also possible L bank mooring under trees below lock but no facilities. Attractive town with shops and launderette up hill.

Pk 22 Bollards above lock and 0.5km upstream stone quay with bollards.

Germigny (pk 21.8) Good quay with rings on R bank. Village with restaurant and boulangerie close by. Only one chamber of former double lock in use, depth 5.4m.

Pk 27.2 Restaurant quay R bank, 1m. depth.

Pk 28 Bollards above lock, R bank.

Flogny (pk 31) Good R bank quay with water but only 0.9m depth. Boulangerie in village.

Charrey (pk 34.7) The R bank basin in front of the striking old canal building (recently converted into flats) has no facilities, but good depth (1.7m).

Tonnerre (pk 44.5) Port de plaisance, Tel 03 86 55 00 94. Good quay with water & electricity but shortage of rings and electricity points. €8.60 for 10m in 2012. Interesting small town. Water level fluctuates, and deeper draught craft need to allow for this when mooring. Watch rocks/depth at end nearest Lock 96Y. Small hire base. Market on Saturday in town.

Pk 47 Bollards L bank

Pk 51.5 Two bollards R bank below bridge, and R bank above bridge.

Tanlay (pk 53) 80m stone quay at which hotel barges have priority over middle part. Free halte with water & electricity and basic showers, and another quay without facilities opposite. Good recycling facilities. Bar/restaurant at end of quay. Beautiful chateau at centre of town. Shops including good bricolage, and small supermarket.

St-Vinnemer (pk 56.5) Bollards on R bank, depth uncertain.

Lézinnes (pk 63.4) Bollards on L just after lock 85Y. Watch depth. Another mooring L bank upstream of lock.

Ancy-le-Franc (pk 74) Good 30m quay with water & electricity. Depth 1m upstream, and 1.5m downstream. Hotel boat has priority on Tue, Wed & Thur. Bollards on bank opposite. Shops & restaurants in town. Magnificent Renaissance château.

Ravières (pk 82.7) Good 90m stone quay with free water & electricity, basic toilet and shower block. Depth varies between 1m and 1.5m. Small supermarket and other shops in village about 800m up hill by church. Restaurant (Tante Lisette) at southern end of quay, closed Sun. Mon & Thurs evenings. VNF depot at end of quay has used oil disposal facilities.

Cry (pk 86.9) R Bank basin with picnic table. Depth 1m. Possible water.

Pk 95.7 La Grande Forge. Tourist attraction with good quay and bollards. No facilities.

Montbard (pk 102)
- In the basin below lock 64 is a 70m quay with 2 pontoons (one with priority access for disabled), water & electricity. €10 in 2012. Bicycle hire. Locaboat have a temporary hire boat base here for 2012 & 2013 which may become permanent because of difficulties with water levels in the Canal du Nivernais
- Long quay in basin above the lock. Water & electricity. €15 in 2012. Shops, restaurants and supermarket close. SNCF station 5 min walk with occasional TGVs to Paris. Laundrette 10-15 mins away. Friday market beside supermarket near lock 64.

Vedette service from station to tourist attractions from July 1st.

Venarey-les-Laumes (pk 116) Basin and low stone quay administered by Nicols. €3 for water, €3 for electricity in 2012. Showers and toilet block administered by commune, not open in June 2012. Part of quay owned by barge Horizon, check arrival dates on noticeboard. No shops in Venarey. Good supermarket, shops, banks and railway station in Les-Laumes – 20 min walk. Reasonable restaurant *L'Hydomel* on road to Les Laumes. .

Pouillenay (pk 120) Quay on L bank with water (apply at the Mairie). Pleasant village with one of the *Plus Beaux Villages de France,* Flavigny-sur-Ozerain, 5km up hill (used in film 'Chocolat').

Marigny-le-Cahouët (pk 125.7) Bankside mooring, L bank above lock 27. Under 1m depth. No electricity. Water at lock. Excellent restaurant in old lock-keeper's cottage (lock26), catering for 6 or 8, booking necessary.

Pont-Royal (pk 137) Stone quay but beware shallow section Watch slipway half way along. Water & electricity – apply at La Maison du Canal opposite or phone 03 80 84 28 27/06 62 14 43 76. myswelle@live.fr. Bread can be ordered. Cost of mooring varies with length. In 2012 €3 per stay for 10m, €3 for electricity, and €3 for water. Bus to Semur from opposite the restaurant.

Gissey (pk 148) Bollards in basin, R bank. No facilities.

Pouilly-en-Auxois (pk 155) Port de plaisance with long quay. Water & electricity. Washing machine €4, dryer €4 and showers €1 at capitainerie. In 2012 mooring + water €3 per night for 10m boat + €3 for electricity. €3.50 over 12m. WiFi. Supermarket with fuel at 200m. and small town with shops and restaurants 1.5km north.

This is the summit level and the start of the 3.3km long tunnel, height 3.1m. You must book your time of passage with the lock keeper who will ensure that nothing is coming the other way and will want to see your lights and life-jackets as well as issuing a radio and permit to be handed in at the first lock after the tunnel. The tunnel is now lit but only southern half was functioning in May/June 2012. The roof is lower inside than at the entrance and the sides curve so it is important to keep in mid-channel. Use of CCTV system allows controller to track passage of boats during transit. Boards recommended for protection against safety line on northern wall.

Escommes (pk 160) R bank quay with water & electricity.

Vandenesse-en-Auxois (pk 163) Mooring in canal basin in beautiful surroundings. Water & electricity (both €4in 2012) collected by Mairie (ignore sign on post). Bread can be ordered from Salon de Thé (Charolly) 03 80 49 22 71, closed Wednesdays. Depth between 1m and 1.4m. Visit village of Châteauneuf with its castle on a hill overlooking the canal, another of the *Plus Beaux Villages de France*.

From here to Dijon the canal runs down the lovely valley of the R Ouche.

Ste-Sabine (pk 166.3) Grassy quay close to restaurant, above bridge. No bollards.

Crugey (pk 169.5) Quay in basin with bollards. No facilities.

Pont-d'Ouche (pk 173) Port de plaisance, *Chez Bryony,* (06 13 37 13 08) with 6m finger pontoons and bankside mooring for barges. English owner has basic foodstuffs on sale, bread to order, and small café/bar. In 2012 - €6.80 per night for mooring on pontoons, including water & electricity. Toilets. Washing machine €3.60, dryer €3.00, showers €2.60. Book exchange. Guardiennage €3 per night. Bike hire. Restaurant, L'Auberge du Renard, with WiFi, over bridge. Bus to Dijon, and to Bliny (nearest supermarket, and market on Wednesday mornings) also doctor, pharmacy and vet.
Bankside moorings upstream of bridge and downstream of aqueduct (hotel boats have priority).

Pk 173.25 Quay with posts and water, L bank.

Veuvey-sur-Ouche, (pk 176) L bank quay with rings. No facilities.

La Bussière-sur-Ouche (pk 180) Good mooring above lock. Below lock mooring for hotel boats only. Village shops, boulangerie at 100m. Cistercian Abbey converted to 1* Michelin restaurant, run by English couple. Commonwealth war grave in part of cemetery containing graves of 8 crew of a Lancaster bomber which was shot down in the hills near here.

Pk 181.5 Bollards L bank below lock.

St-Victor-sur-Ouche (pk 182.5) Mooring posts on R bank after bridge – watch depth. No facilities.

Gissey-sur-Ouche (pk 186) Halte on R bank, but may be filled by 'live aboard' *péniches*. No facilities. Mooring posts on L before bridge but watch depth.

Ecluse du Banet (pk 189) at Lock 34. Long R bank quay with electricity. €3.50 electricity. Mooring free for 1 night, second night €3. Former lock cottage converted into restaurant, with small shop and bread to order, gîte and bicycle hire. Water by arrangement. Restaurant closed on Tues and Wed.

Pont de Pany (pk 193) Quay. Restaurant.

Fleurey-sur-Ouche (pk 197.4) Free moorings between lock 42S and bridge. No facilities but water tap on R just after lock.

Velars-sur-Ouche (pk 201.8) Good mooring on posts above lock and on rings at quay below lock Supermarket 3 mins away, with fuel.

Bruant (pk 208.5) Bollards on L bank before lock.

Plombières (pk 207) On R bank is quay with no facilities except picnic tables. Hire boat base closed and facilities vandalized. Electricity available with difficulty.

Dijon (pk 212) Port de plaisance and hire base in canal basin liable to be crowded and expensive. Hazardous, wobbly pontoons with sharp metal ends. (Repairs promised in 2012) Water & electricity. Showers from July to Aug. Cost varies with length, and in 2012 was €11.60 (10m) per night inclusive of water & electricity. Reports of bicycle thefts from boats and general mischief, e.g. flower displays from boats thrown into water. Boulangerie across bridge to south, butcher and good supermarket 100m further on. Large city with fine public buildings and TGV rail services.

Pk 215. Mooring at loading quay. No facilitieis.

Pk 224. Mooring on bollards. No facilities. Picnic tables. Shops.

Longecourt-en-Plaine (pk 228.3) Free mooring posts L bank downstream of Lock 69S.

Brazey-en-Plaine (pk 237.4) Quiet, free mooring R bank in basin below lock 74S. No facilities. Large supermarket, post office, and other shops in village (5 mins walk).

St-Jean-de-Losne (pk 242) Mooring is possible in basin before last lock. More facilities including diesel just below lock on R Saône. (See **R Saône**.)

MARNE
River Marne

| Paris to Epernay | 178km 18 locks | 1.8m water 4.4m air | Fluviacarte/Navicarte) 3 Breil 19 or Chagnon formerly Vagnon) 4. |

The first part of the river includes two man-made cuts, each about 10km long, and two short tunnels. Communities along the Marne are working to make the river an attractive cruising area with a number of new pontoons between Paris and Meaux in 2010 and 2011. Above Meaux the scenery is more varied and the river becomes very pleasant. Most locks are electrified; the three nearest to Dizy have sloping sides but most with floating pontoons or bollards. Locks 1 – 10 remote controlled pick up télécommande at either end. Many locks now use VHF. Enquire at first lock for up to date details.

Repairs and chandlery (see individual entries for details)
Hire base at La-Ferté-sous-Jouarre (pk 90)

Maisons-Alfort (pk 176.5) Halte nautique on L bank above St-Maurice lock. Shops near. In 2006 water & electricity not working.

Joinville-le Pont (pk 174) Mooring possible in unprepossessing basin between tunnel & lock 17. Above the lock is a municipal port with large new pontoons installed in 2007. Water, electricity, pump-out etc. Tel 06 11 71 83 00.

Nogent-sur-Marne (pk 171) Good port de plaisance with all facilities.
Tel 01 48 71 41 65 or 06 07 62 94 01. Fax 01 48 71 44 39. Advance booking recommended as visitors pontoon occupied by liveaboards and no access to shore from pontoons without key.

Neuilly-sur-Marne (pk 165) Municipal Port de plaisance on R bank just upstream of entrance to lock 16. Tel 01 43 08 51 35. All facilities except fuel. Tel 01 43 08 21 21.
Also good bank mooring above lock.

Vaires-sur-Marne (pk 157.5) Quay and pontoon shown in Navicarte are not there.
Depth on lock downstream waiting pontoon <1.0m.

Lagny (pk 151.5) Port du Touring Club de France, refurbished in 2006 with water & electricity upstream of bridge. Also good pontoon moorings and quay L bank between the 2 bridges. Bus stop for Eurodisney close!

Lesches, lock 13 – shallow patch 1.0m on inside of the turn when approaching from downstream.

Esbly (pk 142.3) L Bank – new halte in entrance to disused side arm. Depth uncertain.

Pk 142.5 R Bank quay close to shops with fuel station at 100yds.

Meaux (pk 134.5) Halte nautique above lock no 12 in the barrage loop of the river just above the old bridge, ignoring 'No Entry' sign. Pleasant surroundings. Convenient for town. Useful hourly bus to Charles de Gaulle airport from station. Electricity at €4.50 per night.

Basse-Ferme (pk 128.7) Halte at quay of old lock – rural & no facilities.

Poincy (pk 125.1) Harbour with Michelin listed restaurant close.

Mary-sur-Marne (pk 111) Pontoon & quay, R bank close to railway bridge.

St-Jean-les-Deux-Jumeaux (pk 100) Good quay above lock 10, shallow 0.5m. Village shops 1km. Pontoon at downstream end of island with water & electricity.

La Ferté-sous-Jouarre (pk 90) L bank quay with depth ca 1.8m by supermarket, so beware submerged trolleys. At **pk 90.1** is a small Halte nautique R bank behind island upstream of the two bridges. 1.4m at entrance shallowing to less than 1m.
At **pk 91** new pontoons with electricity downstream of the Pont de l'Europe, by the confluence of a small river, shallow <1.2m . Hire boat base with pontoons. Access across current difficult when current running.

Courtaron (pk 87) L bank quay above lock 9. Rural.

Nanteuil (pk 74) Good quay R bank above bridge, water & electricity. New pontoon (2012) with water & electricity. Auberge and village close.

Charly (pk 66.5) Good R bank quay between the bridge and lock 7. Auberge on quay. Supermarket with fuel ½km.

Nogent-l'Artaud (pk 63.4) Small halte nautique L bank above bridge. Get key for water & electricity from Railway Station!

Château-Thierry (pk 50) Stone quay with less than 1.5m, no facilities. Better mooring at closed hire base on R bank. Shops and restaurants near. Fine view from ruined château.

Mont St-Père (pk 42) Good quay R bank above lock 5.

Mézy-sur-Seine (pk 41) Good quay wooden quay.

Jaulgonne (pk 37) Halte with water & electricity,key from Mairie. Bar/tabac with limited menu in town.

Courcelles (pk 30) Lock 4 mechanised. Waiting quay above lock.

Dormans (pk 26.4) New municipal pontoons but limited spaces. €7 for 12m boat in 2012.. Quay with water & electricity on R bank upstream of bridge, adjacent to camping site. Little used L bank silo quay also available.
Good place for visiting the WWI memorial (one of 4). Informative and worth the walk – reportedly more uplifting than Verdun.

Pk 17.7 Locks 3, 2 and 1 all have sloping sides and are provided with floating pontoons.

Vandières (pk 17.7) Good waiting pontoon (>1.5m) and picnic area.

Reuil (pk 11.8) Halte with water & electricity, long cable needed. R bank downstream of bridge. Café/bar in village.

Port-à-Binson (pk 15) L bank pontoon next to park (1.5m).

Pk 8 Rural quay downstream of lock (1.5m)

Damery (pk 5.5) Pontoon with water & electricity. Theft from boat reported here.

Pk 3 Rural quay upstream of lock 1 (1.5m).

Cumières (pk 1.7) Free pontoon for 3 boats with water & electricity.

Epernay The Canal Latéral à la Marne branches off left at Dizy lock but river is navigable a further 5km to Epernay. About 1km up river from the canal junction, L bank are moorings in front of a sports centre Further upstream there are shallows between the L bank and the island. Just below town bridge on L bank is a hypermarket with fuel outside which it is possible to moor. Depth varies from 1.2m to 2.0m, and there is little to tie to, so mooring spikes will be necessary. 700m further upstream, is the Société Nautique d'Epernay, port de plaisance with welcoming capitainerie. Bread delivery in morning and free *apero* on first night. Good security and space for vehicle parking. Except at times of flood this is a good place to leave a boat for a few days or even weeks. Tel 03 26 54 90 47. Fuel from small tanker. Shops, restaurants and many world-famous champagne cellars 10 mins walk. Good rail link to Paris.

Canal Latéral à La Marne

Epernay to Vitry le François	66km, 15 locks	1.8m water 3.5m air	*Fluviacarte/Navicarte 3 Breil 19*

Inspector Maigret fans should note that Georges Simenon who cruised the French canals extensively around 1930 set 'Le Charretier de la Providence' (English translation as 'The Crime at Lock 14') on this stretch of canal. The first murder took place L bank about 200m upstream of the first lock and the denoument above the lock at Vitry. Many locks automated with a mix of radar and poles to twist. (See **Locks**). A lot of commercial traffic. From Châlons to Vitry all locks are automatic and function every day.

Mareuil-sur-Ay (pk 59) Paying halte on R bank. Good depth. Water, electricity, showers & laundrette. Pleasant surroundings & supermarket close. €9.90 over 10m in 2011. New quay between Mareuil and lock L bank before waiting pontoon (1.5m)

Bisseuil (pk 55.5) Quay.

Tours (pk 53) Quay above lock close to restaurant.

Condé-sur-Marne (pk 49) Junction with Canal de l'Aisne à la Marne. Halte. Electricity and water. Crowded but there is also room on silo quay and alongside the bank just after the halte towards lock.

Châlons-en-Champagne, (pk 32) formerly **Châlons-sur-Marne** and many signs unchanged. New municipal halte off main navigation, opened 2011. Water, electricity, showers etc. Open summer only. Interesting town with fine cathedral.

Chepy (pk 23.5) Rural mooring with picnic tables.

Pogney (pk 18) Public quay.

La Chausée-sur-Marne (pk 14) Moor to R bank above bridge. Pleasant village with basic food shop and restaurant.

Soulanges (pk 9) Quay L bank above lock 4.

Vitry-le-François
- Just above Vitry lock the canal forks left. The right fork leads to a dead end with long quay where mooring is possible if not full up with barges.
- After 2km there is a T-junction with the Canal de la Marne au Rhin to the left . Turn right into the small port de plaisnce (pk 0) with 1.5m depth and space for 10 boats up to12m. Water, electricity, rubbish, and showers. Very tight for manoeuvring. Convenient for town centre with shops, restaurants and main-line railway station.

Canal entre Champagne et Bourgogne (formerly Canal de la Marne à la Saône)

| Vitry to Heuilley | 224km 114 locks | 1.8m water 3.5 air | Fluviacarte/Navicarte 198 |

Little traffic, perhaps about 1 *péniche* per day. South of the Balesmes Tunnel, some locks are being automated. Others are worked by travelling lock operators and for these you will be asked to state for the following day when you wish to start and how far you intend to go. It is important to stick to your plan; otherwise you may miss your turn and have to wait a long time. If you intend to stop in a chain of automatic locks you should keep the VNF/lockkeepers informed. A few locks fill to overflowing – set fenders low and be ready to fend off. Good mooring places on this canal are scarce because of the bad state of the banks. Few of the locks have water – in May 2005, only no. 22 and possibly no. 29.

Main line railway stations at Vitry-le-François and Langres.

Good mooring quay upstream of lock 68 Ecriennes (1.6m).

Orconte (pk 13.5) Good paying halte above lock 66, with water electricity and showers. Person who takes the money will unlock the showers.

St-Dizier (pk 30) Just below lock 59 (La Noue) small port de plaisance and boatyard with chandlery in basin, with 1.5m depth. (Reported closed in 2012). Better depth at long free quay just above lock 58 (St-Dizier) and good quay opposite Centre Nautique after lock 58. Industrial surroundings but reasonably close to town with shops and restaurants.

Ancerville (pk 36.5) R bank mooring with 1.5m after lock 56 but opposite disco – no good at week-ends.

Chamouilley (pk 38.5) Wooden quay on R bank between bridges, approx. 1.5m depth. Lots of weed but good stop. Another quay on L bank downstream of lock 55.

Bayard-sur-Marne (pk 46.3) Concrete quay upstream of lock 52 (need stakes) and another upstream of lifting bridge (need stakes).

Chevillon (pk 51) Low quay downstream of lock 50 (need stakes). Lock 50 has a water hose. Restaurant near.

Autigny-le-Grand (pk 56.5) Concrete quay upstream of lock 47. Bollards and picnic table.

Joinville (pk 63) First quay on R bank belongs to the gîte but offers overnight stops, water & electricity, showers, laundry. Town halte a bit further on with water & electricity, pay at machine.

Donjeux (pk 72) Concrete quay with water & electricity. Shops and bar in Rouvray (800m)

Villers-sur-Marne (pk 77.9) Picnic halte L bank.

Froncles (pk 84) Halte nautique with water & electricity and laundry. Range of shops and restaurant within 1km.

Vouécourt (pk 89.7) Picnic halte downstream of lock 34.

Viéville (pk 93.2) Halte with water & electricity. (Note halte is upstream of lifting bridge, not downstream as indicated in Fluviacarte).

Riaucourt (pk 101.5) Small quay by old dove-cote on R bank.

Chaumont (pk 109) Paying halte. All facilities including laundrette. Restaurant near. Steep 20 mins walk up leafy lane to town centre with station. Supermarket and bricolage nearer.

Foulain (pk 125) Mooring R bank between locks 16 and 17. Water. Depth about 1.2m. Restaurant and a few shops in village.

Rolampont (pk 139) Free halte. Toilets, water & electricity.

Langres (pk 149) Free halte between locks 2 and 3, with 110m of stone quay and about 1.2m depth. Limited electric sockets, just 2 at each end of quay, but rather more water points.

Main line railway station 10 min walk from quay. Beautiful old walled town 3km up steep hill or bus from station. Fine 12th century cathedral. Good shops and restaurants, some close.

Peigney (pk 151) New picnic halte (2012). Hotel/restaurant nearby.

From here to the Saône (74km 44 locks) there are practically no facilities. Most villages very small and have no shops but there are lots of bankside stopping places.

Balesmes. The tunnel starts about 5km beyond Langres. In principle there is one-way traffic at fixed times, but when traffic permits the lock keepers can give permission to pass through at any time. Do not attempt to go through without checking!

Heuilley-Cotton (pk 162) L bank mooring above lock 1, depth 15m.

Villeguisen (pk 167.5) Good L bank mooring above lock 9. 100m quay with rings. Depth 2m. Boulangerie van calls at 09h00 in village.

Piépape (pk 169.5) R bank above lock 12. 35m quay, 1.2m depth. Bakery/general store 5 min in village.

Dommarien (pk 174) Small stone quay that may be occupied by fishermen. No facilities.

Cusey (pk 181.5) L bank quay after bridge with water & electricity. Contribution if asked.

Pk 190 Silo quay.

La Villeneuve-sur-Vingeanne (pk 192) Possible mooring by old silo, R bank between locks 27 and 28. Quay 40m long, depth 1.5m. No facilities.

Pouilly-sur-Vingeanne (pk 195) superb rural village.

St-Seine-sur-Vingeanne (pk 197) New short quay R bank above lock 29.

Pk 207 Between locks 35 and 36 silo quay with 1.5m depth.

Oisilly (pk 211) Small R bank quay above lock 38. Shallow- barely 1m.

St-Saveur (pk 220) worthwhile stop to visit Talmay castle.

Maxilly (pk 223) and 2km from junction with R Saône). 50m quay above lock. The village about 1km with Boulangerie, small general grocers and basic bar/restaurant.

Heuilley-sur-Saône Junction with R Saône.

SAÔNE AND RHÔNE
River Saône

Corre to St-Jean-de-Losne,	165km 19 locks,	1.8m water 3.5m air	Fluviacarte/Navicarte 10 Vagnon 6 Breil 3
St-Jean-de-Losne to Lyon	200km 5 locks	3m water 3.5m air.	Fluviacarte/Navicarte 10 Vagnon 6 Breil 3

The Saône is a beautiful river flowing in a broad green valley. Below St-Jean-de-Losne the hills to the west form the Côte d'Or with its famous vineyards, followed below Chalon by those of Mâcon and the Beaujolais. Pike and perch are local fish. As will be seen from the map, five canals join the Saône that eventually enters the Rhône at Lyon. The km marking of the Saône is confusing. Works have shortened the river but the pk posts and published charts still show the original distances and they are used here too. Above Gray several loops have been by-passed by straight lock cuts. Barrages generally at the upstream end, and pleasant moorings are on the downstream approach. Check depths when navigating out of dredged channels. Pontoons for visiting boats have been installed at various places on the upper Saône, generally in backwaters or other pleasant spots. Usually no facilities except sometimes a water tap.

When the river is in flood some sections of weirs are opened and navigation is through them instead of through the locks. Such sections are clearly marked. Remember that headroom *may* be reduced at bridges. For daily water level readings telephone: 03 85 38 02 02 (Mâcon) or 04 72 56 59 20 (Lyon).

There are underwater training walls, and navigation requires care although the channel is well marked with buoys and beacons. Dredgers are often encountered. (See also section on Signals)
Following a fatal accident at the Bollène lock on the Rhône in 2001, Saône lock keepers may insist that all crew on board wear lifejackets during locking. As with many rules in France, this is enforced with varying levels of vigour, but keepers wishing to enforce it simply do not operate the lock until all crew comply.

Where locks are manual they close for lunch, 12h30 – 13h30. Otherwise locks open 09h00 – 19h00.

From Chalon-sur-Saône southwards on both the Rhône and the Saône, you will meet or be overtaken by large hotel ships. They usually have reserved mooring places at many of the larger towns. Also they have priority at locks, but since the locks are typically 185m long, and the hotel ships only 125m, there is usually room for you astern of them. In the presence of other craft, they may use the CEVNI sound signals, or VHF 10 to advise of their intentions. Give them priority and manoeuvering room, especially in the vicinity of bridges or other restrictions. Finally, do not assume that where they go you can safely follow. In spite of their size, most of them draw less than a metre.

Repairs and chandlery (see individual entries for details)
Seveux-Savoyeux (pk 314), Scey-sur-Soâne (pk 366), Pontailler (pk 251), St-Jean-de-Losne (pk 215), Suerre (pk 187), Gigny (pk 123), Pont-de-Vaux (pk 97.5), St-Germain-au-Mont-d'Or (22.5), Albigny-sur-Saône (pk 18), Lyon (pk 0-7). St-Symphorien (pk 0 on Canal du Rhône au Rhin)
Hire boat bases at Port-sur Saône (pk 366), Gray (pk 283), Tornus (pk 112), Loisy (pk 18 R Seille).

Good rail connections by TGV at Dijon, with frequent service to Auxonne.

Corre (pk 407) Junction with Canal de l'Est (Branche Sud). Pontoons with water, electricity and fuel and quayside moorings above 1st lock on Canal de l'Est. Off the river just below the lock is a large R bank marina. €12 for all boats in 2012. Most boats have to berth stern to pontoons, with the bow secured between two vertical posts. Many berths also have a 6m finger pontoon. Each berth has its own electricity point. Several water points. Capitainerie with good facilities and restaurant in 2012. There are basic shops and restaurant in pleasant village, and Camping Gaz available from TV shop!

Cendrecourt (pk 392) Jetty adjacent to camp site in arm on R bank.

Montureux-les-Baulay (pk 384.5) – L bank – 30m quay

Fouchécourt (pk 381) 40m wooden quay – no facilities. Restaurant.
Further down stream are 4 finger and one single hammerhead pontoons at Petit Port de Fouchecourt (03 84 68 77 74). €13 for 10m boat. Water & electricity, washing machine, WiFi, café/restaurant. Access difficult for over 12m length.

Baulay (pk 380) L bank – 20m Wooden quay is now private. In village boulangerie and café/crêperie/restaurant.

Conflandey (pk 372) Possible bank side mooring L bank above lock and bridge, and on R bank below lock 30m wooden quay with bollards and rings close to caravan site which was closed in 2012 but has new ownership and may open in 2013.

Port-sur-Saône (pk 366) Good long quay on L bank just below the narrows through the town. €4 per night, but no facilities (fees not collected in 2012). Further downstream on R bank is hire boat base has all facilities including fuel, but is crowded. Tel 03 84 91 76 36. €13 for 10m boat in 2012. Lift out facilities. Supermarket up hill on busy main road.Town has several good restaurants.

Scey-sur-Saône (pk 356)
- Hire base, and 40 places in port de plaisance managed by commune in basin just upstream of lock 7 and 1km from town. Tel: 03 84 92 72 12. €10 for 6m boat in 2012. 40 places. Water & electricityon each pontoon. 8 tonne crane. Bins and showers temporarily at hire base, but new capitainerie being constructed which will have showers, washing machine, dryer, WiFi, tourist information, chandlery and small workshop and children's play area. 2km from town via footpath/cycleway. Shops, post office etc. in town.
- To moor close to town centre, continue up canal after lock 7, then turn left downstream into river, which has quay on R bank but depth barely 1.2m. Town supermarket offers delivery to boat. Reports of boats grounding in river approach to village.

Soing (pk 332) 40m wooden quay with water & electricity of L bank.
(pk 333) Immediately opposite the pk mark, 18m jetty L bank. Depth over 1.5m.

Charentenay (pk 328) Yacht moorings in poor condition on L bank in R fork just upstream of the lock cut. Water 80m away in middle of little used camp site.

Ray-sur-Saône (pk 325) Small halte with water. Shallow – marked 1.0m. Few shops and restaurant. Splendid castle on hill.

Seveux-Savoyeux (pk 314) New port de plaisance and hire base. Tel 03 84 67 00 88, on R bank with water & electricity, fuel, repairs, winter storage and pump-out station. €10 water and €10 electricity in 2012. Village with supermarket which will deliver, + good restaurant 1km away.

Rigny (pk 288) small quay above lock 15. Small café/restaurant 500m away.

Gray (pk 283) Hire base and halte L bank above lock. Electricity & water, and fuel. Tel 03 84 65 44 62. 1.5m depth. €5 in 2012.
Quay on R bank above lock has good depth. Beware of shelf at new fixed pontoon. Long quay on L bank below lock has limited depth 1.0m signed but shelves fast, so deeper draught boats may be able to use,

but bottom rocky so approach with care. It also offers 6 free electricity and water points. Supermarket 2 minutes walk; town 5 minutes walk.

Arcs-les-Gray (pk 281) - Some 2km south of Gray, 6 finger pontoons. Water & electricity – free.

Velet (pk 279) Small quay for single boat on L bank.

Mantoche (pk 276) Quay with rings. Best depth at upstream end. Attractive location in front of small château.

Pk 260.5 A 30m quay L bank with taxi service to restaurant/pizzeria advertised.

Pk 260 L bank pontoon for single boat.

Heuilley-sur-Saone (pk 256.5) Just below bridge on R bank, small pontoon for 1 boat.

Pk 254 Junction with Canal entre Champagne et Bourgogne (Canal de la Marne à la Saône). Below lock 18 (Heuilley) keep to the R bank side of the channel to avoid shallows at the mouth of the river arm.

Pontailler (pk 251) Excellent quayside mooring on R bank just below the road bridge, although water skiers may disturb especially at weekends. Port de plaisance and hire base with all facilities through narrow bridge on R bank just above the road bridge. and small chandlery. Depth in entrance 1.3m but dredging promised for 2013, and 1.6 to 1.8m in Port. Good reports of assistance and repairs organized by helpful Dutch manager, who can also provide limited fuel supplies in needy cases. Restaurants and shops in small town.

Lamarche-sur-Saône (pk 246) Quay with water & electricity combined available on purchase by debit/credit card of tokens. €3 for 2 hrs. Campervan halte. Supermarket, boulangerie, and cafes 5 mins walk.

Pk 245.5 R bank quay for 3-4 boats. Water & electricity appear to be for campers only.

Auxonne (pk 233
- Pontoons on L bank just above the road bridge with good (2m) depth, water & electricity . €4 for 8 hrs water & electricity.
- Stepped quay on L bank below the bridge.

Both convenient for shops and restaurants. Attractive small town. WiFi at tourist office €1.
- **New marina – Port Royal** L bank, 500m upstream of road bridge at the foot of the Vauban military barracks, indicated by yellow flags. Opened in 2010, run by H$_2$O of St. Jean de Losne. 150 berths. WiFi. Showers. Guardiennage. Use of power tools not allowed causing much concern as owners cannot work on boats. English capitaine & wife, Roy & Carol Sycamore Tel 06 02 34 40 75.

Auxonne station is on the Dijon-Besancon- Mulhouse line and offers much more useful services than that at St-Jean-de-Losne.
Busy lock in season. Water Skiers.

R. Tille entrance (pk 222) Avoid very shallow gravel bank.

Junction with the Canal du Rhône au Rhin (pk 219)

Mailly-le-Port (pk 221.7) Stone quay R bank, watch depth.

St.-Jean-de-Losne (pk 215) A new refueling pontoon has been installed, which offers petrol as well as diesel. Self service out of hours with payment by credit card, and a rather low credit limit, which in August 2011 only allowed about 50 litres per transaction (but accepted multiple transactions using the same card).

Canal de Bourgogne joins the river on R bank below bridge. At the junction is the entrance to the Gare d'Eau, old commercial basin now mainly used by pleasure craft. Depth about 1.5m. Soft mud. All facilities at two yards and cruiser hire base.
- On L of entrance is **Joel Blanquart** with all services, €10 for 10m in 2012. Chandlery, repairs, washing machine €5, dryer €6. WiFi. 15 tonne crane and secure moorings (if there is room), but no fuel. Guardiennage. Agents for Volvo Penta. Tel 03 80 29 11 06.
- On R of entrance is H_2O, repairs, maintenance, *gardiennage*, chandlery, brokerage, WiFi etc.. Water & electricity but no showers or washing machine. Many reports of poor security and very unsatisfactory service. Tel 03 80 39 23 00.

Hire base is at north end of basin.

Repairs at **Atelier Fluvial**, Saint Usage, close to the first lock on the Canal du Burgogne. Takes boats up to 40m specialist in steel welding and metal work. Tel: 03 80 27 03 00. Also moorings to work on own boat.

Bouba Meca Boat at St-Jean-de-Losne who operates a breakdown service 7/7. Tel: 03 80 39 29 38. www.appelboubal.com

Quayside mooring just above fuel point. Tabac on bridge has free WiFi. Laundrette on quay. Book exchange in museum on main street. Tourist office opposite museum in Mairie.

Good Auberge at east end of bridge in Losne, other restaurants on quay. Shops in town and supermarket. Marine upholstery & sewing services – Catherine Rassalle, 13 Quai de la Hutte, 21170 Losne. Tel 03 80 29 10 92 (crassale@yahoo.fr. – English spoken).

Seurre (pk 187) Large port de plaisance L Bank just below Seurre lock on L bank between lock and road bridge. Capitainerie du Confluent, 03 80 20 31 05. Water, electricity, showers, washing machine, WiFi and pump-out station. €13 for 10m boat, incl. water & electricity, in 2012. Basin for smaller boats immediately after lock L bank. Superb 17th century organ in St-Martin's Church.
Boat repair yard on R bank after bridge.

From Seurre the old course of the river is navigable for 10km upstream. Attractive, but the only feasible moorings are at the head of navigation, Le Châtelet, where there are finger pontoons just below the disused lock. They are probably inaccessible with a draught of over 1.5m but there is room to anchor.

On R bank leaving Seurre, after the bridge is a boatyard offering repairs.

Verdun-sur-le-Doubs (pk 167) Entrance to the R Doubs is just above the bridge over the Saône. Port de plaisance in picturesque surroundings on L bank of the Doubs below ramparts of old town with good capitainerie (with restaurant). Tourist office next door. Hire of bikes, electric bikes, and boats. Boat-trips available. Slip-way. Mostly bow- or stern-to mooring but there are two pontoons, and a small quay at upstream end for longer vessels (shallow at downstream end).
Best depth, about 1.4m at the upstream end of the pontoons. Access to shore via steep ramp. €12.50 per night (in 2012) for boats up to 12m, including water & electricity. WiFi. Washing machine and dryer €10. Showers €2.50. Small supermarket on quay, shops and restaurants in town.

From Verdun, a 7km stretch of the river Doubs is navigable by boats drawing up to 1.8m. It is much used for sand extraction. Beware dredgers with submerged cables.

Gergy (pk 159.4) Halte with 60m pontoon for boats under 12m. Water & electricity on application to adjacent restaurant €10, only open July – Sept. but village shops and restaurant about 800m away. Very restless mooring at week-ends because of passing speed boats.

Chalon-sur-Saône (pk 144) Yacht Club for small sailing boats appears not to have any facilities for visitors.

Chalon-sur-Saône (pk 142) Port de plaisance in eastern arm of river behind island. Arm is one way – upstream traffic only. All facilities including laundrette, fuel (petrol & diesel) and used oil disposal. €14 for 10m inclusive of water, electricity & showers in Sept. 2012. Reluctant to accept craft longer than 15m. Tel 03 85 48 83 38. Hypermarket across main road behind capitainerie. Adjacent sports shop exchanges Camping Gaz cylinders. Large town with picturesque old quarter and Museum of Photography. Many good restaurants, especially in the Rue de Strasbourg on the island.

Pk 129.5 Small pontoon L bank above bridge and wooden quay below bridge. No facilities. Watch depth.

Gigny (pk 123) Rural halte nautique in disused lock and on pontoon downstream. Water & electricity, washing machine, dryer, book exchange, boat repairs, WiFi. Limited diesel. Restaurant open April - Sept. Bread can be ordered from campsite. Section of pontoon reserved for hire boats Friday 16h00 – Saturday 18h00, and Sunday 16h00 to Monday 18h00. Heidi & Stephan Werndli, 03 85 44 76 84.

Tournus (pk 112)
- Quay upstream of bridge for vessels over 15m. Limited electricity from box at top of stairs (with long lead). May be submerged when river high, but normally offers 1.8m depth in middle and 1.4m at ends. Look out for large rock in middle.
- Downstream of bridge is excellent R bank 90m long pontoon with water & electricity, for boats under 15m. Hire boats have priority at upstream section from 6pm Friday to 6pm Saturday. Supermarket downstream of pontoon and one street in, can be accessed from quay – ring the bell. Bricolage at 10 mins walk in direction of La Poste.

River Seille (pk 106) Small pretty river enters on L bank. Navigable 39km. 4 locks to Louhans, a lovely old town. Minimum depth 1.3m but less in dry summer. Of the two branches of R. Seille entering the Saône only the downstream one is navigable.
- **La Truchère**, (pk 0.75) Long pontoon with water & electricity managed by restaurant. €8 mooring but free to restaurant customers, €2 electricity and €3 water in 2012.
- **Cuisery** (pk 13) Halte nautique managed by campsite. 35 places. €9 night in 2010.
- **Loisy** (pk 18) Hire base with space for visitors. In 2010 €5 including water & electricity for first night, subsequent nights according to length of boat, but only on Fridays, Saturdays and Monday when personnel are there.
- **Branges** (pk 35) Port de plaisance for boats under 13m. €10 in 2010.
- **Louhans** (pk 39) Port de plaisance for boats under 15m. Water & electricity, showers.

Pont-de-Vaux (pk 97.5) Branch canal 3.7km with entrance lock from Saône, hours 08h00 – 21h00, (9h00 – 19h00 out of season), port de plaisance has been enlarged and encourages overwintering. 225 places. Tel 03 85 30 99 10. Repairs. Pump out facilities. 13t crane. Chandlery. Washing machine. Free showers. WiFi €2 per 24 hrs. €10 per week, but signal poor. Free WiFi at tourist office beside capitainerie (closed Sun & Mon). Hire base, diesel available. Depth 1.2m. Supermarket with gas bottles close. Large market on Wednesday mornings.

Asnières (pk 90) Small pontoon with water and 1.6m depth indicated. Good auberge.

Vésines (pk 87) Small pontoon with water, but 1m depth indicated.

Mâcon (pk 83)
- The yacht harbor has been completely rebuilt over the last 2 years, and enlarged to accommodate over 400 boats. However works have been delayed, but it should be fully operational in spring 2012. €20 for 12m boat in 2012, electricity, and 20c per person tax, extra. Tel 06 71 90 95 72.. All facilities including fuel and crane. Hypermarket 10 mins walk. Town centre 3km; good cycle path.
- (pk 80.5) L bank pontoon (3 boats) close to small shops and good restaurants just upstream of road bridge. Laundrette close.
- (pk 80) Pontoon (about 80m long) downstream of road bridge on R bank. No facilities, but a water tap on quay above. Max stay 3 nights.

Pont d'Arciat (pk 73) Pontoon R bank downstream of bridge. Water & electricity and access to swimming area at adjacent campsite. €7 + €6 for electricity. Approach squarely from abeam, not obliquely – rocks reported. Restaurant near and shops 2km. Bread from quayside snack bar.

Pk 69 Stone quay, L bank, 1.8m, no facilities. Between here and Lyon several small yacht harbours, but most shallow and full of local boats. Not usually for visiting yachts.

St-Romain-des-Iles (pk 66) Small halte. No facilities.

Thoissey (pk 63) On L bank are remains of 1930s concrete bathing area which have been converted into moorings for small boats. Space for 1 or 2 larger craft but no water or electricity.

Pk 57. 'Nature' mooring L bank, good depth.

Belleville (pk 55) Pontoon R bank downstream of bridge. Water & electricity, good depth. Do not approach from upstream. Restaurant close, but shops 1.5km.

Montmerle (pk 52) Pontoon L bank downstream of suspension bridge. Depth 1.8m and deeper at downstream end. Water & electricity. €10 . Small supermarket and shops close.

Pk 43 Nautic 01 Port de plaisance. Only small boats & very shallow.

Villefranche-sur-Saône (pk 40.5) Pontoon L bank in former commercial basin adjacent to camp site. Free mooring for 72 hours. Water & electricity and reasonable depth on outside of pontoon. Usual shops and supermarket.

Trévoux (pk 31) Pontoon upstream of suspension bridge with water & electricity. Stay limited to 72 hours in season. Passenger ships have priority on quay beneath bridge (summer depth 1.6m). Their scheduled arrival and departure times are usually posted near the bridge abutment. Attractive town.

Pk 30 Belles Rives restaurant pontoon, about 20m.

St-Germain-au-Mont-d'Or Nautic Auto, L bank at pk 23.8 is very crowded, but is reported to have a 20 tonne crane.(Tel 04 78 98 24 24). Yachting 69, R bank at pk 22.5 offers repairs, service etc and is reported to have an 18 tonne crane. (Tel 04 72 08 96 77)

Neuville-sur-Saône (pk 20.5) L bank quay just downstream of roadbridge 2m depth. Shops, restaurants and laundrette close. Electricity on quay and water tap under small manhole cover beneath tree at upstream end which doesn't always work.

Albigny-sur-Saône (pk 18) R bank pontoons, water & electricity , chandlery, service and repairs. Depth 2m. Tel 04 72 08 83 97 Convenient for bus or train to Lyon, and Rochetaillée Motor Museum. Until the opening of the new port in Lyon this was the most secure mooring from which to visit the town.

Pk 18 Small Halte L bank, no facilities and near busy road. Small port with facilities R. bank.

Couzon (pk 17) Mooring is possible L bank above the lock by agreement with the lock-keeper. It is also possible to moor inside a rather unusual structure about 500m below the lock on the L bank, the outside being reserved for passenger boats.

Fontaines-sur-Saône (pk 14.5) Small L bank halte, but reports of night-time hassle from local teenagers.

Collonges-au-Mont-d'Or (pk 12.3) Small R bank halte very close to famous *Paul Bocuse* restaurant.

St-Cyr (pk 12) Small pontoons and dolphins.

Île Barbe (pk 10) Apparently shallow restaurant mooring on R bank, approached from downstream of the Isle Barbe, may be free if not required by trip boat. Good mooring in old lock.

Lyon (pk 0 to 7) Interesting city with much to see and excellent restaurants. L. bank Saône quay just upstream of road and rail bridges at about pk 2.5, overhung by willow trees, with space reserved for pleasure craft only. But be cautious if mooring to quays in Lyon, they have reputation for disorder, vandalism and theft. It is not a place to leave a boat unattended for any length of time.
Overnight consider the bend above Fourvière, close to the Pont de Feuillée (pk 4.5), where mooring rings in the wall are accessible from boat but not the street. Fuel available from L bank barge at Saône pk 1. This is about 1km downstream of the VNF offices and quay, is cheaper than most waterside fuelling points and also offers limited chandlery, wine and nautical antiques. It is closed on Sundays. Fuel also available about 1½km up the Rhône.

Bassin de la Confluence (pk 0.8) A new marina (2011) L bank in a newly excavated basin,. Currently around 20 berths on floating pontoons, but more might be added if demand justifies. Nominally for boats under 16m with maximum permitted stay of 4 nights but neither restriction appears to be rigorously enforced. Very busy at beginning and end of season.Temporary capitainerie with showers, toilets, pump-out and WiFi. Entrance is via a lift bridge on the Saône upstream of Port Rimbaud. Secure access. €12 for 12m boat and €20 above this including water & electricity in 2012. Frequent tram service from end of basin to city centre

At times of flood, alternating traffic flow is imposed on the Saône between pk 1 and pk 7, and at such times, mooring in this stretch may be prohibited. Illuminated boards indicating the alternate traffic times have been improved, and are now reasonably easy to see.

River Rhône

Lyon to Port-St-Louis-du-Rhône	310km 12 locks	3m water 6m air	*Fluviacarte/Navicarte) 16 or Vagnon 5*

Above its junction with the Saône, the Rhône shallows to less than 1m in about 5km and with strong currents is not suitable for cruising. About 1km upstream of the junction is a left bank harbour that may have space for one or two visitors.

Below Lyon the Rhône current is normally well below 4 kts. In wet seasons and spring, up to 6 kts is possible, making the river dangerous. Either the Mistral, a strong north wind that blows down the Rhône valley, or a south wind blowing against a fast current, can both produce conditions that are unpleasant and even dangerous. Sea-going ships and enormous barges will be encountered. Keep well clear of them. The deeper draughted ones exert a powerful suction effect drawing small craft towards their sterns. It is usual to share locks with commercial craft unless they are carrying flammable or otherwise hazardous cargo. Keep careful look out for logs and whole trees in the river.

Beware of strong currents above locks especially when hydro-electric generators are running. Dangerous cross-currents may be met near the start of the dividing wall between the lock approach and the barrage. When approaching, keep well in the lock channel and away from the dividing wall. Provided all this is understood, in normal times any yacht capable of 6 kts should have little difficulty in navigating in either direction. All locks now have waiting pontoons very close to the gates with No Parking signs (*Sauf Plaisanciers*). These are reserved *for* pleasure boats,.

Hotel ships – (see earlier note under Chalon-sur-Saône).
A chart is essential. Rhône locks are impressively large with negligible turbulence. Floating bollards make mooring easy. Yachts may be required to await the arrival of commercial craft before being allowed through but any delay should not be more than ¾ hour. Obey the traffic lights on the approaches. These are not always easy to see. The journey time for a yacht cruising at 6 kts is likely to be a minimum of 4 days downstream and 7 days upstream.

All locks are equipped with VHF 19, 20 or 22 and you should contact lock keepers 15 to 20 minutes before your estimated arrival time by VHF or telephone. In October 2009 the VHF channels allocated to the locks were changed and are as follows, Pierre-Bénite 19, Vaugris 22, Sablons 20, Gervans 19, Bourg-lès-Valence 22, Beauchastel 20, Logis-Neuf 19, Châteauneuf-du-Rhône 22, Bollène 20, Caderousse 19, Avignon 22, Vallabrègues 20, Port-St-Louis 19.

The CNR (Compagnie National du Rhône, the Navigation Authority) website www.cnr.tm.fr. provides both current and historical information about the '*débit*,' the flow of water in cubic metres per second and a comparison with the typical figures shown in **Fluviacarte/Navicarte 16** gives an indication of the current likely to be encountered. It also provides details of VHF channels and other contact information. The CNR has a programme to control most of the 13 locks remotely, providing 24 hour operation for commercial vessels and 5am to 9pm operation for pleasure craft. Another excellent website is www.inforhone.fr that gives twice daily reports on current flows and well as other very useful information.

The *débit* can be very roughly converted to a current in km/hour by multiplying it by 0.0072 for the upstream reaches near to Lyon, and by multiplying it by 0.0036 once one is downstream of Bourg les Valence (more than 100km downstream of Lyon). For example a flow rate of 2000 cubic metres per second at Viviers, (just over half the flow rate at which navigation is stopped) would give a current of about 7.2km per hour or 4 knots. The *débit* figures are shown on illuminated signs at Pierre Benite, Bourgles-Valence and Beaucaire locks, and are also available from the lock keepers.

There are some long stretches without good mooring places. Plan in advance where to stop for the night. If there are difficulties in finding moorings, note that there are landing stages or pontoons above and below most of the locks. Some of these are nominally reserved for vessels of the CNR, and others for waiting for the lock, just a few having no restrictions. Lock keepers who are aware of scheduled traffic movements are usually able to permit overnight mooring to them. If weather is bad, just below the lock is more comfortable and safer than just above. Anywhere on the Rhône be cautious about rafting off other boats unless weather is very calm and stable.

There are a few canalised sections that are relatively dull, but along much of the original river the scenery is magnificent. Passenger and hotel boats have priority on some quays, so read any notices carefully.

Repairs and chandlery (see individual entries for details)
Valence Port de l'Epervière (pk 112), Port Napoléon (pk 323)

Lyon (on Rhône) (pk 1) Halte nautique on L bank upstream of first bridge. Shell garage complex. Fuel. Not recommended for reasons noted in previous section, plus water skiers.

St-Fons (pk 3) Run-down halte just above lock Pierre Bénite on L Bank.

Givors (pk 18.4) Halte and small harbour on R bank. All services.

La Roche (pk 26.5) Small halte without facilities, R bank in old arm, above motorway bridge.

Vienne (pk 29) Public quay L bank, partly reserved for tourist boats, and small pontoon R bank, below downstream bridge and staging 250m further downstream. Principal shops, restaurants and Roman buildings on L bank, small supermarket, shops and laundrette on R bank.

Le Port (pk 35.4) New pontoon – pleasure craft moor to inside.

Les Roches-de-Condrieu (pk 41) Good yacht harbour. Pontoon moorings with depth 3m or more. All facilities, including laundrette. Tel 04 74 56 30 53. Diesel available 7 days a week in season. €17 per day, €82 per week for 11m. Shops and good restaurants on both sides of river. Lake for swimming and water sports.

Chavanay (pk 47) R bank halte for 1 boat just upstream of old suspension bridge pier.

Andancette (pk 68.5) Small free pontoon on L bank. Good depth, out of the current..

Andance (pk 68.5) Sloping quay on R bank. Only useable in settled conditions, upstream end probably best.

St-Vallier (pk 75.5) Small (2 or 3 boat) pontoon with no facilities, but convenient for shops, new in 2011. Report of grounding on rock or concrete at 1.7m depth,10m from approach to pontoon from downstream, 10m off bank.

Pk 78 L bank public quay with no facilities and sheltered from north.

Tournon (pk 91) Small yacht harbour on R bank, but crowded with only 1m in entrance and shallows inside. Depth 1.4m or less alongside quay. Heavy wash from passing barges.

La Roche-de-Glun (pk 98) Free pontoons with electricity in R bank old arm, but the 3 finger pontoons have limited depth due to weed (perhaps 1.2m). Village with restaurants & small supermarket close. Anchoring also possible in this arm of the river as no commercial traffic allowed.

Valence (pk 110)
- Good quay, L bank. No facilities and close to urban motorway. Access town through small underpass.
- Valence Port de l'Epervière (pk 112) Large yacht harbour, with all facilities including WiFi, petrol & diesel and 30 tonne boat lift. Entrance channel has now been dredged, visitors pontoon just inside entrance. Call on VHF9, or tel 04 75 81 18 93. Big marina with no wash and secure. Restaurant in club house. Fuel pumps are self service with credit card payment. Chandlery with reasonable stock. Hypermarket 1km. south along busy road. Pleasant town centre 2km north. Good rail acces, but note that TGV station is about 10km from city centre (served by shuttle bus.)

Le Pouzin (pk 133) Short high quay with electricity on R bank upstream of bridge. Hotel boats have priority. Strong current. Also a little used factory quay at pk 133.6

Cruas (pk 145) New R bank marina which should be approached from downstream – course to enter is shown on a plan on the downstream red beacon. €12 per day inclusive for 12m boat, €73per week. Open all year. Town about 1km away with interesting buildings and basic shops. Tel 04 75 96 48 79. Sloping quay on R bank with bollards & rings upstream of marina.

Pk 148 to pk 149.5 Be aware that there are several shallow and rocky areas just to the east of the starboard channel markers.

Montélimar (pk 160) Public quay on L bank below bridge, about 3km downstream from town. Adequate mooring if not occupied by barges.

Viviers (pk 166) Good yacht harbour. €12 per night. inc. electricity & water. Enter from downstream passing between faded red pile and red/green pile, effectively behind the hotel ship jetty. Do not 'cut the corner' from downstream - there is a (usually) submerged training wall. Up to 2m depth alongside rather unstable finger pontoons, but for deeper draught boats the pontoons directly ahead of the entrance offer best depth.

Public quay has 2 dolphins for hotel barges at deep water end of wall, making mooring difficult at times.

Alternatively good sheltered anchorage outside buoyed channel in old river that enters on R bank. Old town well worth a visit. Good restaurants in square.

Bollène (pk 190) Pontoons above and below the lock.

St-Etienne-des-Sorts (pk 204) Small pontoon on R bank has been removed following flood damage, and there are no plans to replace it for 2012.

Port de l'Ardoise & Port 2 (pk 213.6) about 5km up old Rhône. It is possible to anchor in old river at pk 218.5 downstream of Caderousse lock. Sheltered. Port 2 has all facilities including *gardiennage* and 10 ton boat lift. Tel 04 66 50 48 48.

Roquemaure (pk 225) Deepwater quay on R bank. Shops including supermarket and restaurants in village, 10 mins walk. Very exposed especially in Mistral.

Avignon (pk 241) At pk 242, after passing through Avignon lock, turn sharp L back up the old river channel, past the end of the famous bridge. Very close to the Pope's Palace and the historic centre of Avignon with much to see. Mooring on quay with water & electricity. €18 per night or €72 per week with discount if electricity not used. Rafting off will usually be necessary in summer. Capitainerie has showers, laundrette and fuel (diesel & petrol). WiFi and Internet available in the Place de Pie.Tel 04 90 85 65 54. Poor report of "Sud Maintenance" (mechanical problems) which was recommended by capitainerie but expensive and questionable competence.

Vallabrègues (pk 261) Pontoons, with electricity and water, €23 per night. 20 or so pontoons, 19 reportedly reserved for permanent residents. Exposed to wash and wind. Pleasant small town.

Beaucaire As a result of the changes in water level when the river was canalised, there is currently no access from the Rhône to the Canal du Rhône à Sète at Beaucaire, but works to restore the link are being considered.

Pk 269 Just below the junction of canal and river south of Tarascon, high quay wall on R bank.

Arles (pk 282) Halte with pontoon on R bank about 100m upstream of the central road bridge was removed for underwater archaelogical survey and bank repair work in 2009 and has not been replaced. Stone quay (with new steel structure) upstream on L bank is reserved for hotel and passenger cruise ships. Currently the best mooring option is to lay alongside the restaurant barge 'La Péniche' R bank just upstream of the road bridge. The barge owner allows this, and will loan a key to provide access along the gangway from ship to shore at times when the restaurant is closed. No charge, but you are (gently) encouraged to eat at his restaurant. Check in advance by Tel: 04 90 93 31 10

A fine old town with spectacular Roman amphitheatre and subject of many paintings by Van Gogh. Intermarché and other shops about 200m inland of halte on same side of river. The canal from Arles to the Golfe de Fos with reconstructed lifting bridge painted by Van Gogh is entered from the L bank at about pk 284, but is blocked by an anti-salt barrier near its southern end. It may be navigated only from June to September. It is shallow and suffers from being used as a rubbish dump on the edge of Arles. Marina is planned in Canal d'Arles à Fos but may be a long time materialising.

Port-St-Louis-du- Rhône (pk 323) VNF office by lock which does not sell vignettes. Small quay on R bank before lock where masts can be stepped.
Lock only at limited times for pleasure craft, although it may be possible to lock through with commercial craft at other times. Locking times are displayed on lock gates. In 2009 they were as follows:-
Entry from Rhône   06h00, 08h15, 11h50, 16h05, 18h45
Entry from Port   06h20, 08h45, 12h20, 16h35, 19h15
To check times Tel 04 42 86 02 04
- **Port de Plaisance** in basin at west end of Canal St-Louis. Storage in water only.
- **Navy Services Boatyard** in Canal St-Louis has moorings with electricity and water. The yard offers craneage and 50 tonne boat lift, dry storage only, transport and a range of other services.
Tel 04 42 11 00 55.
- **Port Napoléon**, a well equipped, secure and protected marina, as well as moorings there is space for 4000 boats on hard standing, also covered storage. It is reached travelling east along the Canal St-Louis into the Golfe de Fos, leaving the Phare St-Louis to starboard then turning southwest to enter the buoyed channel beyond the east end of Digue St-Louis. English spoken. All facilities for boat repairs and huge chandlery, Store Marine, and Boat Repairs ,MMarine. 06 18 46 09 35. Car hire and taxi service to airports. Discount for CA members. Tel 04 42 48 41 21. www.port-napoleon.com.

Masts can be stepped or unstepped at either Navy Services or Port Napoléon. See **THE SEINE** for note about mast transport..

Canal du Rhône à Fos leaves Rhône at about pk 316 but is for commercial traffic only. If westbound in the Med, follow the Petit Rhône from north of Arles, and then the Canal du Rhône à Sète.

Canal de Caronte entered on the western side of the Golfe de Fos. This was originally part of a canal that ran to Marseille by way of a 7km tunnel that collapsed in 1963. Now a stretch about 8km long links Port de Bouc to Martigues, and provides access to several harbours in the Etang de Berre, a substantial very shallow lake. Because the canal is used by large ships, tugs and passenger boats, it is essential to call Fos Port Control on VHF 12 before entering it. Crowded port de plaisance at Martigues popular with power boaters. VHF 9.

Canal du Rhône à Sète

Beaucaire to Sète	74km 1 lock	2.2m water 5m air	Fluviacarte/Navicarte) 4 or Breil 7

Access via Petit Rhône that leaves main river at pk 279 just upstream from Arles. The channel down the Petit Rhône is narrow in places, but well marked by pillars and buoys. Beware training walls and near submerged piles in stream. After 18km take channel to starboard into lock leading to Aigues Mortes.

Whilst it is possible for small craft (water draught less than 1.2m and air draught less than 2.5m) to reach the Mediterranean by continuing south down the Petit Rhône to Grau d'Orgon, this is not recommended without local knowledge and settled weather.

Pk nos. on this canal have changed and are now taken from where the canal joins the Beaucaire branch which is still measured 1 – 29.

Repairs and chandlery (see individual entries for details)
Sète (pk 98), Aigues-Mortes (pk 51).
Hire boat bases at Beaucaire (pk 1), St-Gilles (pk 24), Bellegarde (pk 13), Lattes.

St-Gilles (pk 24) 1km beyond lock, turn sharply to starboard. 3km to village with port de plaisance, Tel 06 71 22 88 54 and hire base. Most moorings are end on. Modest shops and restaurants near.

Beaucaire (pk 1) The St-Gilles canal is open to navigation for about 29km as far as a point close to its former junction with the Rhône. 1 lock (automatic). Port de plaisance in large basin. For visitors' moorings need to go under the bridge – height approx. 3m – but can be raised by contacting capitainerie. Tel 04 66 59 02 17. Avignon-Nîmes bus stops just across road beside port. Since mooring is impossible on this stretch of the Rhône, mooring here is the only way to visit Beaucaire and Tarascon, across bridge. Fine castles. Magnificent views. Shops, restaurants, boatyards. Hire bases. There is a long term project to re-establish the link to the Rhône.

Bellegarde (pk 13) Hire base. About 1km from pretty village.

Gallician (old no. pk 39) (new no. pk 12.5) Halte nautique. 2012 - 15€ for 12m inc. water, electricity and showers – digicode acess. Small village – basic shops.

Aigues-Mortes (old pk 51) (new pk 22) (detour around Aigues-Mortes now numbered separately PK 1 – 5). Port de plaisance under fortifications of 12th century walled town. Expensive (€37 for 12m) and liable to be crowded. Boatyard with facilities for stepping masts but depth only 1.2m. Easy access to sea with 3 marinas close through the Canal Maritime to Le-Grau-du-Roi. Depth 2m. Overhead cable 16m and 2 bridges, one lifting and one swinging en route to Le-Grau-du-Roi open 4 times Monday to Friday; 3 times Saturdays; and twice Sundays and holidays. Bridges can be contacted on VHF73 or Tel 04 66 51 91 86. Mast stepping and all other facilities available at yacht harbours at Le-Grau-du-Roi, La Grande-Motte and Port-Camargue. Train to Nimes.

Palavas-les-Flots (old pk 75) (new pk 46) Half fishing port, half holiday resort, with excellent Port Fluvial with all facilities except fuel, on channel running from canal to sea. Boats need to *moor bows-dto due to shelf below quay that quickly becomes shallow. Also, if the river is flowing quickly, mooring can be difficult and you can end up mooring diagonally + several pontoons in need of repair.* (Limited headroom and depth make sea access impossible save for small craft.) About 1km up the Lez from Palavas is R bank landing stage which backs onto a supermarket car park, with a waterside petrol (only) pump operated by credit card. Can be very busy at weekends.

Lattes North from Palavas the R Lez is navigable for 6km as far as **Port-Arianne,** a modern residential, restaurant and office development built around a harbour on the southern side of Montpellier. There is a single lock operated by the capitainerie in Port-Arianne Tel 04 67 81 86 07. Maximum air draught 3.3m and water draught 1.4m. Hire boat base. Tramway to Montpellier (railway). Direct flights to UK. Shops and restaurants.

Pk 91 (new pk 62) About 1km before Frontignan, is a recently constructed channel, about 2.5km long, which passes through a small fishing harbour and then enters the Mediterranean (where a breakwater is being built to protect barge traffic to Sète in event of heavy weather). The sign forbidding the channel to pleasure craft is to keep the many hire boats from venturing into the Med and does not apply to privately-owned craft.

Frontignan (old pk 92) (new pk 63/64) Quays on both sides of lifting bridge. Bridge opens, only if there is a boat waiting to go through, at about 08h30 and 16h00 every day from 1st April to 10 November, and over the winter months, only on request at 16h00. This must be requested before 12h00 by telephone to 04 67 01 06 40 for weekdays and to 04 67 67 67 67 at weekends and on holidays. Water and electricity – jetons

- on W. side of bridge. 2€ for 5kwh or 100 litres. Small town, more attractive than appears from canal. Convenient shops, restaurants and railway station. Short train ride to Sète.

The long quay on the Sète (west) side is the most convenient for an overnight stop, but there are no facilities on either side.

Sète (old pk 98) (new pk 69) Access to the sea via lifting bridges. Open at about 0900 and 1700, not Sundays or holidays; possibly at other times on request to capitainerie Tel 04 67 74 76 21. Mooring in yacht harbour, but water very dirty and much disturbed by wash from fishing boats. All facilities. Crane for masts. Reports of vandalism to foreign boats left for the winter.

Marina just inside the port on the Étang de Thau side (opposite station), run by La Royale Languedocienne.

THE MIDI – BISCAY - TO THE MED

| The Gironde to Bordeaux | Breil 16 | 'Gironde Estuary' a new guide published in 2008. |

CA HLR for Bordeaux is happy to brief members on the seaward approach or departure, current navigation situation and mooring possibilities. (See the *CA Almanac or website*.)

Low bridges start at Le Pont de Pierre, Bordeaux. Masts can be unstepped at Royan, Pauillac and in the Bassin à Flot in Bordeaux but not at the Point du Jour, Bordeaux. If making landfall at Royan be alert to the possibility of buoyage changes in the approach. Pauillac is recommended. Other estuary harbours include Mortagne and Meschers, both approached up drying channels on the eastern side of the estuary.

The **R. Dordogne** enters the estuary at Bec d'Ambes, and is navigable with suitable draught craft for over 50km upstream. Substantial pontoon some 16km upstream, at Cubzac-les-Ponts, and others downstream at Bourg & Ambés. River is tidal for about 40km, up to Castillon-la-Bataille. Navigation information available from the DDE at Libourne, Tel: 05 57 51 06 53.

Bordeaux: On approaching from seaward, the Port Control should be contacted about 4km from the Pont d'Aquitaine, the first bridge, (which has over 50m headroom.)VHF 12 or Tel: 05 56 31 58 64 or 05 56 90 59 34.

At the second bridge (stone bridge) avoid arches nos. 9, 10 and 11 (counting from L bank) as there are submerged railings when tide is in, also arches 2 & 16 (shallow). There can be cross currents at low water.

About 200m upstream of Pont d'Aquitaine at Lormont on R bank are municipal pontoons and on L bank, a small marina Point du Jour, both with all facilities.

Access to **Bassin à Flot** needs booking (Bordeaux Port Control Tel:05 56 90 59 34) – English spoken. Operates around HW and is quite slow – about 2 hours overall. The waiting pontoon is upstream of lock just before a major new bridge (scheduled for completion 2012) after which the whole Bassin area will be improved/redeveloped. Marina/boat yard in the inner basin now run by Compas Marin (Tel:05.56.50.60.02; www.le-compas-marin.fr.) Winter storage, boat maintenance, mast stepping. No shore facilities but restaurants and supermarket close by, and laundrette 10 minute walk. Excellent cycle access along river front to central Bordeaux. Also tram and bus stops.

A new pontoon, le ponton d'honneur, just downstream of the Pont de Pierre, has water & electricity and is right in the centre of town; all shops close by. Ring the Mairie Tel:06 44 18 87 37 to check availability.

The tide rushes strongly through the many arched Pont de Pierre but the arches are wider than they look. Best to approach as near to slack water as practicable. The centre arch, with reinforcement to its base, is reserved for the Airbus transport barge.

River Garonne

| Bordeaux to Castets-en-Dorthe | 54km 0 locks | tidal water 3.5m air | Fluviacarte/Navicarte 11 (which also contains useful tidal information.) Breil 16 |

The river is tidal, largely unbuoyed, and with extensive sandbanks. Be alert for changed and missing buoys and fishing boats with nets stretching across the river. In normal conditions Castets-en-Dorthe can be reached on one tide, but when the Garonne is in spate this may not be possible. A tidal bore of 1m or more high may be experienced at spring tides. Moor securely, the current runs very fast. Alternatively ask permission to moor alongside a sand barge.

Bègles (pk 66) Left bank marina, offering 20 visitors places and fuel. Beware strong current – safer not to enter inside pontoons until slack water. Access to Bordeaux centre by bus.

Portets (pk 50) Pontoon.

Cadillac (pk 35.5) Modern pontoon upstream of bridge. Beware of fast current.

Castets-en-Dorthe (pk17) The lock is to starboard, just above a high road bridge. Consult lock keeper for daily time Tel: 06 62 99 63 91.Small waiting pontoon L bank. Lock operation around local high water. Capitainerie of port in canal 06 77 89 66 34.

Canal de Garonne (Formerly Canal Latéral à la Garonne)

| Castets-en-Dorthe to Toulouse | 194km 53 locks | 1.8m water 3.5m air | Fluviacarte/Navicarte 11 Breil 7 |

The canal is quieter than the Canal du Midi, following the course of the R Garonne and rising gently to Toulouse. There is no commercial traffic and hire boat traffic in only a few areas. A first class cycle path runs along the whole canal from Castets to Toulouse and on to the summit at La Ségale.

The locks are generally quite shallow. They are automatic and entirely operated by the boater. An intercom is available to summon help if necessary. The lock cycle is started by turning a pole overhanging the canal just before a lock. Once moored in the lock, a button ashore needs to be pressed to set the lock in motion. Ladders are provided but there is no consistency about their side or position in the lock, nor the side of the operating button. When going upstream, it can be better to land a crew member at the platform in advance of the lock; this is particularly so at the deeper locks at Agen where it may be easier for that person to also take a line with them and drop it down to the boat. The position of mooring bollards is not consistent; some of the deeper locks have floating bollards or poles round which a rope can be looped. There is generally a by-pass swashway for overflow water when the canal is full. Look out for its exit just below the lock; there can be strong cross currents. Currents can also occur above the lock. Water can also flow over closed gates; this is quite normal. Some locks have rough edges and there are occasional corners and recesses which can prevent fenders working effectively. Planks across fenders can be helpful.
Air services to the UK from Bordeaux and Toulouse. TGV and local tains run from Bordeaux to Toulouse, largely following a similar route to the canal, with stations within walking distance at Agen, Valence d'Agen, Moissac, Montauban, Castlesarrasin, Dieupentale, Grisolles and Toulouse. Stations are also easily accessible by bus or taxi from Castets-en-Dorthe, La Réole, Pont des Sables, Buzet. Check timetables as small stations have limited trains, mainly aimed at morning and evening commuters.

Castets-en-Dorthe (pk 192,5) No mooring between locks 52 & 53. Just above lock 52 are pontoons for 50 boats stern to; water & electricity, WiFi. New shower facilities and waterside café planned (2012). Winter mooring. Capitainerie Tel: 05 56 27 44 21..12m €14 pn (2012) Bread, butcher, small general store. Locks

52 & 53 (to R Garonne) operate at around local HW; consult lockkeeper for daily time Tel: 06 62 99 63 91. 2km to Caudrot for railway to Bordeaux.

Repairs and chandlery (see individual entries for details)
Moissac (pk 64), Castlesarrasin (pk 55).
Hire bases at Meilhun (pk 175.5), Pont-des-Sables (pk 165.5), Les Mas-d'Agenais (pk 155), Damazan (pk 140), Buzet (pk 136), Agen (pk 107), Montauban (Montauban branch canal).

Fontet (pk 183) Halte in basin off canal; water & electricity. Limited availability as many permanent moorings. 3km to La Réole for railway.

Meilhan (pk 175.5) Halte close to R Garonne with water & electricity, toilet; showers at adjacent campsite. Wifi. . British managed. Reservations possible 05 53 94 30 04. Bread, butcher, general store, restaurants, bar. Bus to Marmande for railway.

Pont-des-Sables (pk 165.5) Halte with water & electricity; good depth. Bread, general store, restaurants. Hire base. Bus to Marmande for railway.

Fourques (pk 164) Mooring, no facilities. Small store, café.

Le Mas-d'Agenais (pk 155) Quay with jeton operated water & electricity, showers and pump out. Water, showers and fuel at hire boat base. Bread, butcher and general store.

Caumont (pk 160) Mooring, water & electricity. Small store.

Pont-de-Ladonne (pk 153) Pleasant rural halte with water, electricity and café/restaurant.

Villeton (pk 148.5) Quay, water & electricity. Pizzeria. Restaurant Le Chope & Pichet (05 53 83 13 49) at La Gaulle lock (pk 147.5)

La Falotte (pk 146) Rural halte, mooring to bank, no facilities. Small lapidary museum.

Damazan (pk 140) Hire boat base. Diesel.

Buzet (pk 136). Moorings both sides of road bridge. Hire boat base, water & electricity. Junction with River Baïse with link by R Garonne to R Lot. Bread, butcher, general store, restaurants, bar, large wine cave. WiFi. 7km to Aiguillon for railway station.

Feugarolles (pk 130) Mooring pontoon, no facilities.

Auvignon lock (pk 125) Mooring quay upstream, no facilities.

Sérignac-sur-Garonne (pk 119) Quay with water & electricity. General store with butcher and bread. Restaurants.

Agen (pk 107) The canal crosses the Garonne on a fine aqueduct. Quay (no facilities). Hire base with pontoons. Water, electricity and fuel (expensive). WiFi. Laundrette nearby. Main railway station. For the connoisseur of prunes, those from Agen are magnificent. Festival at end of August. Farmers market Sunday morning.

Boë (pk 101.5) Water & electricity. Hypermarket 5 minutes walk.

Saint-Christophe lock (pk 97) Restaurant Le Poule au Vélo, open May-Oct, closed Wed. Reserve 05 53 63 41 17.

Valence d'Agen (pk 81) Pontoons with water & electricity. Pleasant town with large supermarket, shops, restaurants, bars and railway station. Market Tuesday.

Pommevic (pk 77) Small quay with water & electricity.

Malause (pk 74.5) Moorings with water & electricity close to small railway station. Bread, butcher, general store, pizzeria.

Moissac (pk 64) Long quays. Depth 1.8m. Water & electricity. British run Capitainerie with water, electricity, toilets, showers, fuel, pump out, washing machine and WiFi. Winter mooring. Noble Marine offers; service, maintenance and repairs. Some chandlery. www.cepnoblemarine.com Tel: 05 63 04 09 89. Restored double lock down to R Tarn; quay with water & electricity and further cruising area for about 9km upstream and 9km downstream of lock. Town boasts the beautiful abbey church of St-Peter, supermarket, shops, restaurants, bars and an excellent food market on Sat. & Sun. mornings. Railway station.

Pk 58 Mooring by road bridge convenient for large Intermarché supermarket.

Castelsarrasin (pk 55) Quay and pontoons in large basin with water & electricity. Laundrette in capitainerie Tel 05 63 32 01 39. Winter mooring. Repairs and chandlery at Chantier Navale Castlesarrasin Tel 05 63 32 01 39. Railway station.

St-Porquier (pk 49) New quay with bollards; no facilities.

Montech (pk 42) Short quay just above the branch to Montauban; also a paying halte with pontoons with water & electricity. Tel 05 63 64 23 92; open Apr to Oct. Supermarket across bridge away from town. The *Pente d'Eau* (water slope) here is a remarkable structure that hauls barges (not yachts) up an incline, so bypassing five locks. It is currently out of action.

Montauban branch canal. Completely renovated (2011) 11km, 9 locks,branch has a depth of about 1.4m and the locks are operated by a *telecommande* issued (and collected) at the first lock. Ring lockkeeper to advise arrival; Tel: 05 85 75 71 38.
Lacourt Mooring about 1km above the first lock, water & electricity, but a depth of only about 1.2m.

Montauban Capitainerie with pontoons, water & electricity, winter mooring. Hire base. Tel 05 63 20 55 24. Bread nearby; town with all shops about 15 minutes walk. Railway station.It is now possible to lock down onto R Tarn; navigable about 9km upstream to the unrestored Corbarieu lock. Some pontoon mooring.

Dieupentale (pk 31) New (2011) 50m long staging opposite railway station. Shop.

Grisolles (pk 27) Small quay upstream of road bridge and small staging downstream. Railway station, restaurant and shops which include an excellent *quincaillerie*.

Ecluse de l'Hers (pk 18.5) Bank above lock probably last reasonably tranquil mooring before Toulouse.

Saint-Jory (pk 15) Short term mooring above lock. Bread, butcher, general store

Lacourtensourt ((pk 6.5) Reasonable overnight mooring above lock.

Canal du Midi

| Toulouse to Les Onglous | 240km
63 locks | 1.4m water,
3.3m air | Fluviacarte/Navicarte 4
Breil 7 |

The canal rises steeply from Toulouse to the summit at La Ségale and then descends steeply until Argens-Minervois where there is a 53km stretch without locks. Older and more picturesque than the Garonne canal. No freight traffic but hotel barges and numerous hire boats during the season. Some bridges are low and curve down steeply at the sides. Most locks are oval and some locks are 'staircases' with multiple chambers, one directly feeding the next. Can be very busy in Jul-Sept, so fender well. Some locks have rough edges and there are ladder recesses which can prevent fenders working effectively. Planks across fenders can be helpful.

From the Port d'Embouchure in Toulouse, the first three locks are operated remotely (see below). Upstream of Toulouse to the summit, locks are automatic and operated by the boater (except for the multiple locks). Boaters must put someone ashore to operate the button at the lock to set the cycle going. In 2012, there were lockkeepers on all locks from the summit to the Mediterranean.

The Canal du Midi can run short of water and in some years the summit level has been closed for this reason. When it is open the depth may be reduced to less than the official figure of 1.4m. Go slowly through bridges and also past outlets of basins feeding the canal. Shallowest water is often 10-15m downstream of lock and best possibility of mooring a boat close to the depth limit just above the lock. Ask lockkeepers for information or consult the VNF website.

N.B. Many of the plane trees along this canal have been infected by an incurable fungal disease and are being cut down. If mooring with spikes it is important that these are disinfected at the next lock and special containers are provided for this.

Air services to the UK from Toulouse, Carcassonne, Béziers, Montpellier. TGV and local trains run from Toulouse to Monpellier and onwards although the railway moves away from the canal between Carcassonne and Béziers. Stations within walking distance at Toulouse, Castelnaudary, Carcassonne, Narbonne, Béziers, Agde, Sète, Frontignan. Stations also accessible by bus/taxi from Bram, Trèbes, Homps, Capestang, Colombiers, Montpellier. See individual entry. Check timetables as small stations have limited trains, mainly aimed at morning and evening commuters

Repairs and chandlery (see individual entry for details)
Port-la-Robine (pk 168), Grau d'Agde (pk 231)
Hire bases at Ecluse de Négra (pk 33), Castelnaudary (pk 64), Bram (pk 81), Trèbes (pk 117.4), Homps (pk 154), Argens-Minervois (pk 151), Le Somail (pk 166), Capestang (pk 190), Colombiers (pk 200), Port Cassafières (pk223), Agde (pk 231).

Port de l'Embouchure, at the junction of the Canal Latéral and the Canal du Midi is not recommended for unattended boats because of many people living rough.

Toulouse (pk 0-8) Interesting cruising through the city centre. For part of the route, the canal is in the centre of an urban motorway and set rather higher than the carriageways: sailing through a traffic jam is an ususual sensation.

Béarnais, 2 écluses des Minimes, 2 écluses de Bayard (pk 1-4) These three locks are operated remotely by the VNF (2012). Travelling upstream, Béarnais will open on approach; enter and tie up and await the locking cycle. Minimes is deep and has limited mooring points; Bayard has floating bollards. Travelling downstream, there is a pole to attract the VNF operator.

Port St-Sauveur (pk 5) central and secure marina with pontoons. Winter mooring. Water, electricity, toilets, showers (€2), washing machine, fuel, pump-out, book swap, WiFi, local shops; city shopping, restaurants nearby. Capitaine 12m €16pn (2012) open April-October. capitainerietoulouse@gmail.com Tel: 05 61 14 17 25. Reservation advised. Airport for UK and Ireland. Railway station.

Ramonville (pk 12) Port Sud yacht harbour; pontoons with water, electricity, fuel. Bus service into Toulouse from main road, about 1km, with less frequent service to/from a point 300m away. Port technique on opposite bank has workshops, crane but extent of services unclear.

Castanet lock (pk18) From here to Emborrel lock (pk47.5), essential put a crew member ashore to start the lock cycle except at multiple locks where there is a lock keeper. First oval lock, particlarly deep lock (formerly a double).

Montgiscard (pk 25) Quay L bank just above lock. Good depth & water. Pizzeria & basic restaurant close; bread and restaurant up hill to town. Intermarché supermarket accessible from mooring by bridge at pk 27.

Ecluse de Négra (pk 33) Small hire base. Water & electricity.

Gardouch (pk 39) Mooring, water. Bread, restaurant. Many live-aboards.

Port Lauragais (pk 50) Port beside motorway service area, not as noisy as location might suggest. Quay with water & electricity. English speaking Capitainerie on barge Tel:06 03 48 23 06. 12m €12 (2012). Restaurant, toilets & shower. Bread delivered by Capitaine or obtainable in tourist office. Some food in motorway petrol station shop. Canal du Midi museum. 1km to railway station at Avignonet-Lauragais.

Pk 51.3 A couple of hundred metres below Ecluse de l'Océan are two landing stages. They are occasionally used by trip boats, so check with lockkeeper.

Ecluse de l'Océan (pk 52.5) From here to L'Etang de Thau (pk 240.5) the locks are automated and operated by a lock keeper (2012). There may be a gradual move to complete automation in less busy areas.

Summit Level (pk 52–56) Having reached the summit level of the world's first ship canal, bankside mooring above Ecluse de l'Océan provides good access to the memorial to Riquet, its builder, and to the end of the intricate system of feeder canals. 2km further, **Le Ségala** offers a quay and restaurant and the summit level ends at Ecluse de la Méditerranée. From here to Agde, all locks manned (2012).

Castelnaudary (pk 64) Moorings either to town quays or on south side of large canal basin at, or adjacent to, hire base with water & electricity. The town quays, to the west of the large basin, and close to the town centre, accommodate capitainerie with water & electricity, showers, toilets, washing machine. Book swap, WiFi. But fuelling point closed. Tel:04 68 23 69 09. All shops, restaurants, bars. 12m €13 pn (2012) including 2 showers. An attractive town, home of *Cassoulet* and of the French Foreign Legion. Railway station.

Le Peyruque (pk 72) Small café/shop at lock.

Bram (pk 81) Hire boat base; water. No mooring for private boats for 100m from bridge. No facilties. Restaurant by bridge. Shops, restaurants and railway station in town (20 minutes walk).

Sauzens (pk 94) Short stone quay with water and 1.4m depth.

Carcassonne (pk 105) Port de plaisance just above town lock, stern to, or quayside when port is not busy but attracts lots of hire boats midweek in season. Water, electricity, washing machine, dryer, showers, free internet in Capitainerie. port.carcassonne@wanadoo.fr. Tel: 04 68 25 10 48; reservation possible. €17.40

per night for 12m boat in 2012. Railway station, all shops close by. There is also quayside mooring below the Carcasonne lock water & electricity. Flights to UK.
Road bridge below town lock has centre height of 3.3m but very tight and sides have only about 2.4m.The old fortified town is much restored and full of tourists, still worth visiting.

L'Eveque lock (pk 113) When going down stream, do not moor close to down stream gates in lock – hidden protrusions when lock empties.

Trèbes (pk 117.4) Quays up and downstream of bridge on blind bend. Hire base L bank; mooring stern to. 12m €12 (2012) Water & electricity. Bankside mooring R bank between bridge and lock. No facilities. Butcher, baker by port. Laundrette by river bridge. WiFi at café. Restaurants, wine bar. Tourist office with internet access. Large supermarket 10 minutes walk. Bus to central Carcassonne, 25 minutes.

Marseillette (pk126) Mooring to banks in village and short quay upstream of lock. Water. Restaurants/bar, bread.

Puichéric (pk 136) 10 minutes walk from bridge. Butcher, bread, small supermarket, wine shops.

Laredorte (pk 139.4) Quays depth 1.7m with coin operated water & electricity (expensive). Restaurant by port. Bread, butcher and Intermarché (10 minutes) in town.

Homps (pk 145) Hire boat base; stern-to moorings. Water & electricity. Quays both banks, with water & electricity. Quayside restaurants/bars, small store by quay, wine shops, supermarket on main road. Adapters for large electricity points can be borrowed from the Capitainerie (toilet).12m € 20 pn (2012) Tel 04 68 91 18 98. 10km to Lézignan-Corbières for railway station.

Argens-Minervois (pk 151) Bankside mooring L bank above road bridge or in large hire base; water, electricity, toilets, showers. Restaurant. Small shop with fresh bread across bridge.

Roubia (pk 155) Quay with water.

Ventenac-en-Minervois (pk 161) Quay with bollards outside winery. Restaurants. Bread and gas at small stall by quay.

Le Somail (pk 166) Picturesque village with restaurants, antiquarian book shop. Bankside moorings, but crowded with 2 hire boat bases . Small store on barge – fresh bread.

Port Minervois (pk167.8) Quay with café/wine shop that provides water and showers. Open 15 April to 10 November.

Port la Robine (pk 168.3) Small port in small arm north of canal. Moorings with water. Diesel. Winter mooring, repairs, maintenance, chandlery. Cathare Marine www.catharemarine.fr. Tel: 06.84.52.55.31 Bankside mooring with 1.6m depth 500m farther in entrance to the branch canal to Narbonne.

Capestang (pk 190) Picturesque town with the lowest bridge arch on the canal. Bankside moorings, water & electricity. Showers, toilet and washing machine. WiFi/internet access in tourist office. British run capitainerie. Tel 04 67 39 21 66. Supermarkets, bread, butcher, wine shops. Market Sunday morning. Bus to Béziers for airport/railway station.

Poilhès (pk 194) Small halte with coin operated water & electricity points. Restaurant. Very limited shops.

Colombiers (pk 200) Hire boat base in basin, with bankside mooring outside. Low footbridge across basin - 2.4m. Free electricity and mooring for 1 night, thereafter €15 per night for 12m boat. Restaurants, bread, small shop. Bus to Béziers for railway/airport,

Fonsérannes (pk 206) The 7 lock staircase (first opened in 1681) takes typically just over the hour for the ascent and slightly under the hour to descend. Crew should be ashore to handle bow and stern lines as it is normal to "walk" the boat from chamber to chamber. Ascents are from 10h00 to 11h45, and from 16h00 to18h15. Descents from 08h30 to 09h30 and from 13h30 to 15h30. Some 20 years ago, the 7 locks were by-passed by a water slope as at Montech. This has never worked reliably and has effectively been adandoned.

Béziers (pk 208) Good quays in canal basin no water or electricity and longish walk uphill to the interesting part of town. Modern shopping centre nearby, bread and small supermarkets within walking distance. Laundrette uphill past station. Fine cathedral with view from terrace. Birthplace Pierre-Paul Riquet, designer/builder of the Canal du Midi. Airport for UK. Railway station.

Villeneuve-lès-Béziers (pk 214) Bankside moorings below bridge and lock. Good pizzeria L bank near bridge. Facilities of camp site (also L bank) including laundrette, available to boaters

Portiragnes (pk 219) bankside moorings needing spikes but village has small shops and a modest supermarket.

Port Cassafières (pk 223) Hire base. Fuel and other services.

Pk 227 R bank moorings with limited water & electricity give easy access to beach about 1km away, just downstream of a funfair.

Agde (pk 231) Bankside mooring usually possible in the canal west of the round lock though busy in season. Basin withhire base; water & electricity. Large fruit stall by lock. Bread by river bridge to town. Close to mainline station; Wifi in brasserie opposite station. Other shops and restaurants across in town (10 minutes walk).
Unusual round lock with 3 sets of gates. The eastern exit from the round lock leads into the R Hérault upstream of the weir. The southern exit leads into the R Hérault and to the sea. Contact lock keeper in advance to take this exit; operating times are 09h00, 11h15, 14h15, 16h15, 18h00 for exit, a little later for entry. About 1km up river from the eastern exit, canal continues to the right towards the Etang de Thau. The Hérault remains navigable upstream of this junction for about 5km. Attractive scenery but no mooring. If wintering boats at boatyards along the River Hérault, beware swift changes in water level - rise and fall can be 1m in half an hour at town quay.

Les Onglous (pk 240) Mooring to quay outside Glenans Sailing School usually possible. The canal comes out here into the Etang de Thau, a large shallow salt lake, with extensive oyster and mussel beds, unlit at night. *Fluviacarte/Navicarte 4* has useful chart of the Etang. It can be rough in strong northerly winds.

Note that the discharge of toilets and holding tanks is strictly forbidden in the Etang de Thau and in the waterways that feed it.

When crossing the Etang de Thau, look out for shell fish divers, who often work alone from anchored dinghies. Some but not all indicate their underwater position with a small cigar-shaped float. This practice also continues for the first few km along the Canal du Rhône à Sète.

Marseillan: good small yacht harbor and town quays. Water & electricity, showers, toilets at harbour office. Fuel, shops, restaurants. 5 tonne crane.

Mèze: small fishing port now developing as a holiday resort. Good yacht harbour with most facilities (no electricity) and small crane. Fuel pumps here are for fishing craft only.

Bouzigues: Small but pleasant harbor with only room for about 12 visiting boats. Restaurants, but limited shops in village. Pump-out boat. If full it is possible to anchor outside in calm weather.

Sète (See Canal du Rhône à Sète).

Access to the sea
1. Port-la-Nouvelle (pk 168.7) The Canal de Jonction branches off the Canal du Midi leading to the Canal de la Robine and Narbonne. Exit into Mediterranean at Port-la-Nouvelle (yard with crane), so giving a short cut if bound for Spain. This route involves crossing the R Aude which has rocks and shallows although these are well marked. Depth is shown at first lock in the Canal de Jonction. Depth further downstream, especially below Narbonne, may be no more than 1.2m. Check with lock keeper. Entrance to sea from Canal de la Robine can be shallow, 1.0 to 1.2m.
Sallèles-d'Aude is a good stopping place in modern basin. Mooring both banks above lock. Water on R bank only. Shops near.
Narbonne Hire base near bend midway between Gua and Narbonne locks. Good mooring at quays below both Gua and Narbonne locks, the latter after passing under the old Roman bridge with houses built over it. Narbonne harbourmaster Tel 06 11 71 27 19. Headroom under lowest bridge, 3m. Quay being modernized (2012). Fine city over 2000 years old, with outstanding covered food market. Roman relics everywhere. Beware of cross currents below Narbonne lock.

2. via Le Grau-d'Agde (pk 231) - take southern exit from Agde round lock (pk 231.4) with three entrances. See Agde above. Short stretch of canal into R Hérault. Navigable depth about 1.6m out to sea at Le Grau-d'Agde, about 4km. In addition to the low bridge over the Hérault in Agde, there is also a road bridge with clearance 12m about 1km downstream. Boatyard on L bank below this bridge. No accommodation for yachts at Le Grau-d'Agde, but Chantier Allemand just before the river mouth has a full chandlery and workshop. Short waiting pontoon. Winter storage ashore, mast stepping and short term cranage ashore for antifouling etc. www.chantier-allemand.com Tel: 04 67 94 24 19. About 3 miles east of the river mouth is the yacht harbour of Cap d'Agde with every facility

3. via Etang deThau at Sète - take eastern exit from Agde round lock then up the R Hérault for about 800m and thence turn east into Canal du Midi.

River Baïse

Buzet to Valence	57km 20 locks	1.2m water and 3.5m air up to Lavardac and 1m water and 3m air above Lavardac	Fluviacarte/Navicarte 28 Breil 7 or Vagnon 7

From Buzet on the Canal Latéral à la Garonne it is possible to travel south (upstream) on the very attractive R Baïse to Valence sur Baïse. Being a river prone to flooding (which can quickly silt up locks and their approaches) and a source of irrigation water in dry periods, significant summer water depth reductions can be expected. Official depth figures must be treated with scepticism. The locks are small (31m by 4.3m) and there is no commercial traffic. There are haltes at Lavardac, Nérac (hire boat base), Condom (hire boat base) and Valence. Comparitively little hire boat traffic.

5km downstream from Buzet, the Baïse joins the R Garonne for 4.5km, to a junction with the R Lot at Nicole. For hire boats, a tug is provided for the Garonne section, where the current can be strong. The channel is narrow and shallow, although fairly well buoyed. Private craft may use it 'at your own risk and peril' (literally translating the official rules) and will normally be provided with a pilot boat to follow. The depth may vary from day to day, and the navigation authority will advise on the feasibility given an accurate figure for the boat's draught.

River Lot

| Nicole to Fumel | 78km 8 locks | 1.0m water 5.5m air | *Fluviacarte/Navicarte 28 or Breil 5 or 7 (Breil 7 only as far upstream as Villeneuve)* |

Whilst this water draught is an official maximum, for much of the year there are few problems with a greater draught, and a CA member reported no problems with 1.27m draught as far as Villeneuve (then head of navigation) in June 2001. Along the river are several small villages with free pontoons.

Aiguillon (pk 3) Quay above lock, with water.

Clairac (pk 10) Town quay R bank above lock. Water & Electricity.

Castelmoron (pk 23.4) Town quay R bank downstream of road bridge.

St-Livrade (pk 32.5) Quay L bank with no facilities.

Port Lalande (pk 23.7) Upstream of the fine new stone lock (9m rise with floating bollards). Hire base R bank.

Pk 47.8 Caution. Channel through rocks past abandoned lock reported (2002) to be badly buoyed.

Villeneuve (pk 50) Attractive and interesting town, Both banks very noisy when concerts held on stage that projects out into river. Especially at times of festivities, be cautious about mooring on R bank (free) below hotel terrace and bridge, where you may be vulnerable to bottles and other missiles lobbed from above.

St-Sylvestre and **Penne d'Agenais** (pk 60) Two hire bases on opposite banks.

Fumel (pk 78) Dam – present limit of navigation. There is an isolated, but impressive, navigable stretch of the Lot around Cahors, some 64km and 14 locks between Luzech and Crégols, which can currently only be reached over land and on which several boat hire firms operate. (*Fluviacarte/Navicarte 27* or *Breil 5*)

Plans have been drawn up for the re-opening of the still unnavigable length of 43km between Fumel and Luzech, but no timetable has yet been given for the work.

For the latest information on Baïse and Lot, contact the Lot et Garonne Conseil General at Agen, Tel 05 53 69 33 33. The Baïse and the Lot are under regional control, not the VNF.

BRITTANY

Given the time and a boat of suitable dimensions, the Brittany canals can be a delightful alternative to slogging round the north-west corner of France to reach the Biscay harbours. There is now virtually no commercial traffic on the waterways between St-Malo and Redon.

Apart from Rennes, there are only a few villages en route. Some of these will have a base nautique which may be little more than a quay with perhaps showers at a nearby camping site, and a few local shops. Thus, one has the choice of spending the night at a base nautique or simply tucking the boat alongside the bank with no signs of civilisation for miles. Apart from the R Loire (Nantes - Bouchemaine), these waterways are not controlled by the VNF and use is free. Chômages list and other advice from Service de la Navigation, 1 Avenue du Mail, 35000 Rennes, Tel 02 99 29 66 66 or the Nantes office 02 51 82 55 55.

CRUISING THE INLAND WATERWAYS OF FRANCE & BELGIUM

Will your boat get through?				
Waterway	Draught m max (tirant d'eau)	Height m max (tirant d'air)	Locks No.	Distance km
Channel Biscay Link				
Rance Maritime	1.9	3.25	23	
Châtelier lock-Dinan	**1.4/1.6	15/16	1	6
Dinan-Rennes	1.2 max	2.5	47	79
Rennes - Redon	1.2 max	3.2	13	89
Redon-Sea	1.3	27	1	48
* Enquire at Châtelier lock where the level is controlled.				

Nantes à Brest Canal				
Nantes- Redon	1.2	2.5	17	95
Redon – Pontivy	0.8	2.4	90	110
Blavet River	Tidal below Ecluse Polhuern			
Pontivy- Lorient	1.4	2.6	28	70
Aulne River/Canal	1.1	2.5	46	112
Brest- Châteaulin	3.0	3.1	1.0	42
Châteaulin- Port Carhaix	1.1	2.5	33	72

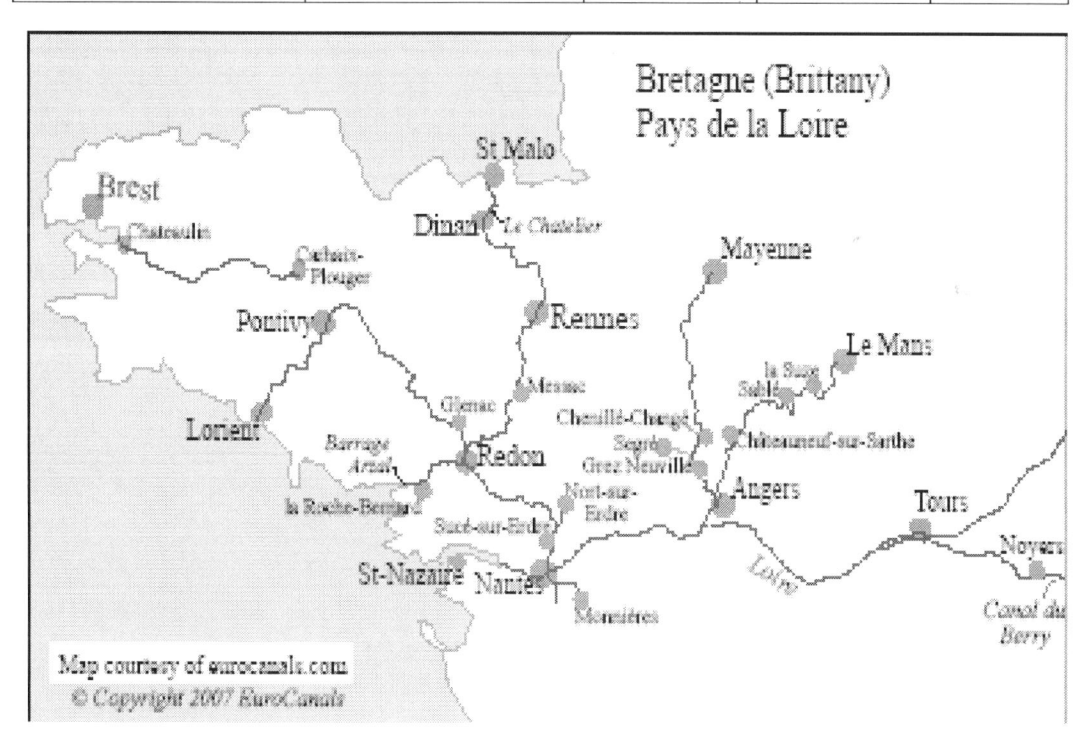

** **CAUTION** In summer there may be severe shortages of water in the Canal d'Ille-et-Rance and the River Vilaine. On occasions, the maximum permitted draught may be reduced to as little as 0.9m. With severe water shortage the I'lle-et-Rance canal may open only at weekends and require craft to pass through locks in groups. Water level timetables from HMs/marina offices in St-Malo, Les Bas Sablons, Dinard, or at the

Rance Barrage. Tel 02 99 46 21 87 32 (Barrage); 02 96 39 55 66 (Châtelier lock); or Rennes above. The smallest locks on the waterways are 25.8m by 4.5m.

River Rance

| St-Malo to Châtelier lock | 22km 2 locks tidal | 1.80m water 3.0m air | Fluviacarte/Navicarte 12 |

There is a barrage upstream of St-Malo. Barrage lock operates on the hour for upstream traffic (hour + 20 mins downstream). Not worked around low water (less than 4m). Entry between 20h00 and 04h30 on request only. Châtelier lock operates between 06h00 and 21h00 over a 4-5 hour period when water level in Rance is being maintained at 8.5m (see CA Almanac for notes on the passage between St-Malo and Dinan).

Canal d'Ille-et-Rance

| Châtelier to Rennes | 79km 47 locks | 1.2m water 2.5m air | Fluviacarte/Navicarte 12 Breil 1 or Vagnon 10 (This applies to the next 4 Brittany routes.) |

Below Dinan power lines above the Châtelier lock give a maximum air height of 15/16m. Châtelier lock controls depth over range 1.4/1.6m. First low bridge just upstream of Dinan quayside. Mast can be lowered in St-Malo's Bassin Vauban or at Dinan

Distances that follow are km from Rennes

La Vicomté-sur Rance (85km) Port de plaisance above Chatelier lock.

Dinan (79km) Port de plaisance with L bank pontoons. Diesel unavailable in 2008. Halte nautique at Lanvallay opposite on R. bank.

Evran (66km) Halte fluviale above Ecluse 42

St-Domineuc (57km) Halte fluviale below Ecluse 38.

Tinténiac (47.4km) Halte fluviale below Ecluse 33.

Les Onze Ecluses Eleven locks (31-32) all in a 2km stretch of canal. To save water lock keepers usually wait for several boats to assemble at this staircase.

Hédé (42.8km) Halte fluviale between locks 29 and 28.

The summit level of the waterway is between locks 21 and 20.

St-Germain (23.9km) Halte fluviale with toilets and cold shower, below lock 11.

Betton (13km) Halte fluviale about 800m above lock 6.

Rennes (pk 0) Facilities for yachts are poor for such a large town. The basin downstream of the Ecluse du Mail offers little but water and crude toilets, although it is reasonably close to the city centre.

River Vilaine

| Rennes to Arzal barrage | 131km 15 locks | 1.2m water, 3.2m air | Fluviacarte/Navicarte 12 etc |

Locks: apart from the barrage, locks on the I'lle-et-Rance and Vilaine are supposedly operated between 08h00 – 12h30 and 13h30 – 19h30. These times are not adhered to. Alongside ladders in the locks. Crews expected to assist the lock keeper.

A useful free guide to the Vilaine, revised annually, is available from Institution d'Amenagement de la Vilaine, Boulevard de Bretagne, 56130 La Roche-Bernard, Tel 02 99 90 88 44.
Diesel also from Crown Blue Line at Messac.

There is a swing bridge at Cran with an air draught of 5.8m when closed, which opens by arrangement in Winter and at fixed times in Summer (VHF 10). Opens for small ships between sea and Redon, ship has priority but can be followed through. Two fixed but very high bridges near La Roche-Bernard.

Repairs and Chandlery (see individual entries)
La Roche-Bernard, Redon, Arzal, Foleux.
Hire base at Messac.

Redon has excellent train connections and is a good place for crew changes. Paris is €58 away via Rennes by train and takes about 3 hours.

Downstream from Rennes, the waterway Authority office is close to Ecluse du Mail (lock 1) which is the start point for the distances given below. Outskirts of Rennes are industrialised, so best continue to halte nautique at –

Pont- Réan (18km and below lock 6).

Boel (21km to lock 7),

Guipry-Messac (47km and above lock 12). A hire boat base and more extensive than the others.

Beslé (69km)

The last lock is no.13, some 52km from Rennes

La Roche Bernard (123km) Just under 4 mile up river from Arzal. Substantail port de plaissance with 563 berths and 56 visitor berths. Navi'Net has a breakdown van and promise to cover the whole of Brittany. Tel 02 99 90 66 76.

Beganne About 12 miles up river from Arzal (to the left going upstream), a new simple tie up pontoon approx 25 metres long. No facilities, 2km hike to the village. No charge for over night.

Foleux (115km) Just under 8 mile up river from Arzal. Port de plaissance with new pontoons and capitainerie (2012) for 42 visitors (to the left going upstream) with water & electricity, toilets and showers. Chandlery. Depth at least 2 metres. No fuel available.. Small cafe with fair food/prices stops serving food at 22h00.
Possible to over winter eg of cost for 10metre boat (8 months on hard with crane lift in and out and shoring up with pressure wash approximately €920) yard is run by Jean Francois on 00 33 299 918 140
Transport to and from station or air-port not good.

Pont de Cran Swing road bridge published opening times in summer season 9 / 10 / 11 / 14h30 / 16h30 / 18h30 / 19h30. Pontoon either side of bridge to tie up to. On the sea side pontoon possible to step ashore and try the highly recommended (but untired) restaurant by the bridge.

Rieux Just under 18 miles up from Arzal, left hand bank, two sets of pontoons approx total legth 100 metres. cost per night for 10 m boat €7 in 2012. Water & electricity on pontoons at top of walkways. Clean toilet and laundry facilities. 5 minute gentle walk up to village (2 bars, boulangerie, auberge offering B&B / meals). Fresh produce van and Gaz offered from van on Saturday mornings.

Redon (89km) 21 miles up river from Arzal and as far as you can go without de-masting. The Vilaine crosses the Canal de Nantes at Brest, and entry to the yacht harbour is only possible from the South. It has good facilities, sells diesel and masts can be raised there. Cost per night for 10 metre boat €15 in 2012. Depth at least 2 metres. Facilities with showers €1.5. Market day Monday.
Daily Telegraph daily, other UK papers following day. Fuel available in basin or 3 minute walk away from Total Garage. Wifi internet in basin near to Harbour Master. 2 internet cafes in Rue Notre Dame where there is also a good cafe called Little Bistro. 3 small supermarkets in town and bigger slightly further out. Good french cinema with 5 theatres. Poor public transport facilities. Poor chandlery services but excellent technical assistance possible from the hire boat company opposite the Harbour Master (spare parts delieverd within 24 hours) Possible to lift out or de-mast.

Arzal,(131km) Two marinas, one with fuel and chandlery. Here the yellow 'dinner boat' requires access to the concrete quay just inside the barrier and has priority.

From Redon to the Arzal Barrage all marinas use VHF 9, and intership traffic uses VHF 10. The Arzal barrage, built in 1970, provides a freshwater cruising area for 42km up to Redon. The sea lock at the northwestern end of the barrage operates 6 to 12 times a day depending on season and tides but not when there is less than 1.5m in the sea approach.

Canal de Nantes à Brest

Nantes to Pontivy	144km 106 locks1	.1m water 2.5m air	*Fluviacarte/Navicarte 12 etc*

(The river stretch from Nantes to Nord sur Erdre has a depth of 1.45m with air draught of 3.8m.) At Redon the Canal crosses the R Vilaine. Quays and 2 hire bases.
From Redon, the Canal de Nantes à Brest is now diverted onto the R. Vilaine for a few km then runs south-east to connect with the canalised but attractive R. Erdre. Bretagne Fluvial hire base at Sucé-sur-Erdre. An 800m tunnel has to be negotiated beneath the city of Nantes. There are bankside moorings and a good port de plaisance just before the tunnel. At the other end is the St-Felix lock that provides access to the tidal Loire. The lock is worked between 06h30 and 19h30, for 2 hours before and 3 hours after HW Nantes. Masts can be raised downstream of the fifth bridge, preparatory to the 64km passage down the river, past St-Nazaire and out to sea. In a north-westerly direction from Redon, the canal runs through Malestroit and Josselin to Rohan and Pontivy. Lowest official depth 0.8m between Pontivy and Rohan, and at least 1m elsewhere. The section north of Pontivy was blocked with the building of a hydro-electric dam at Guerlédan in 1920. There is a local movement to re-open it, possibly by providing a boat lift. The extreme western end of the canal is the canalised R Aulne (See below).

River Blavet

Pontivy to Lorient	72km 28 locks	1.4m water 2.6m air	*Fluviacarte/Navicarte 12 etc*

Tidal below the sea lock just upstream of Hennebont (pk 58). Important notes about navigation and timing in Fluviacarte/Navicarte 12. Reports that some rock markings may be missing. Below lock be aware that all dangerous rocks may not be marked. In locks when descending moor well clear of the top gates if the indicating line for lock sill is not obvious.

River Aulne

90km 33 locks	1.1m water 2.5m air	*Fluviacarte/Navicarte 12* gives no useful detail. Check with Aulne Loisirs for current information.

It is 30km up the beautiful Aulne River from Landévénnec in the Rade de Brest to the Guily-Glaz lock that is worked 2 hours before and 1½ hours after HW. The Admiralty Chart of the Rade de Brest (3427) finishes at the Pont Térénez. Between Térénez and the Guily-Glaz lock, the general rule is to keep to the outside of the bends, otherwise in the middle. The current reaches about 2.5kts in the river and it is difficult to anchor out of the tide. There are moorings off Trégarvan. Once beyond the lock, yachts use the quays at Port-Launay and Châteaulin. With 3m of water in the canal and no headroom restrictions, large yachts can reach Châteaulin. The section between Châteaulin and Port Carhaix has self-operated locks, and is restricted to boats of 1.1m or lesser draught. Aulne Loisirs hire-boat base (Tel 02 98 73 28 63) at Châteauneuf-du-Faou, 43km upstream from Châteaulin. The Aulne is navigable as far as the Goariva lock, about 37km farther upstream, but in December 2007 concern was expressed locally that the upper reaches may not have adequate depth for navigation during the summer months.

Rivers Loire and Maine

| Nantes to Angers | 92km 0 locks | tidal water 4.5m air | *Fluviacarte/Navicarte 13 Vagnon 11 Breil 10 (This applies to the next 3 routes.)* |

The channel is typically 100m wide, and is tidal up to Ancenis. Depth is maintained by training walls and varies with season and rainfall. It is buoyed and in parts also marked with stakes which cover at high water. VNF offices will give advice and also provide a useful free guide. Nantes office, for downstream of Ancenis, Tel 02 40 44 20 20. Angers office, for upstream of Ancenis, Tel 02 41 74 16 30. VNF Vignette required. Just upstream of the canal entrance at Nantes, is an interesting footbridge which rises and falls with the tide maintaining headroom of 3.8m. Limited water depth at times of drought. Low key work is underway on further training walls to improve navigation, with the target of a minimum depth of 0.5m during dry summers.

Maine Basin

Attractive countryside with frequent haltes nautiques in small towns and villages, although moorings at Angers are limited. Beware cable-hauled ferry to Isle-St-Aubin, north of Angers. Authorised depth 1.4m but may be less than 1.1m in dry summers. Where noncanalised, depths vary with season and weather. No commercial traffic, but busy with hire boats at height of summer. Locks are small and some are operated by boat crews.

River Mayenne

| Angers to Mayenne | 130km, 45 locks | 1.4m water 2.8m air above Laval 3.4m below | *Fluviacarte/Navicarte 13 etc* |

Navigable north from Angers through Château Gontier and Laval to Mayenne. Distances below are from boat harbour opposite the Castle in Angers.

Grez-Neuville (22km) Hire base with water & electricity.

Chenillé-Changé (35km) Hirebase and municipal pontoon. Attractive village, restaurant.

Daon (42km) Hire Base. Water, and restaurant in village.

Château Gontier (55km) Municipal halte, with water, electricity & showers.

Laval (91km) Halte with water & electricity and quay.

Mayenne (125km) Halte with water.

River Oudon

| Angers to Segre | 18km 3 locks | 1.4m water 4.1m air | *Fluviacarte/Navicarte 13 etc* |

Leaving the Mayenne 28km north of Angers runs through countryside to Segre. Being a river, depth can be reduced to below 1m in dry summers.

River Sarthe

| Angers to Le Mans | 132km 20 locks | 1.4m water 3.4m air | *Fluviacarte/Navicarte 13 etc* |

Navigable through Sablé-sur-Sarthe (hire base) to Le Mans.

Distances below are from the boat harbour opposite the castle in Angers.

Châteauneuf-sur-Sarthe (34km) Pontoons with usual facilities L bank. Town with shops, restaurants etc R bank.

Sablé (62km) Hire base, pontoons & quay.

Arnage (121km) Private club (Maine Marine) with small quay, and also moorings about 3km downstream.

Le Mans *(134km)* Port close to town centre with usual facilities. In dry summers depth may be less than 1m.

NORTH EAST FRANCE
Canal du Rhône au Rhin (Doubs)

St-Symphorien to the Rhine	236km 114 locks	1.8m water 3.5m air	Vagnon 2 or Breil 9

Fluviacarte/Navicarte 32 is a single sheet map with limited information. Especially for a deeper draught craft the guidance as to channel position given in *Vagnon 2* is very useful.

Most of the first 186km are the canalised river Doubs and are extremely attractive, particularly the latter part where it rises to over 340m through fine mountain scenery and deep gorges. Some tricky shallows, usually marked by buoys. Two tunnels, both short. Little commercial traffic. When heading downstream on the R. Doubs sections, take great care at the approach to locks to ensure that the channel has been correctly identified. The weir is often alongside the lock and not marked in any way. In some conditions it is almost impossible to see it.

Repairs and chandlery (see individual entries for details)
St-Symphorien (pk 0).
Hire boat base at Dole (pk 18), Montbelliard (pk 164), Mulhouse (pk 31.6)

St-Symphorien (pk 0) Junction with R Saône. Good mooring basin run by **Bourgogne Marine** Tel 03 80 39 25 63. Maintenance, repairs, gardiennage.

Abergement-la-Ronce (pk 7) 50m concrete quay for 3-4 boats. 1.3m depth. Bread nearby.

Choisey (pk 15) 50m long pontoon with 1.6m depth. Shops in village 1km uphill from pontoon. Water tap some 60m down bank.

Dole (pk 18) Good port de plaisance on R bank between locks 66 and 67, €13.70 for 10m boat in 2012. Tel 03 84 82 65 57. Congested at hire boat changeover times. Depth about 2m. Water & electricity. At times of strong river flow, you are advised to use pontoons at upstream end to minimise risks from inexperienced hire boaters unused to current.
Opposite is L bank quay alongside a busy road and hence noisy with no facilities. Picturesque town, birthplace of Louis Pasteur.

Rochefort-sur-Nenon (pk 26) Pleasant 25m pontoon mooring on R bank just above weir but no facilities.

Ranchot (pk 39) Small concrete halte. Depth 1.5m. Water & electricity. €8 for 10m boat in 2012. Boulangerie close and indifferent restaurant, (June 2012).

St-Vit (pk 48.5) Very small halte in old river downstream of lock 58A, and possible bank mooring above lock.

Pk51.5 Downstream from Osselle, upstream of bridge – quay 40m, depth over 1.8m. No facilities.

Thoraise (pk 59.5) Pontoon mooring for 2 boats above lock, with water & showers, picnic table, barbeque and small children's play area. The Thoraise tunnel, just upstream of the lock has been artistically floodlit.

Besançon (pk 73) Concrete quay and pontoons on river L bank just above lock 50. Attractive town centre about 1km.

During the summer, for boats drawing not more than 1.3m it is possible to continue up river (not through tunnel) for about 1km, carefully following buoyed channel. Just after 3rd bridge, Pont-Battant, there may be moorings in high season.
Continuing to the right (south) of the island, just before the lock (St. Paul) is the halte Moulin-St-Paul, which has good facilities including pump out facilities. Tel: 06 71 17 91 29. It is close to the heart of the old city, but has very limited space for boats longer than 13m. The river buoyage is only maintained over the summer and this route should not be attempted without it. At other times the port de plaisance can be reached by passing through the tunnel, and then turning left and heading 1km downstream to the lock, which unusually for France, is operated manually by the boat crew. Above the manual lock there is a new L bank pontoon, also administered from Moulin-St-Paul, with the downstream end reserved for hotel boats. (The loop around the city was closed for bridge repairs to facilitate use of trams in centre of city, in 2012.)

Novillars (pk 86.4) Pontoon on R bank. Basic shops 10 minutes walk.

Pk 91. Stone quay above Deluz double lock.

Deluz (pk 93) L bank below bridge, halte with finger pontoons, water, electricity & pump out station. €7.40 for 10m boat in 2012 Little space for visitors, and badly designed bank side needs careful fendering. R bank above bridge – 50m stone quay limited water & electricity points. Basic shop in village.

Laissey (pk 95.7) R bank pontoon. Village only has a butcher's shop. Tricky lock to enter due to water outflow and eddies.

Ougney-la-Roche (pk 100) Restaurant with small pontoon on L bank of L arm above lock 43. Advance booking required.

Baume-les-Dames
- (pk 110) Good halte near bridge, with about 150m of quay, water & electricity - €10.20 per night for 10m in 2012. Restaurant adjacent to quay.
- (pk 112.5) Pontoon on R bank at campsite. Electricity. Water is a long way from pontoon.

Pk 125.5 – 126 Underwater obstruction reported in middle of river (2012). Course close to R bank recommended.

Clerval (pk 127) Single pontoon on L Bank. Watch depth. Water and electricity. Beware strong current when mooring. Single pontoon on R bank above lock – no facilities.

Isle-sur-le-Doubs (pk 140) R bank quay, 80m long opposite supermarket 500m downstream of lock 26. Fuel 200m from canal. Noisy, near main road. Above road bridge and lock 76 is a halte with about 120m quay, water & electricity €8.50 per night (2012). Depth less than 1.5m at upstream end of quay. Town has all shops and several restaurants. Laundrette in square and Bar-Restaurant du Palais has WiFi. Station with trains to Besançon, Mulhouse and Belmont.

Colombier-Châtelot (pk 147.9) Piled quay 300m upstream of lock 23.

Colombier-Fontaine (pk 151). It may be possible to moor at VNF yard just upstream of lift bridge. Both noisy. Village with restaurant near.

Bavans (pk 157.2) R bank quay.

Montbéliard (pk 164) Pontoons in old canal basin. Outer ones have 1.8m depth, which shelves to 1.2m at quayside. Mooring €10 plus €3 ea. for water & electricity. Pleasant town with impressive new gardens upstream of road bridge. Good shops and a handsome château. Good rail communications.

Vessels heading north are advised to telephone the Navigation Service at Valdieu (Tel 03 89 25 18 21) not later than 3pm on the preceding day to advise of their intention and agree timing. Locks are automatic up to lock 9. Other locks were manual in 2012, although work has started on the automation of some of them. It is possible to get from Montbeliard to Dannemarie (pk 9 on Rhine side of the summit) in 10 hours.

Belfort branch (pk 172) Begins just above lock 9, with a pleasant rural mooring stage with space for 4 or 5 boats and 1.7m depth. Branch is 14km long and 1.6m deep. Trévanans (6km along) port de plaisance run by *Association pour les Voies Navigables de Franche-Comté*. Contact Service de la Navigation de Montbéliard for latest depths etc. Tel 03 81 91 17 32.

Bourogne (pk 178) 40m quay on L bank with bollards and good depth alongside a factory. Rather industrial but convenient.

Morvillars (pk 179) – Between locks 7 and 6 – 50m above lock 6, 15m stone quay on L bank; further upstream 100m stone quay on L bank alongside warehouses.

Montreux Château (pk 185.6) R bank halte above road bridge and lock, with space for about 6 boats. In 2012 €5 including water & electricity, paid by credit card into a machine at the entrance to the tourist office by the bridge. It is necessary to insert the number of the power point into which you are plugged.

Pk numbering starts again from 0 just above lock. Beware of shallow patches at summit.

Valdieu (pk 5) Canal maintenance depot. Some locks past summit are automated or mechanised. 2 lock keepers take boats down to lock 15. Here 2 others take over until lock 27. Then 2 more take over to Mulhouse. When possible boats must travel in convoy. Stopping is discouraged at other than changeover points, but it is possible by prior arrangement. It is essential to tell the lock keeper one's plans well in advance.

Dannemarie (pk 9) Substantial port de plaisance on L bank – 6 sets of pontoons and several finger pontoons - €10 per night including water & electricity (2009). Dannemarie a small town with shops and restaurants across bridge.

Between Dannemarie and Mulhouse, locks 17 to 39 are a mixture of manual, part-mechanised and mechanized. With two teams of lock-keepers it is possible to get from Dannemarie to Mulhouse in 6 hours.

Hagenbach (pk 13) Between locks 22 and 23 L bank 60m wooden-edged quay with bollards. Water & electricity.

Spechbach (pk 20.2) Between locks 28 and 29 R bank 50m quay. Restaurant close by.

Zillisheim (pk 26) Bankside mooring is possible on L bank below the lifting bridge after lock 35, immediately in front of large Catholic college. Edge rather shallow, but soft mud. Shops in village.

Pk 31.6 Boatyard with crane and limited chandlery about 200m upstream of lock 39.

Mulhouse (pk 33) In the vicinity of lock 31, significant civil engineering works involving both road and rail crossings of the canal were under construction in summer 2012. When these are completed the boat yard that was displaced by the works will be reinstated and moorings provided, although these will not be as central as the port de plaisance in the old basin, about a km further downstream. This is convenient for the town centre, station and efficient modern tramways. Popular, and from June to September it may be prudent to book. Tel: 03 89 44 48 25. Interesting town with good shops, restaurants and a number of very impressive museums, including what is claimed to be the world's largest motor museum.

Vessels leaving Mulhouse are required to telephone the Navigation Service at Mulhouse (Tel 03 89 44 48 25) not later than 3pm on the preceding day to advise of their intention and agree a start time. This requirement may change, so check with the Mulhouse Port de Plaisance.

A few km east of Mulhouse the canal expands from *péniche* sized waterway to one capable of handling 3000 ton Rhine vessels.

Between Mulhouse and the junction with the Rhine at Niffer are two 12m pontoons for pleasure craft, set in a pleasant forest area – Halte de Homburg at pk 7.4 and Halte de Petit Landau at pk 4.6. If overnighting at either of these display a white all round light, for the large barge traffic operates through the night.

Niffer (ca 18km from Mulhouse) Junction with Grand Canal d'Alsace. Two locks, with the lock building for the newer and larger northern one designed by famous architect Le Corbusier.
In the approach to the southern lock are pontoons and a small yacht club, and there is access to the **Canal de Huningue**. This is a small canal that once ran alongside the Rhine all the way to the Swiss border, but currently only the first 2.5km to Kembs are navigable. It is narrow and there is some current, so passing other craft requires care.

Kembs Port de plaisance (with restaurant) at head of navigable Canal de Huningue, close to a small village with limited shops.

Grand Canal d'Alsace

Niffer to Strasbourg	102km 7 locks	2.1m water 6.7m air	*Fluvio-carte no.1 Naviguer en Alsace* available locally or use *Rhein 1* published by DSV Verlag (in German)

Some sections are the canalised R. Rhine. The canal is wide and runs between stone banks. The current in the main channel is considerable, 2-4 knots. Traffic is heavy. Passenger ferries and huge barges make uncomfortable wash. Locks are very big and yachts may be kept waiting for barges with which they can enter. There are waiting quays above locks.

Niffer (Rhine km. 185) Junction with Canal du Rhône au Rhin. (VHF Ch.20)

Ottmarsheim Lock (Rhine km 193.4) (VHF Ch. 22)

Fessenheim Lock (Rhine km 210.3) (VHF Ch.20)

Vogelgrun Lock (Rhine km 227) (VHF Ch.22)

Neuf Brisach (Rhine L bank France). Just below Vogelgrun lock is the junction with the Canal de Colmar.

Colmar 23km & 3 locks up a side canal is worth visiting. Depth 1.8m. In low season call 03 89 74 57 44 before lunch on the previous day to arrange for the locks to be operated.
There is a halte nautique with water & electricity at **Kunheim**, about 6km from the Rhine, and a mooring stage about 3km from Colmar, but otherwise few possibilities to moor.
Colmar is an attractive town set at the foot of the major Alsace vineyards, It offers excellent food and drink, plus a good music festival around the beginning of July and a museum devoted to one of the town's most famous citizens, Bartholdi, who designed the Statue of Liberty. Port de plaisance in Basin de la Batellerie with all facilities including laundrette. Tel 03 89 20 82 20.

Breisach (Rhine R bank Germany). Alsace Canal rejoins R Rhine below Vogelgrun lock. About 300m back up river on the west is Port de l'Ile de Rhin, a large yacht harbour with good depth and facilities, and set in the eastern bank is MYC (Motor Yacht Club) Breisach. The former is in France and about a 2km walk from the pleasant German town of Breisach, whereas the latter is very close to the centre of Breisach, but has only about 1.5m depth and is crowded; it has water & electricity (€1 coins required and expensive). There is a clubhouse with showers, toilets and a soft-drinks vending machine.

Markolsheim Lock (Rhine km 240) (VHF Ch.20)

Rhinau Lock (Rhine km 256.7) (VHF Ch.22)

Rhinau. Just over 1km below Rhinau lock L bank is the junction with the Canal du Rhône au Rhin, Branche Nord.

Strasbourg lock (Rhine km 288) Over the 3km downstream of Strasbourg lock are L bank commercial harbours, and the one at Rhine km 290 offers moorings for pleasure craft, although it is too far from the city centre (5 or 6km) to be a preferred choice of mooring for Strasbourg.

Canal du Rhône au Rhin (Branch Nord)

Rhinau to Strasbourg	35km 13 locks	1.8m water 3.5m air	*Fluviacarte/Navicarte 17*

Part of the old route to Strasbourg, this offers an agreeable alternative to the canalised Rhine. Little traffic and pleasant rural surroundings. An interconnecting canal from the Grand Canal below the Rhinau lock joins its original route north, at about pk 102. South of this point the old route is unnavigable, but restoration of a 25km stretch to the point at which it joins the Canal de Colmar has started but is not yet completed (2012). This will permit hire boats to cruise from Strasbourg to Colmar, something they cannot currently do since they are not permitted to use the Rhine.

Boats planning to enter the canal at Ecluse du Rhin, early in the season (before June), are advised to contact VNF in advance, preferably the day before planned arrival.

Boofzheim (pk 105.5) Hire Base. 80m stone quay on R bank. Bollards, water & electricity.

Krafft (pk 116) L bank quay 2.2m depth at former hire boat base. Further upstream on R bank, concrete quay; appears to have water & electricity . Pleasant village with good restaurant.

Plobsheim (pk 121) Quay

Strasbourg (pk 131 etc.) (See Canal de la Marne au Rhin). At about pk 133 is the Bassin de l'Hôpital noted below under Strasbourg.

Canal de la Marne au Rhin

| Strasbourg to Vitry-le-François | 312km, 157 locks | 1.8m water, 3.5m air | Fluviacarte/Navicarte 17 Breil 4 |

Although some of this canal runs through industrial areas, there are many beautiful stretches, especially the first 75km from Strasbourg where there is some of the best canal scenery in France. There is some commercial traffic and a large number of hire boats, even early in the season. Canal is generally in good condition. Locks are a mixture of manual and automated. Mooring is usually easy. Several tunnels and one inclined plane. Some locks are automatic, operated by a remote control télécommande which is provided on loan at the start of the automatic series. http://projetbabel.org/fluvial/rica_marne-rhin-canal.htm - see for photos and information about this canal, and a website that covers all waterways in France

Repairs and chandlery (see individual entries for details)
Strasbourg, Toul, Lagarde (pk 209).
Hire boat base at Saverne (pk 269), Lutzelbourg (pk 259.7), Pk 258, Niderviller (pk 246.5), Hesse (pk 241).

Strasbourg An exceptionally beautiful city with a large commercial port. The number of interconnecting channels and canals are confusing; *Fluviacarte/Navicarte 17* has useful plans.
Société Koejac, Quai des Belges, on the L (north) bank of the Bassin Dusuzeau. Fuel, repairs, 20 ton boat lift and good chandlery, €18 for 12m in 2012, plus €2.40 for electricity. 2km SE of city centre. Limited shore facilities.
The central mooring at the Quai des Pêcheurs in the River Ill is largely occupied by static *péniches* save for a passenger boat landing stage at its centre. It may be possible to lie alongside one, but they are used as bars, so can be noisy. The approach is from the Canal de la Marne au Rhin at its junction with the R Ill by the Palais de l'Europe.
The current is strong and there are many passenger boats, so care is needed.
In spite of the encouraging notes in Fluviacarte/Navicarte 17, sailing through the 'Petite France' area should not be undertaken without a careful check of bridge clearances and depths. (The official figures are 1.4m water and 2.75m air draught, but as part of the route is free flowing river, both may vary day by day.) Other moorings are in the **Bassin de l' Hôpital** (pk 133), about 1km south, which is a private boat club. There is secure mooring with locked gate, water & electricity. €10 in 2011. Quiet spot near centre of town. Both of these are reasonably close to stops on new and efficient tram routes. If sight-seeing invest in 3-day pass from tourist office which gives savings in museums and other services including transport.
For alternative mooring lock down onto the Rhine, and head for Kehl, on the German bank at **pk 293.7** which has a yacht harbour with fuel and restaurant just downstream of the road and rail bridges. (Nearby railway station makes Strasbourg visits easy.)

Souffelweyersheim (pk 307) Halte nautique. 50m quay immediately above lock 50 about 6km N of Strasbourg with water & electricity. Small restaurant close and supermarket 600m. Good frequent bus service into Strasbourg.

Vendenheim (pk 302.5) – 50m quay (but little space for visitors in May 2009)

Pk 297 Basin with good stone quay on R bank, set in forest area. No facilities. *Auberge de la Foret* close to road bridge but limited opening times.

Pk 294 Rural mooring above lock 46 is close to an isolated restaurant, *Les Jardins du Canal*.

Waltenheim (pk 290.9) R bank immediately above lock. 60m quay with bollards. Depth 1.5m. Village close by.

Hochfelden (pk 286.4) 100m low stone quayside outside VNF workshop downstream of road bridge, and grass bankside upstream of it, with no facilities. Shops and brewery about 1km.

Pk 278.7 Bankside mooring with bollards on R bank

Dettwiller (pk 276.8) 100m on bankside mooring with bollards on R bank

Steinberg (pk 273.8) 100m on bankside mooring with bollards on R bank

Saverne (pk 269) Hire base. Long quay and pontoons opposite spectacular Château which is town museum and art gallery. €10 per night, including water & electricity (2011). Picturesque town, good supermarket and laundrette. Internet in Tourist Office. Frequent rail service.

Pk 264.7 Bankside mooring with bollards and picnic table on R bank between locks 27 and 28.

Pk 260.8 Z shaped stone quay on L bank, one arm is 20metres long, the other 30m, fitted with bollards and rings. Water & electricity; coins required. €2 for 15 mins water/3 hrs electricity. A little downstream of the quay is a small dry-dock.

Lutzelbourg (pk 259.7) Hire base which charges for use of pontoons. Several places to moor along the bank with water & electricity. €12 in 2012.
100m further upstream L bank 25m stone quay with bollards but no other facilities.

Pk 258 Halte at hire base on R bank above lock 21, 150m stone quay with water & electricity, mainly taken by hire boats. Beautiful spot with fine walks. Restaurants & limited shops.

Arzviller (pk 255) The Plane Incliné d'Arzviller has cut out 17 locks. A vessel enters a steel tank that is then hauled up a steep incline broadside-on. Most impressive. For sight-seeing moor in wide basin at the bottom. Shortly after the inclined plane is the Arzviller tunnel, length 2.3km, followed after a short crossing-place by Niderviller tunnel, length 500m. One-way traffic controlled by lights. Péniche museum worh a visit.

Arzviller (pk 252) It is possible to moor close to tunnel control office to explore old lock flight.

Niderviller
- (pk 246.5) L bank port de plaisance Le Vieux Moulin re-opened in 2012.
- At pk 245.5 in R bank basin is the hire boat base which has all facilities, including a 25 ton crane. €18 night in 2012 + electricity.
- Also mooring along the bank. Free transport to Altenburger hotel restaurant in forest.

Hesse (pk 241) Hire base. Card access to all facilities, including fuel and a crane. Very busy in season.

Xouxange (pk 235.7) 30m quay with rings. *Auberge* close by will provide freshly baked morning bread if it is ordered the evening before. Madagascan cuisine.

Heming (pk 233) Bankside mooring possible but no facilities.

Gondrexange (pk 230) along Canal des Houillères de la Saar, which joins the R. Saar at Saarbrücken. Large basin with facilities. Local restaurant which provides transport . Bar in a trailer every afternoon at 16h00 and bread delivery in morning. Worth a detour.

Rechicourt lock (pk 222.1) claims to be the deepest lock in the VNF system (15.7m); replaced 6 locks – floating bollards and a speedy descent (30 min). Follow lock keeper's instructions as he will get as many boats in as he can, not necessarily in order of arrival.

Pk 216 Free old quay in basin just before bridge with road access. No facilities. Good depth.

Lagarde (pk 209) Halte and hire base: Tel 03 87 86 85 01 Water, electricity, diesel and a small chandlery. €10 per night (2009) Village has no boulangerie, but baguettes and croissants can be ordered the night before from the epicerie close to the halte.

Xures (pk 205.7) Free bankside moorings in basin, reasonable depth.

Pk 200 R bank immediately below bridge – 80m quay in pleasant surroundings. Water & electricity (requires domestic plug) - €5.50 per night + €3.50 for water & electricity – Adjacent to a camp site.

Einville (pk 191) Quay in small basin on L bank. Shops, restaurants.

Crevic (pk 183.7) 80m stone quay with bollards on L bank. Two doctors and pharmacy in village.

Sommerville (pk 181.3) R bank immediately above lock 21 quay with bollards.

Dombasle-sur-Meurthe (pk 178) Below here some commercial traffic, servicing the chemical plant that spans the canal. On L bank there is a large basin with moorings available. However, basin and surrounding area is very run down. Full array of shops and restaurants in town 1km away..

Varangeville (pk 176) R bank mooring possible near bar/restaurant.

Laneuville-devant-Nancy (pk 168.6) Junction with the Canal de l'Est (Nancy branch). For many years this short cut to the Canal de l'Est (10km and 18 locks) has been in a poor condition and closed to pleasure craft. Although it was extensively renovated in 2004 and was re-opened, it was closed again in 2008 "until further notice" due to landslips. Work to re-open started late in 2012 and it may be open again in 2013.

At about **pk 167** R bank mooring close to *Intermarché* supermarket.

Nancy (pk 163.7) Good port de plaisance in the Bassin St-Georges, Tel 03 83 37 63 70. Fine city, especially the Place Stanislas and the Ducal Palace, both only a few minutes walk from the canal. Wide range of restaurants. Railway station for links to Strasbourg, Paris etc. about 2km. away at other end of town, readily accessible by frequent trams from close to the downstream end of the basin. Fuel from petrol station behind capitainerie.

Leaving Nancy, downstream, there are two lifting bridges within 1km of the marina. One is controlled manually, with traffic lights, the other requires the use of the *télécommande*. Upstream there is large supermarket where it is possible to moor along the bank.

Champigneulles (pk 157.9) L bank 50m quay and 3 pontoons – Limited water & electricity.

Nancy-Frouard (pk 155) Junction with the canalized Moselle. The upper lock (Ecluse de Jonction) is 7m deep and has inadequate bollards. This lock is difficult to see when approaching from downstream, being obscured by a railway bridge.
The lower lock is double, and you may be directed into either chamber.
From Frouard follow the Moselle to Toul to rejoin the canal.

Pompey (pk 347 on Moselle) Halte on L bank.

Liverdun (pk 354 on Moselle) Small halte with pontoon in basin off L bank of river. Restaurant 1km.

Toul: the canal branches off from the river through an automatic lock. Above the lock is **Lorraine Marine**, at a former hire boat base, now run by Duncan Flack, offering fuel, service, and repairs within a 150km radius of Toul. Tel 06 01 85 19 85. 13 Rue de la Champagne, Toul, 54200.

Le Port de France. Good moorings between locks 25 and 26. Depth 1.8m. Water & electricity. Facilities block renewed in 2010 and decking laid down. €9.90 for 11m in 2011. Pleasant surroundings but exposed. Railway station and restaurants near, shops in town and supermarket up the hill beyond the station. Port is now being run by the Mairie. Take care of low bridge with arched profile after lock below harbour.

The flight of locks from no. 26 up to no. 15 are all controlled from no. 26 which is manned. Allow 3 hrs.

Foug (pk 122) 867m tunnel controlled by traffic lights. Good clearance, self-drive. Last lock before tunnel (no. 14) is paired and deep.

Pagny-sur-Meuse (pk 116) Halte with water. Shops.

Troussey (pk 111) junction with Canal de l'Est (Branche Nord), which becomes the Meuse.

Void (pk 104) Moorings by silos and VNF office. The chain of automatic locks between Void and the summit level uses short range 'télécommandes' as an alternative to the difficult swinging arms.

Mauvages (pk 92) Tunnel 4.9km. with compulsory tow. In 2009, east bound at about 08.30 and 13.30, and westbound at 10.30 and 15.30. Transit time about 1½ hours. Follow electric barge but under own power. Then boats sorted into groups for passage down flight of locks. Boards strongly recommended for protection against rubbing strake at side in this and all tunnels.

Demange (pk 85) Pontoon below lock with limited number of spaces.

The locks from Demange (no.1) to Menacourt (No. 17) form a chain, and it is necessary to advise the lock controller by VHF if stopping at any point within the chain. The 21 locks between Longeaux (no. 18) and Bar le Duc are all manual and operated by travelling lock keepers.

Longeaux (pk 67) Bankside mooring just above lock 17. Use ronds (pitons).

Ligny-en-Barrois (pk 62.6) Good halte fluviale.

Bar-le-Duc (pk 47) Quay with 1.5m depth. Close to busy main line station. €11 first night €7 second. Showers, key from capitainerie. Attractive town, worth exploring. It is possible to moor above lock on bankside.

Fains (pk 44) Small free halte before lock. No security or protection.

The 32 locks between Bar-le-Duc and Vitry-le-François all manual and operated by travelling lock keepers.

Sermaize-les-Bains (pk 24.6) Free berth. Bollards L bank, hidden in grass just after double kink under railway bridge.

Pargny-sur-Saulx (pk 19) Halte between locks 63 and 64. Water & electricity. Bar/Restaurant close to canal. Baker and food shop (mornings only) up hill.

Vitry-le-François (pk 132) Junction with Canal entre Champagne et Bourgogne (Canal de la Marne à la Saône) and Canal Latéral à la Marne.

CRUISING THE INLAND WATERWAYS OF FRANCE & BELGIUM

Canal des Houillères de la Saar

Houillon to Saarbrücken	76km 30 locks	1.8m water 3.6m air	Fluviacarte/Navicarte 17 Breil 4

At Saarbrücken the canal crosses into Germany, and joins the R Saar which 80km further on joins the Moselle at Konz.

Repairs and chandlery (see individual entries for details)
Houillon (pk2). Hire base at Mittersheim (pk 20), Saarbrücken (pk 75)

Houillon (pk 2) Hire boat base and pleasant rural mooring with water & electricity, repairs & diesel.

Pk 10.2 Substantial stone quay – no facilities.

Mittersheim (pk 20) Hire base, quay with water & electricity. Shops & restaurant 500m.

Bissert (pk 33) Quay with water & electricity. Other facilities at adjacent campsite.

Wittring (pk 52) Quay with depth 1.2m. Water & electricity at private YC.

Ettring (pk 57.4) Quay with bollards 200m above lock.

Sarreguemines (pk 63) Diesel just above lock 2. R bank port de plaisance at pk 64 with good facilities and new footbridge to town centre.

Saarbrücken (pk 75) Hire base just across border into Germany. About 2.5km further is R bank mooring at foot of grassy slope with coin operated electricity supplies, very close to town centre & shops.

Beyond Saarbrücken it is possible to descend the R Saar to its junction with the Moselle at Konz, and then ascend the Moselle back to Toul, so creating a circular route taking in the Saar, the Moselle, the Canal de la Marne au Rhin to Gondrexange and the Canal des Houilleres de la Sarre, back to the Saar. For this reason, the next section, on the Moselle, now extends beyond the French border at Apach, and lists the mooring possibilities in Luxembourg.

River Moselle

Neuves-Maisons to Apach (frontier)	151km 16 locks	2.5m water 6m air	Good charts though text in German in *Mosel Handbuch* by Karin Brundiers and Gerd Fleischhauer (DSV-Verlag Hamburg)

The canalised river runs from Neuves-Maisons, 24km above Toul. At Apach (pk 242), the L bank becomes Luxembourg and the R bank Germany.
Luxembourg ends at Wasserbillig (pk 206) thereafter the Moselle flows only through Germany and joins the Rhine at Koblenz. The locks below Toul are large, typically 180m by 12m and so you may be expected to wait to share them with other vessels.
Further downstream, the German Mosel is attractive but can be very crowded in summer. Delays at locks are likely. Beside the large locks there are usually small boat locks. These are self-operated and free, but width only 3.4m. Pleasure boats only pay in the large locks (€6) if they use them without commercial craft.

Repairs and chandlery (see individual entries for details)
Toul (see Canal de la Marne au Rhin)

Toul (pk 369.5 on the Moselle) Junction with the Canal de la Marne au Rhin.

Liverdun (pk 354) Small jetty in basin on L bank. Restaurant in village, 1km.

Pompey (pk 347) Halte nautique L bank below the lock. Just downstream of the railway bridge the Canal de la Marne au Rhin branches off southeast.

Millery (pk 340) Small halte in eastern side arm with intermittently working water supply. Only enter side arm from downstream.

Pont-à-Mousson (pk 328) Staging L bank just below the road bridge with 3 hour max stay. Close to good covered food market and town centre with unusual triangular 'square'. In summer 2006 a new port de plaisance was opened R bank about 400m above the bridge. Water, electricity and showers, with other facilities planned. Open all year. Tel 03 83 81 10 68.

Corny-sur-Moselle (pk 311) Camp site with moorings in basin on R bank.

Metz (pk 299) Immediately upstream of the cut to Metz lock is a branch on the R bank with sign to Metz port de plaisance. Turn down here, pass under the motorway bridge and out into a large lake. Continue, keeping about 15m from the L (north) bank, straight across to the opposite side. Yacht pontoons and the Club house of the *Société des Régates Messines*. Water & electricity. Tel 03 87 66 86 03. Picturesque surroundings. Fine city with parks, impressive public buildings and often spectacular 'son et lumiere' or similar free public entertainments in summer months.

Thionville (pk 269) Port de plaisance on R bank downstream of the motorway and railway bridges. Club house of the Société Motonautique de Thionville. Only outer pontoons have adequate depth. Railway station near. Current runs very fiercely here if water level is high.

Thionville (pk 268) Halte near town centre, no facilities and often wash from waterskiers, but very central.

Rettel (pk 249) Quay.

Sierck-les-Bains (pk 246) Small pontoons and quay, semi derelict in 2006.

Apach (pk 242.5) Frontier just below lock. On leaving France, for the next 34km downstream, Luxembourg is on L bank and Germany on the R bank. All the mooring possibilities below are in **Luxembourg.**

Schengen (pk 241.6) Town Quay. Scheduled passenger boats have priority at this, and 3 similar quays downstream, but the times at which they will use them are clearly posted (and the notices showing the times are normally updated every week). They are available for general use outside these times, but it is prudent to add 30 minutes to both ends of the reservation time, since passenger boats may arrive earlier or later than scheduled. If you do use them, moor as near as possible to one end, to allow commercial craft to use the rest, and if overnighting, display an all round white light, since there is round the clock navigation.

Schwebsange (pk 237.5) Large marina and adjacent campsite with all facilities including fuel and a restaurant Tel 23 66 44 60 (prefix with +352 if outside Luxembourg.)

Remich (pk 233.5) Town quay – space usually available downstream of trip boat staging, but again look out for signs indicating reserved times.

Wormeldange (pk 221.5) Town quay – see Schengen above.

Grevenmacher (pk 211.6) Town quay – see Schengen above, but note that there may be some free space at the ends of the reserved length.

Wasserbillig (pk 206.4) There are guest places with water & electricity at the Wasserbillig Boat Club, and there is a town quay just downstream of the busy car ferry ramp at pk 206.1, with the same availability as for Schengen, but in the absence of passenger boats it is heavily used by fishermen so the boat club may be the better option.

Canal des Vosges (formerly Canal de l'Est, (Branche Sud))

Corre to Neuves-Maisons	147km 96 locks	1.8m water 3.5m air	*Fluviacarte/Navicarte 9 Vagnon 8 Breil 17*

Runs from the head of navigation on the Saône to the Moselle and the Marne-Rhine canal. On the Moselle side of the summit, locks 34 to 46 are being automated (2009); locks 33 to 22 are manual. From lock 21 (Plaine de Thaun) to the summit are automatic. On the Saône side of the summit, locks 3 to 8 are still manual (2009); all others are automatic. Water at some locks but few fuelling points.

Repairs and chandlery (see individual entries for details)
Toul (see Canal de la Marne au Rhin).
Hire base at Fontenoy-le-Château (pk 125)

Corre (pk 147) Just upstream of the first lock is bankside mooring and halte nautique with 6 pontoons, water, electricity and fuel. €12 all boats in 2012. (See also 1st entry for the Saône for details of a large port de plaisance, below the lock). Lift out facilities by slip. Moorings shown in Fluviacarte/Navicarte on R bank are non-existent.

 Pk 142 R bank quay with barbecue and picnic tables about 1km above lock 43.

Selles (pk 137.5) Stone quay and small wooden pontoons R bank below bridge. Café/restaurant.

Pk 134.5 20m quay on R bank with picnic table and BBQ – Depth 1.4m.

Fontenoy-le-Château (pk 125) Port de plaisance and hire base. All facilities including fuel and laundrette. €12 per night + €2 each for water & electricity (2009)

Pk 11 Quay with rings on R bank with water and rubbish bins. Depth 1.4m.

Pk 115 Quay R bank, 400m above lock 25 picnic table and BBQ.

Pk 111 Small pontoon R bank above lock 21 in pleasant surroundings.

Uzemain (pk 108.4) Basin on R bank below lock 18. Long quay, but only 50m is useable because very shallow at western end and scraps of concrete at eastern end. Good bank mooring below lock 18 with rings.

Méloménil (pk 107) L bank above lock has rings.

Pk 103 Pleasant VNF quay R bank between locks 8 and 9 with bollards, picnic table and substantial BBQ.

Girancourt (pk 97.5) quay, R bank between locks 1 and 2. Supermarket down hill.

Chaumousey (pk 94) R bank (north bank) 20m quay with bollards and picnic table. However it is on the opposite bank to the village, but there are access tunnels. Also good bank mooring.

After summit level flight down to Epinal automated, some locks with unusual, fibreglass gates.

Épinal (pk 83) Substantial port de plaisance 3km along branch canal that first crosses and then runs alongside the Moselle. Tel 03 29 81 33 45. Branch canal had good central depth (2m) but shelves quite quickly away from centre. In recent years water supply difficulties have led to the depth being reduced to about 1.4m and there are closures from time to time. Port has most facilities and reasonable (1.5m) depth. €5 per night including water & electricity (2009). Good shops, restaurants and excellent covered food market in town.

Thaon-les-Vosges (pk 78) 40m quay on R bank below lock 19 with bollards. Supermarket near. No water or electricity.

Locks 22 (**Igney**) down to 33 (**Socourt**) were still manually operated in May 2009.

Nomexy (pk 71) 40m quay with rings and bollards on L bank with picnic tables above lock. A few shops nearby.

Charmes (pk 60) Pleasant small town with good halte fluviale on L bank. 100m quay below the bridge and 75m quay above bridge. Rings. Water & electricity. However, the quay above the bridge is very popular with mobile homes that compete for the electricity points. €7 per night (2009), including water & electricity; collected at 08h00 the following morning.

Roville (pk 48) Quay R bank just above lock 38.

Richardménil (pk 30) Downstream of lock 45 R bank quay with water, electricity & chemical toilet emptying point.

Méréville (pk 28) Quay L bank above lock 46. (See Junction with Canal de l'Est - Nancy Branch – may re-open in 2013.)

Neuves-Maisons (pk 32) The canal joins the Moselle at pk 392. There is a concentrated industrial area at the head of the large scale Moselle locks but the landscape soon returns to reasonably pleasant countryside. Unlike the rest of the Moselle through France & Germany, this section offers some opportunities to moor to banks which have steel piling. If mooring between the 3 large locks (Neuves-Maisons, Villey le Sec & Toul) advise nearest lock keeper on VHF 20.

The 3 large locks give a smooth and fast ride. When travelling downstream, at pk 372.5 there is a channel leading to the old *péniche* lock, down which smaller pleasure craft are signed. It is a good idea to call écluse de Toul at this point, since the lock keeper may prefer you to use the large lock if this coordinates with other craft movements.

Maron (pk 387 on Moselle) Small pontoon.

Pierre-la-Treiche (pk 377-8) Small landing stage to bar/restaurant R bank just above bridge. (See Canal de la Marne au Rhin)

Canal d'Est - Nancy Branch

Méréville to Laneuville-devant-Nancy	10km 18 locks	1.8m water 3.5m air	*Fluviacarte/Navicarte 9 or 17*

Although reopened briefly, this route that climbs up 5 locks, and then descends 13, to Laneuville-devant-Nancy, all in a 10km length was closed again in 2008, due to a landslip. It is now "closed till further notice". The alternative route via the Moselle has only 8 locks but is about 50km longer. If it ever reopens, it will provide a short cut to Nancy, albeit with 18 locks over its 10km length.

Canal de l'Est - Branche Nord (River Meuse)

Like the Canal de l'Est (Branche Sud), this has been renamed, and some new literature calls the stretch from Troussy to Pouilly-sur-Meuse, **La Meuse Lorraine** and that from Pouilly to Givet, **La Meuse Ardennais.**

Troussey to Givet (frontier)	275km 59 locks	1.8m water 3.5m air	*Fluviacarte/Navicarte 9 Breil 17*

Leaves the Canal de la Marne au Rhin about 20km west of Toul. Most of this route is the canalised R. Meuse. Much of the scenery is beautiful, especially north of Charleville-Mézières where the river runs through the hills and forests of the Ardennes. Commercial traffic is light but there are many pleasure boats at holiday times and accordingly, good facilities for pleasure boats.

Repairs and chandlery (see individual entries for details)
Pont-à-Bar (pk 97)

Euville (pk 266.5) Small halte with water above lock 5.

Commercy (pk 262) L bank pontoon with paying water & electricity points 100m downstream of road bridge, with easy access to interesting town. Also old quay on L bank behind Aldi supermarket has small boat spaced bollards.

Sampigny (pk 252) Rural quay on L bank with picnic tables and rubbish bins.

Lock No. 9, Les Koeurs, A difficult deep lock with no bollards in the wall and no ladder by the operating mechanism.

St-Mihiel (pk 241) Halte fluviale. Water & electricity. Good shops.

La Croix-sur-Meuse (pk 231) Halte with pontoons in basin on R bank. Water but no electricity although this is advertised in Navicarte. Restaurant nearby.

Pk 228 R bank quay with picnic tables & rubbish bins.

Dieue (pk 217) Sloping stone quay (sinkable fenders useful) above lock 15 with water & electricity. Reasonable range of shops about 10 minutes away and helpfully signposted.

Verdun (pk 203) Port de plaisance. L bank near town centre and quayside opposite. All facilities. Noisy music/concerts on quay in July & August. Spectacular fireworks on 14th July. Mooring, including free water & electricity. Supermarkets on edge of town downstream, smaller shops in town. Tour to visit WWI sites from tourist office, and rail tour of Citadel – recommended.

Pk 202.5 Quay with bollards on L bank in old commercial port, before bridge.

Consenvoye (pk 179) Basic halte in R bank backwater above lock 24. Lock has sloping sides, but floating pontoons have been added and it is easy to use. No shops but some local deliveries.

Dun-sur-Meuse (pk 162) Halte fluviale R bank below lock 28. Water, electricity, showers, and washing machine. Pontoons extended in 2008. Fuel station in town, or available from Meuse Nautique at pk 161.

Stenay (pk 149) Halte fluviale in small backwater R bank below lock 31. All facilities including laundrette. Shops and restaurants close, though many now closed. Supermarket on edge of town, 10 mins walk.

Pk 131 Small halte with picnic tables on left bank.

Mouzon (pk 124) Halte in backwater L bank above lock 35. Attractive small town. Showers and washing machine in capitainerie. Water & electricity. €7.80 for 11m in 2010.

Remilly-Aillicourt (pk 113) Remilly-Aillicourt *Hotel du Port*, 1km up old river, approached from below lock 36, has a small pontoon for restaurant patrons.

Sedan (pk 108) Port de plaisance in backwater R bank, above lock 37. Facilities shared with adjacent campsite. Attractive town. €10.80 per night, 11m, in 2010. Supermarket, 10 mins walk. Laundrette in town.

Pk 105 R bank, 2 new 1 boat pontoons.

Pk 103 L bank, 1 new 1 boat pontoon.

Pont-à-Bar (pk 97) (See Canal des Ardennes)

Lumes (pk 88) R bank 100m long pontoon with water. Bakery in village about 1km.

Charleville-Mézières (pk 80) Port de plaisance in pleasant surroundings close to camp site. Branch off canal where it joins river just above lock 43 and head downstream on river passing under 2 bridges to pontoon on R bank. There are further moorings in a large new basin about 300m further along R bank and under an arched foot bridge. The bridge signs indicating that there is 3.1m headroom relate to the full width of the arch, and there is usually 3.5m in the centre – but remember this is a river, so levels may vary. River and basin moorings share showers and other facilities with camp site. Tel 03 24 33 23 60. €23.40 (2 nights) for 11m in 2010.
Town centre 5 mins walk across river by foot bridge. Upstream of the town, lock 42 has high walls – have long warps ready! It is now automatic, but there is usually a lock keeper on duty.

Château-Regnault (pk 63) Pontoon moorings with water & electricity, close to restaurant, supermarket and other shops.

Monthermé (pk 58.6) Marginal L bank moorings upstream of road bridge, to rough sloping wall which needs strong sinkable fenders.

Laifour (pk 50) Quay. Very attractive valley with echo. Small supermarket near.

Revin (pk 40) Approx 1km down buoyed channel, halte fluviale with water, electricity, washing machine and security gates, set in small park. Shops and railway station close. €6.80 per day + €0.20 per person for llm. boat in 2010. €5 without electricity.

Fumay (pk 28) Long quay on L bank upstream of the bridge. Water & electricity. Capitainerie with showers and washing machine. Market on Wednesday

Haybes (pk 25) Moorings downstream of bridge. Best depth at bridge end of quay. Limited shops & pizzeria.

Vireux-Wallerand (pk 14.5) R bank moorings by bridge, with water & electricity. Reasonable restaurant *'La Vie en Rose'* over bridge to L bank, and about 500m upstream. WiFi in Bureau de Tourisme and small supermarket close.

Pk 7. The water level in lock 58 ('les 3 Fontaines') can overflow sides when full – lower fenders.

Givet (pk 4) Quayside moorings L bank up and down-stream of road bridge. (The stretch signed as reserved for commercial craft relates to a time when there was much more freight traffic than now.) Unsubstantial R bank pontoons below bridge with water & electricity, and showers etc in capitainerie in former warehouse on quay. Tel 03 24 42 14 33. (When river is in flood, you will be asked to use the L bank quay rather than the pontoons.) Small supermarket in square behind capitainerie and a good range of shops and restaurant L bank.

NORTH FRANCE

Yachts starting from the East coast of England can conveniently enter the inland waterways at Dunkirk or Calais. The first stretches of the canals run through flat country and are comparatively uninteresting, but they improve rapidly as one goes south and east. The most direct way to the Mediterranean is to make for the Marne route that can be joined at Condé-sur-Marne, south of Reims. Alternatively one can follow the river Oise down to the Seine and Paris and then take any of the three routes south through France. Several attractive circular tours can be worked out. Generally speaking, the further east one goes, the more interesting the waterways become. Water is available at many locks.

Fuel is not easy, so top up whenever possible. Many canal-side fuelling points are for barges only and cannot legally supply yachts. The canals from Dunkirk to the R Escaut are referred to collectively as the Dunkerque-Escaut waterway or the Grand Gabarit. They carry heavy commercial traffic. For approach and entry details for Dunkirk and Calais, see the *CA Almanac*. (See also WEST BELGIUM).

Calais The yacht harbour has facilities for handling masts that can be unstepped and, if required, safely left there. Repairs can be arranged. Water and fuel available. Entry to the canals is through the Ecluse Carnot and the Ecluse de la Batellerie. Arrangements for these locks should be made in advance with the harbour master at the yacht harbour or with the port authority on VHF 10 or 12. After the Ecluse de la Batellerie turn L into the Canal de Calais. The VNF office is across the road on L bank near bridge. There is a mooring pontoon for yachts immediately after the junction. This is not secure so leave someone on board.

Canal de Calais

to the River Aa	30km 1 lock	m water 3.47m air	*Fluviacarte/Navicarte 14*

In some summers this canal gets badly choked with carpet of weed. Cooling water flow should be checked frequently.

Pont-de-Vic (pk 29) Good moorings.

Les Attaques (pk 21) Good moorings.

Automatic Bridges There are 5 automatic lifting or swing bridges with detectors that must be passed slowly. Currently the automatic operation is not in use and VNF operator can be called as follows:-
Vic, Cuire, Coulogne and Les Attaques bridges VHF 22 or Tel 03 21 36 27 98.
Hennuin Bridge and lock VHF 18 or Tel 03 21 35 38 07.
Operating hours are from 08h30 to 11h45 and 14h15 to 17h30

River Aa

Gravelines to St. Omer	27km 2 locks	0.8m water 4.45m air	*Fluviacarte/Navicarte 14*(See *CA Almanac* for Gravelines entrance).

The 2 locks are in length of canal close to St. Omer, and from Watten south, the route is subsumed into the Grand Gabarit link to Dunkirk. At one time this canal was disused but it was reported open in 2010.

River Houlle. Halte nautique L bank pk 3.5

Gravelines (pk 29) Possible port of entry. Good harbour, English spoken. Mast removal. Tidal lock – opening times to be checked with VNF.

Watten (pk 120) Halte nautique. Good depth and facilities. Enter through small cut on L bank. Junction with the Canal de la Colme (part of the Grand Gabarit) from Dunkirk.

Canal de Neufossé

St-Omer to Aire	18km 2 locks	3m water 4.48m air	*Fluviacarte/Navicarte 14*

Good moorings on either side of locks. Water at locks. Pleasant countryside. Significant commercial traffic.

Arques (pk 108) On the R bank just downstream of Flandre lock is a basin with a rudimentary port de plaisance. Depth about 1.8m. Modest restaurant at foot of Fontinettes boat lift.

The lock at Fontinettes is 13.1m deep and the bollards are offset into the side which means you may have to move the boat during descent or ascent, it may be advisable to keep engines running.

Aire-sur-la-Lys (pk 93) Moorings without facilities in old canal arm, entrance on L bank at about pk 92 downstream of junction with Lys. The entrance to the arm, and the first moorings are still in regular use by *péniches*. Good depth save for uppermost 200m – arm was dredged in 2007.

La Lys

Aire to Dienze, Belgium	103km 10 locks	1.8m water 3.6m air	*Fluviacarte 14 (Aire to Comines) Navicarte 23 or Geocarte Map 1* for the Belgian section.

The first 40km to Armentières are a canalised river through pleasant country, with péniche sized locks. Downstream of Armentiéres, the boundary between France and Belgium follows the old course of the river, and so crosses and recrosses the present course, for the next 25km down to Menen, and thereafter the route is in Belgium, and its name changes from the R Lys to R. Leie.
The first 4 locks and several lifting bridges are operated by travelling lock keepers. Tel 06 60 06 10 41.

St-Venant (pk 12.5) Both R bank quay and L bank harbour, above the lock have water & electricity. Shops close.

Merville (pk 19.2) Pontoon in old river arm above lock, or moor to L bank just above lock, both with no facilities, but shops (including Aldi supermarket) and restaurants close.

Estaires (pk 26) L bank pontoon about 40m long with no facilities, downnstream of road bridge.

Sailly-sur-la-Lys (pk 30.3) R bank pontoon about 40m long with no facilities just downstream of road bridge.

Bac-St-Maur Lock (pk 32.8) Lock now automated. Télécommande will be provided at lock before and handed back at lock after.

Erquinghem (pk 37) Halte a short way up R bank side arm just upstream of motorway bridge. Depth and details unknown.

Armentières (pk 40.3) Port de plaisance in old river arm with all facilites, but about 2km to town centre and 1km to supermarket.

Deûlemont (pk 48) Junction with the Deûle, a canalised river taking barges of up to 1350 tonnes. What appears to be a yellow buoy at the junction is actually a very faded red channel marker, and the pontoon on the west side of the wide stretch just downstream of the junction is in a depth of less than 0.8m. (There is a port de plaisance on the Deûle about 1km upstream from the junction).

Warneton (pk 50.3) Quay in old arm on north side of river.

Comines Lock (pk 53.8 and 55km from Dienze) Downstream from here the charts do not show pk markings, so below, indicated distances are from Dienze.) Quays above and below Comines lock (which is in the Walloon region.)

Wervik (44km) Yacht harbour with water, electricity and a bar/restaurant in and old arm of river – enter R bank from downstream. New footbridge provides access to interesting L bank town with tobacco museum and a good range of shops and restaurants.

Also a small L bank plaisance pontoon downstream of footbridge, but subject to barge wash.

Menen Lock (40km) Quays above and below lock, which is in Flemish region and so a Flemish licence is required from here on.

Menen (38km) L bank arm best entered from downstream. YH is to port but space is not always available. Long pontoon to starboard. Pontoon electricity points were vandalised in summer 2007. Barges moor to R bank quay in river, close to road bridge, but wash would make this an uncomfortable option for most pleasure craft.

Kortrijk (Courtrai) (26km) The Leie divides into 2 arms with an island between. Several low bridges make the southern (R bank) arm impassable. The northern (L bank arm has a narrow secrion, so there is currently a 3km stretch over which a one way system operated. This is clearly marked by conspicuous signs and traffic lights and the port control can be contacted on VHF. Extensive widening operations are being carried out on this stretch, but they are still several years away from completion.

There are quays with electricity at both ends of R bank arm, and since they are in the 'one way' length the Port Control must be advised when enetereing or leaving them. Both quays have intercoms to the Port Control for anyone without VHF.

The downstream quay is reached under the Nieuw Dam bridge with an indicated headroom of 2.95m, but there is usually 3.2m or more at the highest point. But check- this is a river and levels can vary rapidly with both weather and heavy use of locks. Both quays, which are free, and have electricity can be crowded, and rafting off will often be necessary. Kortrijk ('Courtrai' in French) is an interesting town with excellent food shops and restaurants.

Kuurne (23km) Yacht harbour, primarily for smaller boats, with short finger pontoons, and some quayside space.

Harelbeke Lock (22km) Quays above and below, and about 500m below, a R bank pontoon with electricity.

Ooigem (16km) R bank junction with Kanaal Roeselare – Leie, a 16km arm up to Roeselare with 1 lock at entrance.

Sint-Baafs-Vijve Lock (11km) R bank plaisance moorings in entrance to old arm above lock.

Dienze. About 1km upstream of Dienze is the junction between the Leie and the Afleidungskaraal (bypass canal) and except for the occasional *péniche* the commercial traffic takes the latter.

Mooring possibilities at Dienze and the summary of the R Leie between there and Gent will be listed later in the West Belgium section.

Canal d'Aire

| Aire to Bauvin | 41km 1 lock | 3m water 4.5m air | *Fluviacarte/Navicarte 14* |

Isbergues (pk 89) Just room to tie up in small turning circle. Before using check if barges turn.

Béthune (pk 72) Overnight mooring in arm of old canal which enters on L bank. Water. The halte nautique is mainly a *péniche* mooring point. Well stocked supermarket, 20 mins walk.

Beuvry (pk 67) Pontoon.

La Bassée (pk 60) In old northern arm through the town was a halte fluviale between the 2 bridges but it had been removed by spring 2007. Supermarket and restaurants near should it be restored in future.

Canal de La Deûle

| Bauvin to Douai | 26km 0 locks | 3m water 4.5 air | *Fluviacarte/Navicarte 14* in which it is part of the Grand Gabarit |

Largely an industrial area.

Vendin le Vieil (pk 50) Pontoons in R bank basin.

Carvin (pk 44) Moorings.

Courcelles-lès-Lens (pk 36) A large sheltered basin on the L bank has a leisure centre with a small port de plaisance. Follow buoys across the basin. A notice at the entrance to this inner harbour warns that its depth is only 0.9m but there is a good landing stage outside with depth about 1.5m. Water & electricity. Pleasant surroundings.

Auby (pk 33) Good mooring, all shops.

Dorignies (pk 31-30) Fuel no longer available on long quay.

Douai (pk 28) Old river route through town centre blocked, but reasonably central quays without facilities can be reached by turning off Grand Gabarit under bridge at pk 30, passing south past silted up basin and up river until blocked by non-working old lift bridge. Alternatively the old river can be entered R bank just above Courchelettes lock and it is possible to moor a few hundred metres along, above Corbehem lock. The latter is passable with air draft less than 2.8m and gives access to about 1km more of the old route. R bank above Courchelettes lock is the junction with **Scarpe Supérieure** which is navigable for about 22km, almost up to Arras, an attractive town with large little-used canal basin. The last lock before Arras (St-Nicolas No. 28) is currently derelict and unuseable.

Scarpe Inférieure

| Douai to Mortagne | 36km 6 locks | 1.8m water 3.65m air | *Fluviacarte/Navicarte 14* |

Haltes at Vred (pk 41.5), Marchiennes (pk 46), St-Amand-les-Eaux (pk 58) and Mortagne (at the junction with l'Escaut.)

This route has been closed for several years and no date has been given for its re-opening.

Canal de la Sensée

| Douai to Etrun | 24km 1 lock | 3m water 4.5m air | *Fluviacarte/Navicarte* 14 |

Surroundings more attractive once past the junction with Canal du Nord. Moorings at locks.

Arleux (pk 15) on junction with Canal du Nord. Fuel.

River Escaut

| Cambrai to Belgian Border | 58km 11 locks | 2.2m water 3.8m air | *Fluviacarte/Navicarte* 14 |

(more on the Grand Gabarit section)
1km north of Etrun this route becomes part of the Grand Gabarit, the large scale route that links Dunkirk to Belgium. In 2008 this river was reported as closed at the northern end, buoyed off and silting up.

Cambrai (pk 0) Port de plaisance immediately above lock no 1 in basin, R bank. Good mooring. Shops and restaurants.

Etrun (pk 12) Halte fluviale in the Bassin Rond next to a boatyard (Etrun Yachting). Good pontoon - no facilities. The Bassin Rond is shallow, probably no more than 1.2m. Depth in boatyard basin is less than 1m. After Etrun the route is a mix of canal and straightened river, with much industry.

The 6 following locks are large (144m long and 12m wide), but surprisingly quick and easy. They may be called on VHF, alternate locks use channels 18 & 22, but they are well organised to handle large amount of commercial shipping efficiently and calling will probably be unnecessary.

Valenciennes (pk 22) L Bank mooring behind island above Folien lock (but **caution** depth may be only 1.2m) or R bank mooring with barges which may be noisy being next to railway sidings.

Fresnes-sur-Escaut (pk 31) Last French lock, where ships papers will probably be checked. After Fresnes, there is no possibility of mooring before the junction with the R Scarpe.

Mortagne-du-Nord (pk 44.5) Halte.

The Belgian border is about 1km downstream.

Canal de St Quentin

| Cambrai to Chauny | 92km 35 locks | 2.2m water 3.7m air | *Fluviacarte/Navicarte* 24 |

A fine old canal running through attractive countryside. Formerly a major commercial route, with paired *péniche* locks, usually with one lock of each pair out of service. Two tunnels, Riqueval 5.6km and Lesdins 1km. Locks north of tunnels automated and south of tunnels mechanised.

Honnecourt (pk 23) Halte fluviale below lock 15.

Vendhuille (pk 27) N end of Riqueval tunnel. Stop here to await towage south. Adequate quay, or possible overnight mooring in disused commercial basin, east bank just below road bridge. Modest shops.

Riqueval Tunnel (pk 28.5 – 34.5) Convoys –Check times with with VNF. Journey time about 2 hours and fee payable. There are plans to scrap the towage system, but first the tunnel needs to be provided with ventilation and this will require an extended closure.

Lesdins (pk 45) S end of short tunnel. Overnight mooring. Good quay, L bank above lock 18.

St Quentin (pk 53) Port de plaisance. Good quay and yacht club. Reported to be expensive. Toilets and showers in clubhouse. No fuel but filling station just outside gate. Port gate locked at night; get key from capitainerie if going out. Town 10 mins walk with shops, restaurants, and fascinating art gallery. St-Quentin to Pont-de-Tugney (pk 66) and Jussy lock (pk 77) to Chauny. Often bollards on banks in these stretches.

Séraucourt-le-Grand (pk 62) Halte in L bank basin. Water & electricity. Shops nearby.

St-Simon Junction with Canal de la Somme Island mooring with 1.5m depth on east side by picnic tables, but barely 1m elsewhere.

Jussy (pk 74) Quay by silo. 2 bakers.

Quessy (pk 83) Mooring on L bank after road bridge. Railway yard noisy.

Tergnier (pk 85) Junction with Canal de la Sambre à l'Oise.

Chauny (pk 92) Useful L bank quay close to town centre and main line railway station. R bank halte with end on moorings and 1.5m depth. Water, electricity, showers & laundrette. From here either continue straight down the Canal Latéral à l'Oise to Compiègne or turn L after 3km into the Canal de l'Oise à l'Aisne.

Canal du Nord

Arleux to Noyon	95km 19 locks	2.4m water 3.7m air	Fluviacarte/Navicarte 24

An alternative to the Canal de St-Quentin, running from the Canal de la Sensée to the Canal Latéral à l'Oise. Modern wide canal - heavy barge traffic, particularly at harvest time. Mooring very difficult in the canal which has sloping concrete sides, but there are several public quays. Care is needed at locks 8-12 where inflow is from openings at one side of the lock. When ascending this can cause difficulty if one is moored on this side. There is a 4.5km tunnel about 25km south from Arleux, controlled by lights and closed circuit TV. This is one-way except for the two-way middle section where convoys from each end meet. Traffic lights control the exit from the two-way section. Normally the convoys are timed so that the northbound one arrives first and waits against the starboard towpath. Small craft waiting should fender well and moor securely, so to avoid being sucked into the side or stern of passing barges. Further south, at pk 79 there is also a 1km tunnel, with one-way traffic controlled by lights.

As is noted later, under 'Future Developments', construction of the new Seine-Nord Canal started in 2011. Whilst this will largely run to the west of the Canal du Nord, its construction is likely to affect the Canal du Nord in a number of places.

Arleux (pk 0) Rather overgrown quay R bank at junction with Canal de la Sensée.

Marquion (pk 8) Mooring possible at pontoon or quay downstream of bridge and lock with water. Also a rowing club pontoon. Fuel from garage.

Moislains (pk 37) Public quay.

Péronne (pk 48) Port de plaisance, with buoyed entrance channel, (depth 1.2m) and quay, both on west bank, north of the 2 bridges.

St-Christ-Briost (pk 56) Basin is silted up but mooring on R bank between basin and road bridge gives access to shop.

Noyon (pk 93) Public mooring. Not very pleasant but worth a stop for interesting town.

Canal de l'Oise à l'Aisne

| Abbécourt to Bourg-et-Comin | 48km 13 locks | 2m water 3.5m air | Fluviacarte/Navicarte 24 |

Most direct route from Chauny to the Marne. A pleasant route with 2.4km tunnel and a reasonable amount of commercial traffic. Locks automatic or mechanised.

L'Avaloire (pk 11) Quay.

Anizy-le-Château (pk 25) Good quay above road bridge below lock 6. beside canal with fuel pumps. Restaurant 15 mins walk.

Pargny Filain (pk 35) Attractive rural halte in basin above lock overlooking feeder lake. Do not moor here or between here and tunnel entrance 3km further, without warning lock keeper. After tunnel, automated chain of 4 locks.

Bourg-et-Comin (pk 47.7) Halte at junction with Canal Latéral à l'Aisne.

River Aisne and Canal lateral à l'Aisne

| Compiègne to Condé-sur-Aisne | 57km 7 locks | 2m water 4m air | Fluviacarte/Navicarte 24 |

| Condé-sur-Aisne to Vieux-les-Asfeld | 51km 8 locks | 2m water 3.5m air | Fluviacarte/Navicarte 24 |

An alternative from Chauny to the Marne is to go via Compiègne and then up the R Aisne. The 2 routes join at Bourg-et-Comin. Then follow the Canal Latéral à l'Aisne as far as Berry-au-Bac; turn right into the Canal de l'Aisne à la Marne and join the Marne route at Condé-sur-Marne. There is a good deal of commercial traffic. Mainly rural.

Port Fontenoy (pk 80) Restaurant with 1 boat mooring downstream of road bridge. Depth 1.5m.

Soissons (pk 67) Good long mooring quay reserved for yachts on L bank upstream of the Pont de Mail and downstream of the footbridge. Free water & electricity. Shops, restaurants and launderette close. Trains to Paris (1 hr.)

Bourg-et-Comin (pk 38.4) see Canal de L'Oise à l'Aisne. New pontoon with water & electricity. Town at 1km.

At lock between Bourg and Soissons, ignore signs for new mooring 2.5km up arm of river, depths are less than 1 metre.

Berry-au-Bac (pk 18.5) Quays on R bank above and below Berry 3 lock. Junction with the Canal de l'Aisne à la Marne. Restaurants on N44 700m north of canal bridge. (*Restaurant de la Mairie* hearty & good value.)

Variscourt (pk 11) Piled quay with bollards & water point.

Pignicourt (pk 7) Bank mooring below lock. No shops but travelling baker's van.

Canal de l'Aisne à la Marne

| Berry-au-Bac to Condé-sur-Marne | 58km 24 locks | 1.8m water 3.5m air | Fluviacarte/Navicarte 8, Breil 19 |

Runs from the Aisne at Berry-au-Bac, through Reims to Condé-sur-Marne with a 2.3km tunnel.

The 9 locks from Berry-au-Bac up to Reims are contactable on VHF22.
Water is available at locks 4 and 7.

Loivre (pk 10) L bank quay.

La Verrerie (pk 12.5) R bank mooring and picnic table.

Pk 22.5 Total garage on left just before foot and railway bridges. It is possible to tie up alongside tow path just before foot bridge under trees.

Reims (pk 23.5) Halte nautique. Pontoon moorings. Water & electricity. Tel 03 26 88 55 36. Convenient for town and cathedral but **very** noisy from heavy road traffic alongside. About 2km N of town centre was a good fuelling quay, but it appeared closed in June 2008. Commercial moorings where one can access E. LeClerc hypermarket just north of fuel quay.

Sillery (pk 34) Port de plaisance with pontoon moorings, 1.5m. Good capitainerie. Secure. Supermarket with fuel close by. 10m taxi ride to TGV station at Champagne-Ardennes south of Rheims with 40 min service to Paris. http://www.ccvmr.com/relais-nautique

Condé-sur- Marne (pk 58) See Canal Latéral à la Marne.

Canal lateral à l'Oise

Chauny to Janville	34km 4 locks	2.2m water 3.5m air	Fluviacarte/Navicarte 24

Pont l'Evêque (pk 18) L bank halte in short arm under bridge is nominally restricted to craft shorter than 15m. Limited shops and restaurant.

Longueil-Annel/Janville (pk 34). Possible moorings above (more space) and below (crowded) lock Janville

Canal de la Somme

St Valéry-sur-Somme to St Simon	156km 25 locks	1.2m water 3.5m air	Fluviacarte/Navicarte 24 Breil 15

The canalised river Somme provides another route into the waterways from the English Channel. Its lower stretches run through largely flat country, but the surroundings are mostly rural and very pleasant. There are several interesting towns. Many associations with past wars, especially World War I. There is a little or no commercial traffic but many fishermen. From the sea to lock 7 (Sormont) the canal is under regional not VNF control, and no Vignette is needed.
Because of the lack of commercial traffic the river is silting up and depth is down to 1.0m. in places. There are many hire boats, whose skippers are issued with mobile phones with speed dial numbers for calling lock keepers. The numbers are posted at each lock, and a list of them is available at the first lock. Private craft will need a mobile phone. There are strong cross-currents where a lock-cut rejoins the main river and certain times of year these can be fierce. Be vigilant.
St-Valéry-sur-Somme See the **Cruising Association Almanac** for approach and entry from seawards. Up to date information about the buoyage can be found at www.somme.equipment.gouv.fr.) There is a good yacht harbour with pontoon berths. No fuel except from garage. Chandler and repair facilities. Toilets and showers in clubhouse. Shops and restaurants near. Crane for demasting.

Sea lock into the canal opens on demand from HW minus 1 to HW. Lock staff in house beside lower entrance.

Once into the canal there is a small pontoon on L bank before first bridge. Boatyard on R bank.

Repairs and chandlery (see individual entries for details)
St Valéry-sur-Somme (pk 0)
Hire base at Cappy (pk 50)

Abbeville (pk 142) Just downstream of the town the river enters the canal. About ½km up this branch is a new quay with water & electricity close to town centre. Hypermarket across the road, with fuel pumps.

Long (pk 124) Halte silted up in 1999 but mooring possible above lock 22.

Amiens (pk 90) Good quay in the centre near cathedral. Water & electricity. Depth 1.4m. Can be noisy.

From here to Péronne there are attractive wooded hills and lakes as the canal follows the old course of the R. Somme. Little difficulty about finding overnight stopping places. Fuel and water not easily available. Little commercial traffic but numerous fishermen.

Daours (pk 79) Vile smell is intensive pig production, not the chemical factory.

Corbie (pk 74) Quayside mooring near lock. R bank by campsite is convenient for town centre.

Sailly-Laurette (pk 65) Bankside mooring upstream of lock.

Cappy (pk 51) Pleasant bankside mooring between lifting bridge and lock. Shops and restaurants. Diesel available from hire base at pk 50.

Frise (pk 43) Quay mooring.

Just before Péronne the Canal de la Somme becomes part of the Canal du Nord for about 20km after which it branches off to the left to end at St-Simon on the Canal de St-Quentin. The junction with Canal du Nord is badly silted and a channel marked with yellow buoys.

Péronne (pk 48) Port de plaisance in an arm of the canal on the west bank north of the two bridges. Depth 1m. Free mooring at commercial quay. Shops and restaurants in town centre, about 1km.

St-Christ-Briost (pk 56) Basin is silted up but mooring on R bank between basin and road bridge gives access to shop.

The Canal du Nord leads to the R Oise and so to the Seine.

Currently the 16km stretch of the Canal de la Somme between the Canal du Nord and the Canal de St-Quentin is closed and no date has been set for its re-opening. A detour south is necessary by way of Noyon

Ham (pk 6) The halte above lock 2 is silted up. Mooring on L bank above lock 3 is possible.

River Oise

Conflans-Ste-Honorine to Compiègne	104km 7 locks	2.5m water 5.25m air	*Fluviacarte/Navicarte 24 Breil 13*

The river Oise, which joins the Seine at Conflans-Ste-Honorine, is an important route to northern France and Belgium.

The Aisne joins the Oise just north of Compiègne. It provides a connection to the Marne that avoids Paris, and also a through route via the Canal des Ardennes to the Meuse and Belgium. The river scenery is rural and winding with distant hills. There is a substantial amount of commercial traffic but most locks are large, paired and so there are few delays.

Repairs and chandlery (see individual entries for details)
Compiègne (pk 97)

Cergy-Pontoise (pk 9) Port de plaisance on R Bank. Depth 1.8m. Comprehensive facilities including laundrette. Good for visiting Paris (30 mins by train). Possible place to leave a boat. Very popular and crowded.

Pontoise (pk 14.5) Quays on R bank above and below railway bridge.

Auvers-sur-Oise (pk 21.6) R bank quay just upstream of road bridge.

L'Isle-Adam (pk 27) Halte nautique in attractive situation. Shops and restaurants near.

Beaumont-sur-Oise (pk 34.2) R bank small jetty and at pk 34.7, scruffy, piled mooring upstream of bridge.

Toutevoie (pk 49) Small quay on L bank in front of restaurant. Care needed. Rough bank shallow in places. Restaurant with mooring and at (pk 52) quay, both R bank.

St-Leu-d'Esserent (pk 52) Restaurant with mooring and, at pk 52.7, quay. Both R bank.

Creil (pk 58) L bank quay 300m upstream of Pont de Creil road bridge has good depth, and is close to town centre. Downstream of the bridge L bank near the rowing club is also possible. There is also mooring on the island near the museum and school of music, but considerable wash from barges.

Maxence (pk 71) Marginal mooring to steep bank upstream of bridge. Also space to moor above lock at about pk 71.6.

Verberie (pk 82.7) Space to moor above lock.

Le Bac (pk 87.5) Quay on L bank below bridge in front of auberge.

Jaux (pk 92) Crowded moorings at Marine Oise Plaisance for smaller craft.

Compiègne (pk 97) Useful fuelling point and good chandler *(Max Guerdin et Fils)* on R bank between lock No 1 (Venette) and Compiègne road bridge. Small yacht club harbour, depth about 1.3m, on L bank at pk 97.8. which is free but donation requested, and visitors may stay for 48 hrs.
Alternatively, moor to quay on L bank just downstream of Compiègne bridge or close to the floating Chinese restaurant above it. Palais de Compiègne, one of the great royal palaces of France, is only a few minutes walk from the yacht harbour. The junction with the Aisne is a short distance upstream.

Canal des Ardennes

| Vieux les Asfeld to Canal de l' Est | 88km 44 locks | 1.8m water 3.5m air | *Fluviacarte/Navicarte 8* |

With the River Aisne this is a very pleasant route. There is a small amount of commercial traffic and it is popular in summer with Dutch and German yachts. Satisfactory mooring places can be found at many small towns and villages with adequate shops and restaurants. Water is obtainable at most locks. No convenient fuelling points between Compiègne and Pont-à-Bar, but supermarket with fuel at Attigny.

Most locks now automated. Montgon flight of 26 locks is automated with 2 keepers on VHF 20. Stopovers must be co-ordinated with these keepers. Locks open at 07h00 from Asfeld to bottom of staircase, 09h00 from bottom of staircase to Pont-a-Bar.

Repairs and chandlery (see individual entries for details)
Pont-à-Bar (pk 1)

Asfeld (pk 58.25) Low quay R bank with bollards just upstream of road bridge. On Navicarte as 'tables pour picnique'. 'Shopi' Supermarket at about 600m over bridge.

Rethel (pk 36.5) Medium-sized town with TGV railway station on the main line from Paris. Good quay near centre, with water, a few electricity points and showers. Moor away from toilet block which acts as magnet for local youths. Fuel station on R, 10 mins walk turning left over bridge into rue de Montpellier.

Givry (pk 21) Pretty quay about 1 *péniche* long with 2 bollards and rubbish bins.

Attigny (pk 18) Last convenient stop before chain of 26 automatic locks to summit level of canal. Good halte nautique. Supermarket near with fuel and gas. Occasional disturbances from local kids reported.

Between locks 27 at Rilly sur Aisne and lock 26, the R. Aisne flows across the canal. Be prepared for cross current. From lock 26 up to lock 1 the locks are automatic.

The Montgon flight - from lock 26 up to lock 4 the locks are automatic, can be called on VHF 20.

Above lock 20 (at about pk 35.5) L bank space for 5 or 6 boats, with good restaurant close across canal.

Le Chesne (pk 29) Small free halte and quays with water & electricity, close to the double bridge, near shops, and with a restaurant, *'Le Charrue d'Or'* close by lock.

Pk 28.4 One metre high concrete wall on s side of the canal, east of town bridges – 3 bollards with 40m spacing

Pk 28.2 2m high corrugated steel wall at silo commercial quay with bollards. Good resting spot before or after the staircase locks. VHF 20 for Vallée de Montgon flight.

La Cassine (pk 17) Pleasant rural mooring below La Cassine lock. 3 bollards. Lock keeper sells eggs & rabbits, and may get bread to order.

Pk 14.9 Mooring possible on corrugated steel wall on R bank just upstream of bridge, 3 bollards.

Ecluse Malmy (pk 12) Low quay with 3 bollards on R bank just above lock.

Omicourt (pk 8.1) possible R bank mooring (with spikes) just below bridge.

Pont-à-Bar Junction with Canal de l'Est (R. Meuse).
Boatyard (**Pont-a-Bar Services**), part of Ardennes Nautisme, R bank with water, fuel, small chandlery, cranage, and other facilities. Under cover storage of vehicles whilst cruising. Tel: 03 24 54 01 50.. L bank has little depth. Bar on corner will get bread to order and has gas bottles to exchange.

Below the lock there is a wide basin where mooring is possible, some rings and bollards, but no facilities.

Canal de la Sambre à l'Oise

| **Fargniers to Landrecies** | 71km 38 locks | 1.8m water 3.5m air | *Fluviacarte/Navicarte 24* |

From Compiègne the Canal Latéral à l'Oise continues to Chauny. A short way further on the Sambre-Oise canal starts. It runs through into the R. Sambre which joins the R. Meuse at Namur in Belgium.

This route will be described in detail under **River Sambre** in the **FRANCE TO BELGIUM** section.

SOUTH WEST FRANCE

Sèvre Niortaise

| Marans to Niort | 80km 9 locks | 1.2m water, 2.2m air | *Breil 14* |

Entry from seawards discussed in **Reeds Nautical Almanac.** Map of waterways and area in *Inland Waterways of France* by David Edwards May. (See Bibliography)
Draught may be less in summer. Forewarn of arrival to Marans Sealock, Tel 05 46 01 53 77. Port Tel 05 46 01 10 35,

La Charente

| Rochefort to Angoulême | 160km 21 locks | Water as below, 3.55m air | *Fluviacarte/Navicarte 25) or Breil 6* |

Attractive river scenery, tidal as far as St-Savinien. Up to Cognac depth will be at least 1.5m at low water. In Summer, with barrages at lowest 2 locks closed, depth usually over 2m. Above Cognac depth decreases progressively, 1.5m at Jarnac and as little as 0.8m at Angoulême. Distances given below are km upstream from Rochefort.

Repairs and chandlery (see individual entry for details)
Hire base at Jarnac

Rochefort Entry from seawards up about 10 miles of estuary from Port des Barques, see CA Almanac or Reeds. Marina with access restricted to around HW. Forewarn of arrival Tel 05 46 83 99 96. Boats up to 18m long and 6m wide, draft 2.50m.

Tonnay-Charente (6.5km) Pontoons above and below bridge.

14km above Rochefort is junction with R Boutonne which is navigable for about 28km. (To pass tidal barrier advance notice must be given at Rochefort.)

Pont-de-Houmée (15km) pontoon with water & electricity.

St-Savinien. (28km) Halte and hire base above sea lock. When travelling upstream contact sea lock at least an hour before ETA. Tel 05 46 90 20 91.

Saintes (49km) Halte with water & electricity. Amphitheatre.

Cognac (85km) Quays, halte & hire base. Depth 1.60m.

Jarnac (100km) Hire boat base

Port d'Envaux (pk 43) Depth 1.50m. Floating pontoons and facilities.

Sireuil (127km) Hire base. Public and private port for boats up to 12m. Draft 0.70m.

Angoulême (144km) Head of navigation. Pk 0 Port L'Houmeau, halte fluviale for boats up to 30m, draft 0.80m.

L'Adour

| Bayonne to Dax | 49.5km 0 locks | tidal water 3.5m air |

(See CA Almanac for entrance directions). An attractive, albeit isolated, cruising area. A good summary in Inland Waterways of France by David Edwards-May. (See Bibliography.)
Anglet Port de Brise-Lames 2km from sea. All facilities including fuel. Other ports de plaisance at Lahonce and Peyrehorade. 6 small tributaries. Navigation Service (DDE) Tel 05 59 55 27 97.

FUTURE DEVELOPMENTS

Survey and archaeological work is now underway for a new link, some 105km long, largely to the west of the existing Canal du Nord, to link the Oise from Compiègne to the Grand Gabarit (large scale canals) near Arleux, thereby providing a north-south access for barges of up to 4400 tons. Serious civil engineering started in 2011. Once the work is completed (officially and highly optimistically by 2015) it is likely that the Canal du Nord will be closed. Unlike the existing Canal du Nord, which locks down to the level of the Somme at Péronne, the new canal will cross the valley of the Somme on a large aqueduct.

BELGIUM

Belgium is a country which tends to be overlooked by the majority of the British boating community, to their great loss. Although many of the Belgian canals are heavily used commercially, particularly in Flanders where, for example, the Albertkanaal can take vessels of up to 2,000 tonnes, and several pass through industrialised areas, this is more than offset by scenery that equals anything likely to be seen in France. There are many picturesque towns, villages, châteaux, abbeys and historical sights within easy reach of the Belgian Waterways.

Belgian food is arguably the best in the world, as is their beer. Indeed, the only real drawback to Belgium is the weather, which is more like that in Britain than in France!

There are more than 1,500km of navigable inland waterways in Belgium. As on waterways elsewhere in the world, one will see aspects of the country which are invisible to those who spend their lives on the land. Even in the industrial areas, there is much of interest to be seen, particularly to those with even the remotest interest in the rise and fall of great industries. Belgium has been described as 'the cockpit' of Europe and there is much of interest to the historian, in particular, many battlefields from the Middle Ages onwards lie on, or close to, the canals and rivers.

Facilities for pleasure craft tend to be less well developed than in Picardy and other parts of Northern France but new marinas are being developed in several places, particularly where commercial traffic is declining, notably on some of the smaller canals.

In 2007, the Belgian authorities prohibited pleasure craft from using red diesel for propulsion. Since this means that pleasure craft can no longer use many of the refueling points that primarily serve commercial craft, waterside refueling points are now few and far between. As at 2011 we are only aware of Antwerp, Antoing, Bocholt, Brussels, Comines, Dijksmuide, Givet, Liège, Namur and Nieuwpoort. If and when we become aware of other places we will post them on the CA website.

FRANCE TO BELGIUM

Belgian Meuse

Givet (border) to Liège	114km 13 locks	2.2m water 5.5m air	Fluviacarte/Navicarte 9

The Meuse route from France to Belgium is summarised in the French Section under the French official name of the Canal de l'Est. From the Belgium border to the junction with the Albertkanaal (north of Liège [Luik]) the scenery is spectacular in many parts, but particularly in the 45kms from Givet to Namur (Namen), most of which lies in Belgium. Commercial traffic is moderate from Pont à Bar to Dinant, increasing gradually the further north one goes. From Dinant onwards, there is reasonably heavy commercial traffic. The size of the barges also increases with vessels up to 1,350 tonnes.

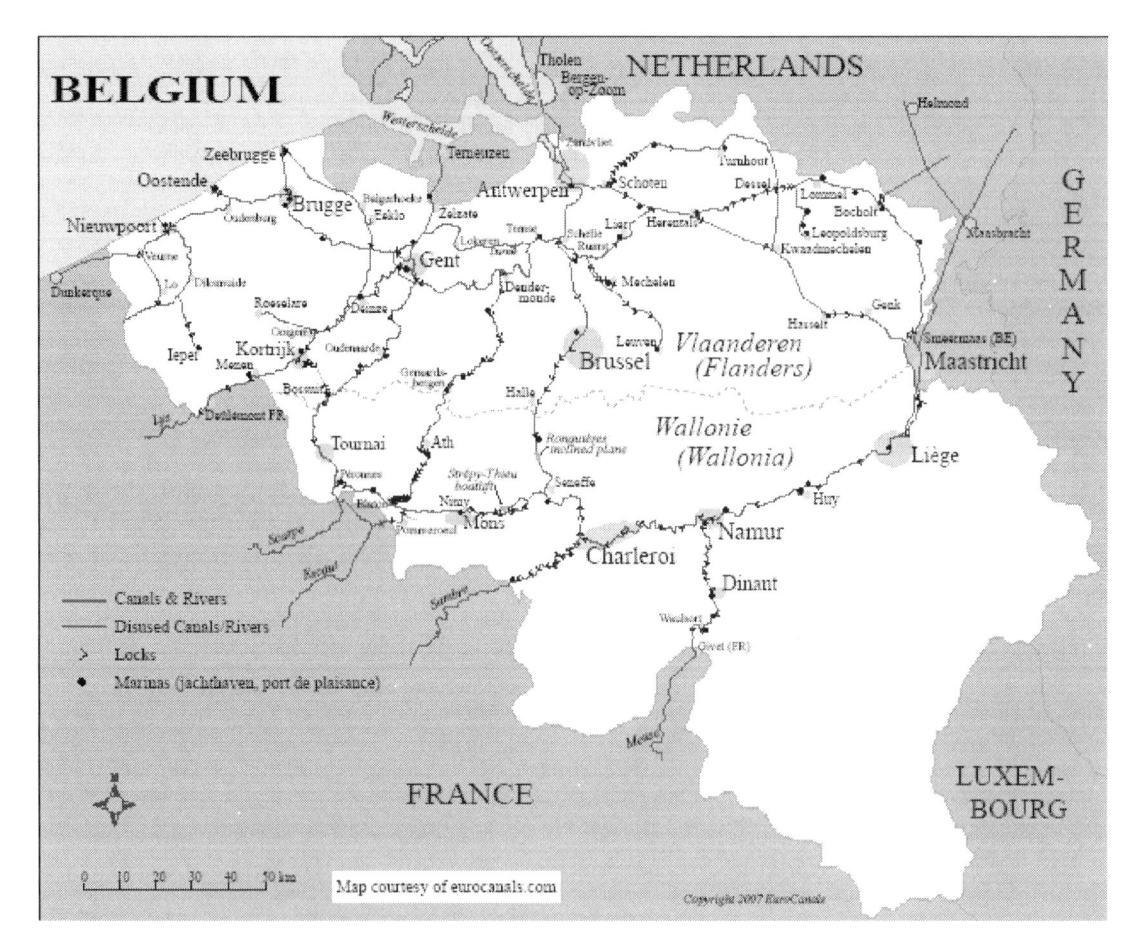

There are rubbish containers at most of the Belgian Meuse locks.

Repairs and chandlery (see individual entries for details)
Heer (pk 0), Liège (pk 110),

Heer (pk 0) At the border, a few metres on the Belgian side, on the L bank, the fuelling point and small chandlers and barge supply shop is still operational.

Ecluse de Hastière (pk 4) mooring possible to R bank in upstream lock approach, with a few electricity points.

Hastière par delà (pk 6) A small number of places are available on the R bank. From April to October, some are reserved exclusively for tourist boats. No water or electricity.

Waulsort (pk 9) Substantial pontoons and quay on R bank below lock, opposite the Hastière Yacht Club. There is a basic bar/restaurant R bank and a free passenger ferry to the L bank. It is possible to winter here, with electricity to most berths.

Anseremme (pk 15.5) Pontoons on the R bank close to the railway bridge immediately upstream of the barrage and Ecluse d'Anseremme. Water & electricity. Upstream of the pontoons there is a small port de plaisance with water & electricity – the R bank entrance through a 3.5m high bridge is easy to miss.

At about pk 16.3 on R bank is the mouth of the R Lesse. This is navigable by kayak, and it is possible to take a train to either Houyet, which is 21km upstream, or Gendron which is 12km, collect your kayak and enjoy the kayak ride down. This service operates from the square in front of the church.

Dinant (pk 19) Boats can be moored alongside on the R bank. Two main areas: one right in town centre, downstream of the bridge, close to busy roads and thus very noisy, the other, about 500m upstream of the bridge, is much quieter. Both have water & electricity. There is also free mooring with no facilities, to the quay in front of the R bank Casino a further 500m upstream. The capitainerie has been moved to Tourist Office next door. Tel 082 22 28 70. Station close.

Houx and **Anhée** (pk 24) On both the R and L banks, upstream of the railway bridge, there are small quays with some bollards, but no other facilities.

Yvoir (pk 27) Restaurant with moorings in R bank side arm. Approach must be from downstream.

Namur (Namen) (pk 46) A marina, Plage d'Amée, R bank above the La Plage lock at about pk 44.6. All facilities, but about 2km from town centre, and run by the same team who run the Port de Jambes. Tel 081 31 39 46. Regular vedette services to town.

More central is the very pleasant R bank **Port de Jambes**, just upstream of the town bridge. Large pontoons with space for 50 boats. Water, electricity, WiFi, showers and diesel. Tel 081 31 39 46.
It is also possible to moor to the L bank quay opposite, except on the days when a market is held on this quay. (A €7 charge is made but there are no facilities).

Beez (pk 52) Port de plaisance de Beez 6km downstream of Namur on L bank. Shops & restaurants 3km.

Sclayn (pk 60) Downstream from the bridge, quays on both banks, railway station on L Bank, limited shops on R Bank.

Andenne (pk 65) On both banks there are long high quays with bollards (at '*péniche* distances' apart), but no other facilities. There is a length of quay on R bank, upstream of the road bridge, suitable for pleasure craft. No facilities, unprepossessing aspect, but convenient for shops.

Wanze (pk 75.7) Port de Statte on L bank with 25 visitor berths opened summer 2000. (Tel 085 23 14 22) Shops about 1m..

Huy (pk 77) Interesting town with cable car to Citadel. Near to bridge. On both banks there are a number of places to secure on bollards. Port de plaisance de Corphalie 2.5km downstream on L bank with water and showers. (Tel 085 21 35 85)

Ecluse d'Ampsin Neuville (pk 82.7) Extensive quays above and below.

Pk 86.7 R bank plaisance quay with no facilities.

Pk 99 Supermarket, Autostop and DIY shop on R bank. Can tie up alongside.

Liège (pk 110) There are several places to moor alongside in Liège. Probably best is the port de plaisance on L bank. Downstream of Pont Albert 1er, and upstream of Pont Kennedy, the entrance is marked by a

prominent metal statue of a diver. VHF23 and tel 042 23 14 04. €25.45 for 3 nights in 2010 incl. electricity and water, and discount token for restaurant.
Recently built ground floor capitainerie, with all facilities including washing machine, and a good restaurant on the roof. Some distance from shops, so for late arrivers, nearest is a small 'open all hours' general store, across the river via Pont Albert 1er, on the road nearest the river, about 100m upstream.

Downstream at pk 112.4 up old arm on L bank are several boat yards, including **Cintec Yachting**, who sell diesel and petrol, offer repairs and chandlery, and have a 15 ton crane on site (and can bring in a larger one if necessary). Open Monday to Saturday all year round. Tel 042 27 49 03.

(There is a plan to create plaisance moorings at the end of this arm, which commercial craft have largely ceased to use.)

There is a good deal of commercial traffic through Liège and delays may be expected at Ecluse de Ivoz Ramet (the first lock upstream of the city). The Navicarte shows the old *péniche* lock alongside the big one as out of service but it is still used when there are problems with the big lock.

River Sambre

| Fargniers to Namur | 88km 17 locks | 2.0 water 3.9 air | Fluviacarte/Navicarte 23 |

The Sambre is a main route between France and Belgium. From France it starts with the Canal de la Sambre à l'Oise at the junction of the Canal de la Sambre à l'Oise with the Canal lateral à l'Oise and the Canal de St.Quentin at Fargniers. At Landrecies the canal becomes the R Sambre in France and crosses the border to Charleroi at the junction with the Canal de Charleroi à Brussels à Rupel and then continues to Namur to join the Meuse.

The route from Fargniers to Charleroi has a limited amount of commercial traffic and passes through some very beautiful and pleasant countryside. It is particularly attractive in the spring and late autumn. The Charleroi to Namur section has heavy commercial traffic, with large vessels of up to 1,350 tonnes (except on Sundays when commercial traffic is forbidden) and largely industrial sites in various stages of decay.

However, In February 2006, the VNF announced that the moving bridge at Vadencourt (12km north of Origny-Ste-Benoîte) was in danger of collapse, and closed the navigation in the pound between locks 18 and 19. Restoration of the aqueduct at Vaudencourt, and another at Macquigny may start in 2012. There is therefore currently no throughway from France to Belgium via this route.

All the French locks are *péniche* size but the Belgian ones are bigger and some at least 110m long. There is a variety of lock types and manning.

From the junction with the Canal de St-Quentin to the lock before Origny St. Benoite the ten locks are automatic and are operated by 'télécommandes'. These are issued at either the Tergnier (32) or the Fargniers (33) lower lock on the Canal de St-Quentin, for traffic towards Belgium or the Origny-Ste-Benoîte lock (25) for southbound traffic. The 'télécommande', which is a radio transmitter, comes complete with instructions in English and several other languages.

From Origny St. Benoite to Etreux (8), the eighteen locks are operated manually. The same éclusier operates several of the locks, travelling ahead to the next lock of his group in a car. He is also responsible for operating the swing bridges in his 'patch'. The seven locks from Etreux (7) to the summit are an automated chain, in which leaving one actuates the next. If you stop between these locks, you should advise the lock keeper so that the automatic system can be reset. After the summit level, the eleven locks from écluse Bois l'Abbaye to écluse de Mauberge are automated, and are also operated by radio 'télécommandes' of a different design, but also with multilingual instructions. The 'télécommande is issued at écluse Bois l'Abbaye. The écluse de Marpent (the last lock in France) is automatic, but manned for 'télécommande return. The first 9 locks in Belgium are all operated manually. Each lock has its own éclusier. The remaining locks on the Belgian Sambre are manned and operated electrically.

Repairs and chandlery (see individual entries for details)
Erquelinnes, (pk 0.3) Péronnes (Canal Nimy-Blaton-Péronnes).

Landrecies (France) to border

| 71km 38 locks | 1.8m water 3.5m air | Fluviacarte/Navicarte 24 |

Moy de l'Aisne (pk 57) Quay on right bank below écluse 32 (Hamegicourt).

Ribemont (pk 48) On the L bank, just below écluse 27, there is a small inlet with a small old concrete edged quay about 30m long fitted with four old very large bollards. It is not a formal halte; rather, it is a place where it is possible to stop. Mooring stakes are required, despite the ancient bollards. The town, with the usual range of shops, is a 20 minute walk away. One boulangerie opens at 05.45.

Origny St. Benoite (pk 44) Immediately below écluse 25, on the R bank is a very large (former commercial) basin. Bollards (at pleasure craft distances apart) have now been installed. However, the wooden 'fender' fixed about 50cm above the water level is old and rotten, with a large number of metal bolts sticking out. No other facilities although fresh water can be obtained at écluse 25. The canalside factory sometimes generates unpleasant smells. Good range of shops in the town, about 15 minutes walk away.

There are few suitable places to stop between Origny St. Benoite and the summit but the travelling lock keepers may be able to advise.

Vadencourt (pk 32) above ecluse 19, R bank mooring with no facilities. See earlier note above about canal blockage at moving bridge above this point.

Tupigny (pk 28) above ecluse 15, R bank mooring with no facilities

Etreux (pk 21.5) On the R bank, below écluse 6, there is a concrete quay with only two bollards, *péniche* length apart. There is often a *péniche* lying there discharging its cargo.

Summit (pk 19) First class halte with pontoons & electricity close to and above écluse Gard 1. Water at the lock. Mont le Gard, a small village with a supermarket is about 5 minutes walk. Bread can be obtained from a van at approximately 0845. There is also a small café/restaurant.

Landrecies (pk 0.5) Relais Fluviale with water & electricity on the R bank above the lock - restored 2003. Bread van.

Maroilles (pk 4.5) Pleasure moorings in landscaped area.

Hachette (pk 7.4) On the L bank above the lock, there is a small relais fluviale in small inlet.

Leval (pk 15) Nature trail and moorings

Berlaimont (pk 18) Either side of the island between the barrage and lock, there are wooden posts for mooring. On the town side, some pontoons, best depth at upstream end.

Pont-sur-Sambre (pk 21.5) On L bank about 200m above écluse Pont-sur-Sambre, there is a concrete quay, about 15m long, separated by a launching slope from a pontoon (about 25m long). Less than 100m from boulangerie (opens 07h.45) and supermarket. Also a pharmacy and post office. The Grill-bar-Tabac is only open at midday and on Saturday pm.

Boussières-sur-Sambre (pk 32) A small quay with some bollards on the L bank, close to the bridge.

Hautmont (pk 35.5) Halte fluviale, capable of taking one small boat, below the lock, near to the barrage.

Mauberge (pk 41.4) In the centre of the town, above écluse Mauberge, a new halte nautique with water & electricity was opened in Summer 2006. Good range of shops and restaurants within easy access.

Boussois (pk 48) Small quay on L bank just downstream of bridge. Well lit moorings with riverside park.

Jeumont (pk 53) Quays both banks plus a new (2011) pontoon with water & electricity, all free.

Border to Charleroi (Belgium)

40km and 11 locks	2.2m water 4.5m air	*Fluviacarte/Navicarte 9*

Repairs and chandlery
Erquelinnes (pk 0.3)

Erquelinnes (pk 0.3) Diesel on the L bank from 'Les *Mariniers',* a pub and fuelling point with a small number of chandlery items. Diesel is still available.

Yacht Club des Frontières (pk 0.6) Entrance under a railway bridge on the L bank. It is located in an old commercial basin. The capitainerie is located in a converted *péniche*. The visitors' berths are immediately to the left of the entrance 'cut', opposite the capitainerie. Facilities include water, electricity and showers. The village, which has a fair range of shops, is 5 minutes walk away. Cost about €8 per night (plus €3 for electricity).

Lobbes (pk 17) Plenty of places to moor, on both sides of the canal, with bollards at pleasure boat distances, in pleasant surroundings. There is a good range of shops 10 minutes walk away (uphill). The restaurant close to the canal is closed on a Monday.

Thuin (pk 19) Limited mooring on L bank above the lock – bollards are at *péniche* distance apart. 10 min walk to town.

There is also a small halte on the R bank close to the town centre. The town has a good range of shops and a barge museum. Good value Chinese restaurant close to station.

Abbaye d'Aulne (pk 28) On the R bank, just above the lock there is a small quay, although it is often occupied by *péniches*. There are three restaurants/bistros close by but no shops.

Landelies (pk 30) Yacht Club Haut Sambre Port de Plaisance in a cut close to the barrage. On the R bank there may be space available with water & electricity but most berths are occupied by club members. On the L bank there is a small quay for three boats but no other facilities. Cost about €9 per night plus €3 for water. The village, 10 min walk uphill, has a small range of shops.

Marchienne au Pont (pk 36.3) L bank mooring in front of castle for plaisance and trip boats. No facilities, but shops and restaurants around square up slope to south.

Charleroi No formal moorings in the centre but in the suburbs both to the North and South of Charleroi there are a number of public quays and basins. Few have amenities close at hand.

Charleroi to Namur

| 49km 7 locks | 2.6m water 5.3m air | *Fluviacarte/Navicarte 9* |

There are a few public quays, usually situated in uninviting surroundings. Probably the best are:

Auvelais (pk 61.6) Quays on the R bank above the lock.

Floreffe (pk 75.5) Quays on R bank below the abbey.

Pont de Loup (pk 49) **Chantier Naval de Vanverkoven**, Closed in 2011 and it is not known whether it will re-open.

Namur (Namen) (See Belgian Meuse).

Haut Escaut/Bovenschelde

| French border to Gent | 86km 6locks | 58m 2.1m water 4m air | *Fluviacarte/Navicarte 23* |

Distances below are approximate from border. Heavy commercial traffic.

Repairs and chandlery available at Péronnes, Antoing, below Tournai and just after junction with Scarpe at **RM Yachting**, Tel: 069 441805

The Walloon licensing system applies to the first part of the route. At Berchem-Kerkhoven lock, you are in Flanders and it is necessary to purchase (or already possess) a valid Waterwegenvignet.

R. Escaut closed at northern end, bouyed off and silting up. All locks manned. VHF 18 or 22.

Antoing (7km) R bank basin for pleasure craft 2.2m depth. Currently no facilities, but improvements planned. Diesel available from Neptune Barge about 300m downstream of basin

Tournai (13km) Narrow channel through town centre and under impressive medieval bridge with one-way traffic under traffic light control.. There is a lifting bridge. L bank pontoons in one way section. It is essential to give notice at start of one-way section if you plan to stop on them.

Hérrines (26km) Commercial quay L bank may have space at ends.

Junction with restored Canal de l'Espierres. L bank above Hérrines lock (30km). This links with the restored and re-opened Canal de l'Espierres and provides a route across the border to Lille.
Small pontoon with facilities and lively café at border.

Bossuit (35km) L bank junction with canal to Kortrijk. Overgrown quay with bollards and vandalised electricity points in June 2007 at junction.

Oudenaarde (54km)L Bank quay between central lift bridge and lock downstream of town. Convenient for town centre.

Gavere (65km) Quay above lock at Asper reported.

Kanaal Bossuit-Kortrijk

| 15km 6 locks | 1.9m water 4m air | Fluviacarte/Navicarte 23 or Geocarte Map1 |

Distances that follow are from the junction at Bossuit. The first lock is large, mechanised and has a rise of 9.5m and floating bollards. Take care when using these for on the ascent they stop well before the lock is full, so be ready to slacken ropes.

Sluis Moen, at about 4.5km is also large, with a 4.5m rise, and leads to the summit level.

Just before next lock, Sluis Zwevegem (at about 10km) are several hundred metres of substantial quay on west bank. Sluis Zwevegem also has floating bollards, and the same warning as for Sluis Bossuit applies.

The next 3 down locks are small (*péniche* sized) and manually operated by a single travelling lock keeper, so there can be delays.
All locks and the travelling lock keeper can be contacted on VHF 20.
On leaving the bottom lock, you enter a part of the Leie in the Kortrijk one way traffic system. the lock keeper will check your destination and advise you when it is safe to leave.

Canal Nimy-Blaton-Péronnes

Péronnes to Mons	39km 2 locks	2.5m water 4.4m air	*Fluviacarte/Navicarte 23 or Geocarte Maps 1 & 2*

Repairs and chandlery (see individual entries)
Péronnes

Péronnes Set in R Bank just upstream of first lock up from Escaut, Péronnes Yacht Club offers a substantial port de plaisance. Tel 069 44 20 81.
There is a chandlery by the disused length of canal to the east.
Above the second lock is a R bank quay with no facilities.

Blaton Public quays, R bank in entrance to Canal Blaton-Ath, which provides a route north to the Schelde at Dendermonde for craft drawing up to about 1.3m. Beware of mini-bore event if tied under bridge before 1st lock at Blaton end. Make sure you have strong ropes. Lock keeper will advise on suitable tide times for exit.

Péruwelz Port de plaisance with moorings R bank both east and west of road bridge. Shops and supermarket about 1km over bridge.

Badour Public quays.

Ghlin Public quays.

Canal du Centre

Mons to Seneffe	25km 3 locks 4 lifts, or 25km 2 locks 1 lift	2.2m water 3.55m air or 2.5m water 4m air	*Fluviacarte/Navicarte 23 or Geocarte Map 2*

Repairs and Chandlery
There is a rudimentary dry dock at Seneffe, Branche de Belcourt. Arrange through yacht club. Reputed to be booked well into the future.

Mons (Bergen) Port de plaisance in the south west corner of La Grand Large, a wide lake that also accommodates a range of watersports. Port offers water, electricity, washing machine, showers and a bar/restaurant. On summer weekends it can become uncomfortable due to wash from a large number of power boats and water skiers. The town of Mons, with its full range of shops and restaurants, is about 3km away and can be reached by bicycle, bus or taxi, and there is a small supermarket about 1km away. Tel 065 87 48 90.

There are 2 locks, Obourg-Wartons about 3.5km east from La Grande Large, and Havre, about 7km. The latter has a 20m rise, and in summer 2007 most of its floating bollards were out of action.

About 4km further the Thieu lock, in the L bank, links to the Historic Canal du Centre. A few hundred metres further down the old canal arm are pontoon moorings at YCDA with water, electricity, washing machine and clubhouse. Tel 067 33 09 21 or 0475 94 52 35.

La Louviere The four hydraulic lifts are a great tribute to the civil engineers at the beginning of the 20th century when work started, although they did not become operational until 1917. The Belgians (assisted by the EU) are spending a significant amount of money to ensure that they are kept in working order- they can take boats up to 38m LOA. All 4 are now operational, the upper one, damaged by an accident in 2003 has been restored by the French Eiffel company and re-opened in 2011. Passage through the 4 lifts must be booked the day before.

Strépy-Thieu There is an alternative, the new Ascenseur Strépy-Thieu, 13km from the Grande Large. This is the world's largest ship lift, with 2 independent tanks, which lift or lower 1350 tonne barges, 73m in 7 minutes. Operating times are 06h00 – 19h30 Monday to Saturday.

There is adequate mooring space below the new lift, including a stretch of R bank quay clearly designed for small craft, but no facilities. It is not possible to moor above the new lift, save when waiting for it, and the top, which is at the end of a very big aqueduct, is very windswept.

The route from the new lift joins that from the old ones about 4km before the junction with the Charleroi-Brussels Canal, R bank. About 1.5km from the junction is a pontoon of Club Nautique de Tyberport, and a pontoon for customers of 'Le Nautic' bar/restaurant, but with a depth of barely 1.3m.

Seneffe. Junction with the Charleroi-Brussels Canal.

Canal Charleroi-Brussels

| Charleroi to Brussels | 70km 10 locks 1 incline | 2.5m water 4.4m air | Fluviacarte/Navicarte 23 |

The scenery through which the canal runs is very varied, part industrial, part urban and part attractive countryside. The trip includes another of Belgium's civil engineering masterpieces - the inclined plane at Ronquières, which can lift vessels of up to 85m length and up to 1,350 tonnes a vertical distance of almost 70m. Passage through the port of Brussels also provides a range of contrasts. Locks and lifting bridges on VHF 20. There is often a lot of rubbish in the canal, particularly in Brussels, so keep a close watch on your cooling system.

Repairs and chandlery (see individual entry for details)
Brussels

Roux Public quays, no other facilities.

Gosselies Public quays above and below the lock, no facilities.

Pont-à-Celles Public quays, no facilities.

Seneffe ADEPS Yacht Haven, part of a water sports centre, 100m up the Branche de Bellecourt (on SE side of canal about 2km SW of its junction with the Canal du Centre). Water & electricity and a friendly clubhouse (cost about €8). No shops nearby.

Ronquières At both the top and the bottom of the inclined plane there are long quays, but no other facilities. It is better to secure at the bottom of the inclined plane rather than the top, where it can be extremely windy with choppy water (for a canal!). There is a restaurant on the R bank a short distance up the disused lock flight.

Ittre R bank above lock, Ittre Yacht Club has a new clubhouse with bar, showers, washing machine etc. Moorings to inside of arm above lock have electricity. There is also a L bank public quay with no facilities.

Tubize Public quays, no facilities.

Halle Can moor to L bank quay above lock, with no facilities, or just though road bridge about 500m above lock, is a L bank quay with coin in slot water & electricity at upstream end. Opposite a supermarket, with a range of other shops within 5-10 min walk. Also close restaurants and a launderette near railway station on opposite bank.

Brussels About 5km north of the city centre. Bruxelles Royal Yacht Club has a large marina. All facilities, fuel and a 25 tonne crane. Pleasant club-house with excellent restaurant. Overnight mooring charge €1.55 per metre. Moorings over the winter months can be arranged. Tel Office 022 16 48 28 and Harbourmaster 022 41 48 48.

Bus and tram stops on road bridge behind club house. (There is a short cut up steps to bridge approach, but gate at top usually locked – key available from club office.) Tram No 4 takes about 15 minutes to city centre. Alternatively club can call taxi or arrange car hire, although Brussels public transport network is cheap and efficient.

Zeeschelde (Sea Canal)

| **Rupelmonde to Brussels** | 32km 2 locks | 3m water 5m air | *Fluviacarte/Navicarte 23* |

Sluis Hingene, the sea lock into the Schelde was opened in 1998; it is twice the length of the old sealock at Wintam, and capable of taking vessels of up to 2,000 tonnes and 200m. At the sea lock, waiting times of up to an hour are not unusual. Call ahead on VHF 68. English acceptable.

Since the Schelde is tidal, timing one's trip becomes important particularly in low-powered boats. HW Rupelmonde (on the opposite bank of the Schelde to the Hingene sea lock) is about 40 minutes after Antwerp (Royersluis), and LW Rupelmonde is the same as LW Antwerp.

There are several lifting bridges, some of them almost 100 years old, although all have fast and efficient lifting systems. These offer a fixed-mast route to within a few km of the centre of Brussels. They lift slightly for barges and other craft without masts but lift more to clear a fixed mast, thereby causing severe road traffic disruption. Yachts may be expected to travel in convoy or possibly follow a commercial vessel. Bridges can be called on VHF 20.

Repairs and chandlery (see individual entry for details)
Brussels

Willebroek About 6.5km upstream of Sluis Hingene, is a R bank arm leading to the Klein Willebroek lock. This lock provides access to the R Rupel for about 3 hours either side of HW, but only between 6am and 10pm (less in winter). Lock-keeper Tel 0497 63 30 76. The arm is entered by a lift bridge which provides about 3.2m clearance in its closed position, and can be called on VHF 20.

On R bank at start of arm is RYAC (Rupel Yacht Club). On L bank nearer to lock is KWYC (Klein Willebroek Yachting Club). RYAC offers water, electricity, pump out and a small café/bar. Tel 038 86 06 06. KWYC offer only water & electricity, but is nearer to free half-hourly passenger ferry crossing to Boom on opposite bank. Tel 0476 29 23 02. Restaurants, but no shops in Klein Willebroek.

CRUISING THE INLAND WATERWAYS OF FRANCE & BELGIUM

Canal de Pommeroeul à Condé

| 12km 2 locks | 2.5 water 4.4 air | Fluviacarte/Navicarte 23 |

The trip from Valenciennes to Mons (70km) could be reduced by about 24km by turning right at Condé instead of turning left and continuing along the Escaut. However, it has been out of use since 1996 whilst the problem of who is responsible for removing Belgian silt from a French canal pound is resolved!

Canal de Roubaix and Canal de l'Espierres

| St-Andre (Fr) to Spiere – Helkijn (B) | 28km 15 locks | 1.5m water 3.3m air | Charts awaited |

This is a newly re-opened link between the French Canal de la Deûle, from a junction north of Lille, and the Belgian Haut Escaut, (Upper Schelde) just upstream of the Hérrines lock. Some €37 million has been spent on restoring the canals and also improving their surroundings. Especially at the western end, the constraints of operating a canal with a number of lifting bridges in an urban area suggest that it will be a slow, but interesting, route. It opened in June 2011 and is under the control of the Lille Métropole Communautée Urbaine (LMCU), not the VNF. It will only be open from 1st April to 15 October, from 08.30 to 12.30 and 13.30 to18.00, although the moving road bridges will not be operated after 16.30.

For access from Belgium, call the first lock, Ecluse de Warcoing a clear hour ahead of your planned arrival on (Belgian) number 0695 56863 or VHF 79. For access from France, 24 hours notice must be given to (French) number 03 20 63 11 39. The Tourcoing arm, which still needs dredging is restricted to a depth of 1.0m. The LMCU plans a website for the new link, which is not yet operational, but an impression of the route can be seen on www.kinette.ch, the website of a Swiss couple who were one of the first to cruise it after re-opening, and which has good pictures, although the text is in German.

WEST BELGIUM

Canal de Furnes and Kanaal Nieuwpoort - Dunkerken

| Dunkirk (Dunkerque, Dunkerken) to Nieuwpoort | 32km 1 lock | 1.8m water 3.5m air | Fluviacarte/Navicarte 14 and 23 |

The link between the Port Est and the canal system is well described by Marian Martin in *The European Waterways – A Manual for First Time Users* and involves a sea lock to dock level and a small lock between Darse 1 and the canal level. It can be slow, so locking between canal and the sea level to use the excellent marinas (Yacht Club de la Mer du Nord, and Marina du Grande Large) is not really an option, unless approaching from, or departing to, seawards. **Call VHF 73** for access and on leaving the lock for bridge opening for entry into Basin du Commerce. There is up to a €5000 fine if you don't.

The Canal de Furnes starts in Dunkirk (Dunkerque, Dunkerken) and becomes the Kanaal Nieuwpoort - Dunkerken at the border. For lock call VHF Ch 73. There are two lifting bridges before the Belgian Border, operated from a single point with CCTV monitoring.

Dunkerque Yacht Club de la Mer du Nord and Marina du Grand Large. All facilities. There is a port de plaisance in the Bassin de Commerce which is at the dock level and so reasonably easy to reach through the small lock. There are also canalside moorings between écluse de Furnes and écluse Jeu de Mail, but no facilities. There is water and rubbish disposal at écluse Jeu de Mail. Bunkering is available at Grand Large.

Veurne (Furnes) A pleasant small town with delightful square and imposing Town Hall, and occasional Spanish features, reflecting its history.

The stop lock, normally stands open but through passage is obstructed by a hand operated footbridge over the middle of the lock, which the lock-keeper must lift. East of the stop lock is the junction with the Lokanaal.

Immediately west is a pleasant small harbour with fingers on the west side for small craft, and alongside moorings for larger craft on the eastern side. Showers and toilets are in the building at the end of the harbour, and there is a pumpout station at the harbour entrance.

There is a single water tap on the west side, and a generous number of electricity points. Electricity supply cards are available from either the lock-keeper or the Tourism Office in the Town Hall. Unfortunately the electricity points use a quite large (32 amp) socket, rather than the usual caravan ones (16 amp.) The lock-keeper will loan an adaptor lead against a refundable deposit of €25, but those with DIY skills can buy the appropriate components from the excellent DELVA hardware store on the quayside and make their own.

There are lifting bridges on all three canal approaches to the town. Those obviously monitored by CCTV are controlled from the lock office and will be opened when there is a gap in the road traffic. For the lifting railway bridge in the Nieuwpoort direction, there is an intercom on a waiting pontoon just downstream of the bridge. The lock-keeper listens, (but may not answer,) on VHF10 for all road bridges, but has no control of the railway bridge.

Wulpen A village about half way between Veurne and Nieuwpoort with a quay and bollards. The lifting foot bridge can be opened with a magnetic card, that should be entrusted to you at either the Nieuwpoort or the Veurne lock, and which you hand back at the other.

Nieuwpoort. There are several large marinas/yacht clubs with full facilities, including fuel, repair-yards and cranes. If entering from seawards, refuel before locking into the canal system. There is a good range of shops and restaurants and a chandlers. Hire boat base in Kanaal Plassendale.

Plassendale Kanaal

Nieuwpoort to Plassendale	21km 3 locks	1.9m water 3.5m air	Fluviacarte/Navicarte 23

The junction between the Kanaal Nieuwpoort - Dunkerke and the Kanaal Plassendale involves locking down to a tidal basin at Nieuwpoort, crossing the basin and immediately locking up again. This tidal basin, known as the Achter Haven is also the means of entering or leaving the canal system from the sea. Generally, the basin can be crossed for about 3 hours either side of high water Nieuwpoort. The locks are not manned outside of 08h00 to 17h00 (somewhat longer in mid-summer), so opportunities to use the route may be limited. There is a third lock out of the Achter Haven, now disused, which leads to the River IJzer. The IJzer can now be reached by first entering the Kanaal Plassendale through the Gravensluis, and after about 1km, just beyond the hire boat base, turning back to starboard through a large new lock, the St-Jorissluis. The channel (unbuoyed) runs close to the **Westhoek** Marina on the west side of the stretch of open water after the lock and then along the south side.

Fuel station at Zandvoorde bridge on L bank, wooden piles available for tying up.

VVW Westhoek is a large marina, with all facilities (except fuel) and a bar/restaurant, about 20 minutes walk from the town centre.
From the lock at Nieuwpoort to the junction with the canal from Oostende to Brugge at Plassendale (where there is another lock) is 21km. The lifting bridges will be operated by a travelling bridge-keeper. Some, but not all of the lifting bridges have waiting piles or pontoons. The canal is very exposed, and whilst central depth is good, it shelves to barely a metre at the sides. In the event of northerly or easterly gales, deeper draught craft could find it very hard to hold their position if required to wait for bridge openings, so unusually for inland waterways, weather forecasts should be checked.

Repairs and chandlery (see individual entry for details)
Hire base in Kanaal Plassendale

Leffinge. About 10km from Nieuwpoort, half-way to Plassendale there is a quay close to a few shops and a restaurant. There is another quay about 4km farther.

Oudenburg. Canal side halte about 18km from Nieuwpoort, on NE bank just before lift bridge gives easy access to town (10 mins), and there is a filling station very close. About 2km farther is a free 24 hour quay with water & electricity, but slightly farther from the town.

Plassendale There is a lock just before the junction with the Oostende to Gent Canal, which normally stands open, and an adjacent lift bridge which is monitored by CCTV so it is usually not necessary to call for it to be opened.

Lokanaal, River IJzer and Kanaal Ieper - IJzer

| Veurne to Plassendale | 45km 2 locks | 1.5m water 3.5m air | Fluviacarte/Navicarte 23 |

An alternative, albeit longer, route which avoids the Nieuwpoort tidal basin, is to take the Lokanaal south from Veurne to Fintelsluis, then turn east to Diksmuide along the IJzer, rejoining the Kanaal Plassendale at St-Jorissluis.

Travelling bridgekeepers will operate the lifting bridges between Veurne and Fintelsluis. About halfway, at Alveringem is a quay with bar/restaurant close. The Lokanaal joins the IJzer just above Fintelsluis lock.

Fintelsluis Small village, with bankside moorings in the IJzer, just above the lock. Two restaurants close.

Roesbrugge In 2006, a stretch of about 7km of the IJzer from Fintele up to a new harbour at Roesbrugge, close to the French border was re-opened to navigation, but only suitable for craft drawing less than 1m, and length less than 10m.

Halfway downstream to Diksmuide is Knokkebrug, a lifting bridge. Contact on VHF20 or Tel 058 28 80 72.

The canal to **Ypres** (Ieper) starts immediately upstream of the lifting bridge. From its junction with the River IJzer, the canal to Ypres runs south for about 15km and has two locks. It ends in a basin about 1km north of the great town hall in the city centre. Owing to lack of dredging, the arm to Ypres may currently not be accessible with a draught of more than 1.1m.

Diksmuide Marina and bankside moorings with all facilities including diesel, with supermarket close. Town with pleasant square, shops, restaurants and a striking war memorial with impressive views from the top, and displays emphasizing the role of the Flemish people. About 2km downstream from Diksmuide a L bank pontoon without facilities gives access to the *Dodengang*, a restored piece of first world war trench, open to the public.

Canal Oostende to Gent

| 66km 3 locks | 2.2m water 3.95m air | Fluviacarte/Navicarte 23 |

The entry from the canal at Oostende is well described by Marian Martin in her book **The European Waterways**. From its junction with the Kanaal Plassendale (some 12km from Oostende) much of the 18km to Brugge (Bruges) is tree-lined and passes through pleasant countryside. There is one lock in Brugge and no further locks in the 40km from Brugge to Gent (Gand). This canal can handle barges up to 2,000 tonnes, so beware their speed and limited manoeuvrability when mooring. Two lifting bridges operate automatically and are CCTV monitored.

Plassendale About 5km from Oostende is a swing bridge, and immediately after it, the junction with the Plassendale Canal There is a quay immediately upstream of the junction.

Stalhille Some 6km farther towards Brugge is a small R bank staging with electricity. Bar/restaurant on L bank, presently reached by free passenger ferry whilst work proceeds on raising height of footbridge.

Brugge is a busy industrial town, as well as a major tourist centre with an impressive mixture of squares, medieval buildings and small waterways. The canal passes under half-a-dozen swing or lifting bridges, which also feed the town centre traffic to and from the busy ring road that runs outside the canal. This presents the bridge and lock operators with the difficult task of balancing the demands of road and water traffic. Not surprisingly, single pleasure craft carry little weight and generally will be required to wait until a convoy can be formed or they are able to follow close behind a commercial craft.

On the approach (from downstream) to the Nieuwe Dam poortsluis is the Verbindingsluis which leads into the Boudewijnkanaall that runs north to Zeebrugge. Much of the commercial traffic uses this route, rather than that to Oostende, so vigilance is required at the junction.

At the Nieuwe Dam poortsluis (north east of the town), the lock is triangular and has three sets of gates – two for the main route and the third to a small, side canal. Provided that a large craft is following the main route and secures along the long (left bank) side, small craft may be able to fit in the 'unused' third corner. Do not stop close to the gates at the other two corners, since lifting bridges carry roads across the ends of the chamber and the lockkeeper will want to lower them unless there is a very large craft to be accommodated.

When following barges into this lock, you may well be waved past by the barge skipper, so that you can enter first and 'tuck in' to the third corner, leaving them the long side. Often there will be a lockkeeper standing at the entrance directing traffic, and they will expect to be obeyed.

None of this should discourage you from visiting Brugge – but do allow plenty of time for the transit. There is a harbour beyond a swing bridge within the ring canal, on the opposite side to the railway station.

Coupure Pontoon moorings with water & electricity in entrance to Canal Coupure on east bank, above a recently restored lock, which marks the beginning of a long-term project to re-open an old route for small craft through the centre. Attractive area 5 mins. walk to city centre for shops and usual tourist attractions. Water & electricity by €1meter. Mooring cost €7 for 8m. boat in 2010.

Recently a lift bridge has been built across the entrance to the Coupure, to carry the foot path and cycle track. The bridge normally lifts hourly on demand for craft to leave, and lifting for craft entry is coordinated with that of the lift bridges up and downstream of the entrance. Waiting piles just downstream of new bridge. Tel 0479 24 63 87.

Flandria Yacht Haven, L bank arm, south of town (close to quay from which hotel and trip boats operate) is further from city centre, but convenient for railway station and has all facilities. Tel 050 38 08 66 or 0477 38 44 56.

About 7km farther is the Stauschleuse Beernem, a stop lock that normally stands open. If you see a green light on approach, so does any traffic approaching from the opposite direction. It does not give you priority.

Beernem L bank Yacht Haven with substantial finger moorings and all facilities, including a good terrace restaurant. Supermarket and baker 5 minutes walk up hill.

About 7km before the Gent Ringvaart is the junction with the Afleidingskanaal van de Leie (Leie diversion canal). A lot of commercial traffic turns in or out of the southern arm, at some speed, so approach with care and listen on VHF 10.

Gent (Gand) To reach the centre of Gent, the easiest route to take is the Ringvaart, a modern and rather dull ring canal to the south-west of the city. A stop lock, normally standing open, on the north-east bank leads to the River Leie and thence to the centre of the city. The lock is inconspicuous and easy to miss. The upstream arm of the R. Leie, which opens off the south-west bank of the Ringvaart goes to Kortrijk (Courtrai), and eventually into France where it becomes the R. Lys.

Three yacht clubs just beyond the stop lock on the River Leie and in the stopped up arm of the old river.

KGWV on R bank with water & electricity, Tel 0475 58 50 38 or 0477 22 66 23.
GLV on L bank opposite KGWV with water, electricity and clubhouse, Tel 0475 75 42 77.
VVW Gent-Leie up old river arm, adjacent to GLV, with water, electricity, clubhouse with restaurant. Tel 092 51 28 36 or 0476 86 41 25. €14 for 8m boat in 2010.

Close to the city centre, about 3km down the Leie, just beyond the St-Agnetabrug there are L bank pontoon moorings with water & electricity, and showers in capitainerie barge. Tel 0479 24 63 88.

Downstream of these moorings, there are several low bridges, which are only lifted or swung on special occasions, but there are alternative routes out of the town centre by way of the Ketelvaart, a narrow canal that runs east and then south until it meets the old course of the Schelde. This continues upstream for about 6km until it joins the Ringvaart at Merelbecke, about 1km above the Merelbecke lock.

Merelbecke Yachting, north of (usually open) stop lock in the Schelde close to the Ringvaart junction, offers moorings with water & electricity. Bar/restaurant and possibility of cycle hire close.

Gent Ringvaart

Evergen to Merelbecke	22km 2 locks	3m water 7m air

The Ringvaart links the dock network and canals north of the city with the routes east (to Ostend), south into France, and the tidal estuary of the Schelde. It takes a roughly semi circular route between Evergen to the north of the city centre and Merelbecke to the south. It has important functions in controlling river flows and preventing flooding, as well as its obvious navigational use. The volume and speed of traffic means that it offers few if any places for mooring.

At its northern end it joins the Gent – Terneuzen canal.

Repairs and chandlery (see individual entry for details)
Gent

About 3km west is Sluis Evergen, a very busy lock, even though the rise is barely 1.2m. In order to reduce delays at this lock, a second lock alongside opened in 2009. Just downstream of the lock in L bank basin is **Gent Boat Service,** who offer repairs and boat storage. Tel 0475 68 53 78.

After crossing the Ostend canal, R Leie and R Schelde, the Ringvaart ends at the Merelbecke tidal lock.

City Centre Route
Good map in book by Jaqueline Jones (see Bibliography)
There still exists a central route across the city centre, with a *péniche* sized lock, and virtually no commercial traffic. From the start of the Ringvaart this runs south through the Voorhaven, at the end of which are 2 bridges. The northernmost Muide Spoorbrug is a low railway bridge, which opens (briefly) about 7 times a day. It may be contacted on VHF20, but only for the five or ten minutes before each scheduled opening, and if boats are not ready and positioned to make their wish to pass obvious, then it does not open. The second is a road bridge with a clear height of 4.2m when closed, also contactable on VHF20.

After this bridge, the route continues south through Handelsdok, a now little used commercial dock, narrows and turns abruptly west by the Gent-Dampoort railway station, and then enters a large basin. On the west bank of this is the Portus Ganda Yacht Haven, with substantial pontoons, and most facilities. The capitainerie is at the north end of the building housing a substantial swimming pool. Access to the pontoons, and payment for water & electricity are by means of a 'smart card' system. The harbour is about 10 minutes walk from the city centre, and there is a good range of shops and restaurants in the area. Tel 0472 41 78 43

Past the yacht harbour, route continues under eastern arch of the road bridge into Visservaart which leads to the Brusselsepoort lock. This lock is operated on demand from 0800 to 1700 Monday to Saturday, and has no VHF. Call on 0477 58 18 04 preferably at least an hour in advance of your arrival. Above the lock the route joins the Schelde. Below the lock take care to pass under the new foot bridge at its higher end.

Turning south about 1km above Brusselsepooort lock takes one through city to Merelbecke, and turning north takes one into the Ketelvaart and onto the R Leie, just downstream of the very central moorings.

Afleidingskanaal van de Leie –Northern Arm

| 13km 2 locks | 1.8m water 3.55m air |

Little commercial traffic.There is a small harbour and a hire base at **Eeklo.**

Afleidingskanaal van de Leie –Southern Arm

| 14km 0 locks | 2.1m water 4.2m air |

Modern canal passing through pleasant countryside to its junction with the R Leie upstream of Dienze. Little industry and no practical moorings.

Kanaal Gent – Terneuzen

| Gent to the Schelde Estuary at Terneuzen | 32km sealock | 4m water 6m air | Dutch Hydrografische Kaart 1803 Westerschelde is recommended |

Very busy with large sea going vessels as well as barge traffic. Largely through areas of heavy industry. From the junction with the Gent Ringvaart, there are 3 lifting bridges all of which have over 6m clearance in their fixed positions. The rules require all craft to hoist a radar reflector.

Distances below are in km from the junction with the Ringvaart, which is about 3.5km north of southern end of the canal.

Repairs and chandlery (see individual entry for details)
Gent

Langerbrugge (2km) Yacht harbour in old arm on west bank has 2 clubs, KYCG and RBSC. Entrance just north of busy car ferry. All facilities including bar/restaurant and it is nearest harbour to Gent accessible with a fixed mast. Visitors welcome.

Moervaart (6km) This is a side canal that runs 27km to Lokeren.

Zelzate (14km) Yacht harbour on east bank about 1km north of Zelzate swing bridge, just on the Belgian side of the Dutch border. Tel 0486 47 65 66

Sas van Gent (16km) West bank, Passantenhaven inside arm is entered about 800m south of the roadbridge, and Jachthaven WSV 't Sas is entered about 700m north of roadbridge, with 2m depth and water.

Terneuzen (28km) At the end of Zijzanaal A (just east of the Oostsluis) are the inner harbour of WV Neusen, with all facilities, and Vermeulen's Jachtwerf & Co. with electricity and water only. Both provide fairly peaceful moorings. Supermarket, shops and restaurants about 500m. Vermeulen's is a family business offering service and repairs, and are a for Bukh, Vetus, Volvo & Yanmar. 50 tonne boat lift and undercover winter storage. (Tel (NL) 011 15 61 27 16).

Access to and from the Schelde is through the Oostsluis and Oostbuitenhaven. In the Schelde outside the sealock, there are 2 marinas in the Veerhaven which is entered about half a mile east of the Oostbuitenhaven. Jachthaven Terneuzen, with all facilities including laundrette, operates the red/green mooring system commonly used in the Netherlands. The visitors berths are usually on the pontoon immediately to starboard when entering the marina.

They are close to the tugs, which can be noisy and cause some turbulence.

WV Neusen with all facilities also has moorings, further away from the tugs. Both are close to supermarket, shops and restaurants.

Moervaart

Mendonk to Lokeren	27km 0 locks	1.3m water 4.3 air

An attractive rural route, and was a river that originally flowed some 50km eastwards into the Schelde estuary, but after the 1953 flooding, its tidal section was dammed, and it is now only navigable as far as the town of Lokeren.

Distances overleaf are in km from its junction with the Terneuzen sea canal.

Mendonk Staging of VVW Mendonk on southern bank at 1.6km. Water & electricity, clubhouse with bar. North bank quay of WSV Spanjeveer at 3.2km just upstream of surviving 1945 Bailey Bridge. Water, electricity and clubhouse with bar, Tel 0477 29 28 00.

Wachtebeke (7.5km) North bank moorings of Watersport Moervaart extend for several hundred metres downstream of the Overleide Brug, the first of 7 lifting bridges. Harbour master usually on boat 'Batavia' Tel 0485 70 79 97. Electricity and a few water points. Town has range of shops, with supermarket and launderette about 500m. Good restaurant *'L'Olivette'* by bridge.

From here to Lokeren the route is narrow with occasional shallows, and so over the summer months from May to September, boats are escorted through the lift bridges in 'convoys' three times a day. The route is managed from a building adjacent to the lift bridge, and craft with a draught of over 1.2m should check that there is sufficient water depth. Tel 0476 20 95 82 or 0476 20 95 84. Out of the summer months 24 hours notice is required. The trip takes slightly more than 3 hours, and there are few if any mooring possibilities before the end.

Lokeren (27km) Attractive market town with moorings to a long quayside alongside a park with electricity and a few water points. Mooring charges are paid and cards to actuate the electricity points obtained from the town tourist office in the market square south of the end of the canal.

River Leie (Lys)

Gent to Dienze	25km 1 lock	1.8m water 4.5m air

The 25km stretch of the river Leie from Gent to its junction with the southern Afleidingskanaal at Deinze is probably the prettiest stretch of navigable water in the Flanders region, making a welcome change from the more commercial waterways. The river winds through meadows and passes small market gardens and beautiful bankside houses and gardens. The single lock, Sluis Asterne, is *péniche* size, so large commercial traffic uses the Afleidingskanaal instead. There are a number of restaurants with moorings for customers.

The following distances are from the junction with the Gent Ringvaart.

Restaurants with moorings at about 2km, 3km, 16km, and 19km.

Repairs and chandlery (see individual entry for details)
Gent

Drongen (4km) LSV Yachthaven (mostly for small boats). €10 for 8m boat in 2010, including water & electricity.

St-Martens-Latem (7km) picturesque village, but most of quay reserved for trip boat from Gent, so only space for 1 other boat.

Leernebrug (13km) MYCG L bank moorings with floating clubhouse, water & electricity above and below road bridge. Limited shops and restaurant 500m in St-Martens-Leerne.

Sluis Astene (19km) normally stands open and there is a hand-operated lifting bridge. Moorings and restaurant downstream of lock.

Dienze (27km) Bankside mooring with no facilities possible downstream of the lifting bridge in town centre and 500m upstream are good but crowded moorings at Deinze Yacht Club with water, electricity, showers and clubhouse. Tel 0495 25 56 20 or 0495 25 56 22.

Dender and Canal Blaton-Ath

Dendermonde to Blaton	85km 34 locks	1.3m water 3.7m air	*Fluviacarte/Navicarte 23 or Geocart Map 2*

(From Dendermonde south to Geraardsbergen, and from Blaton north to Ath, a depth of 1.8m is available, but the middle 20km has not yet been dredged to its original specification.)

This route, which was reopened in 2004, forms a link between the Schelde at Dendermonde and the Canal Nimy-Blaton-Péronnes. Travelling south, the first 65km and 14 locks are river navigation to Ath, and then 20 locks on the 22km canal to Blaton. The distances below are nominal from Dendermonde lock, which is about 2km from the town.

Aalst (13km) VVW Aalst has L bank moorings with water, electricity and clubhouse between the 2 lift bridges close to the town centre.
VZW Aalst, between the second lift bridge and the lock is small and has only space for 3 or 4 boats. A small town with shops and railway station close. There is a new quay just above lock.

Denderleeuw (20km) One boat pontoon below lock.

Ninove (27km) Pontoon with water & electricity R bank upstream of town centre. Also pontoon with 24 hour limit R bank about 2km above lock.

De Gavers Country Park (38km) Quays & pontoon with water & electricity 2km upstream of Idegem lock

Geraardsbergen (43km) L bank pontoon with no facilities between 2 lifting bridges in town centre, or long L bank pontoon of VVW Den Bleek with water, electricity and clubhouse above lock. Interesting town – hill on R bank offers excellent views and is the 'mountain' section of the *Tour de Belgique* cycle race.

The 20km stretch between Geraardsbergen and Ath is the shallowest part of this route. In late summer 2007, the least observed depth was about 1.5m, but this was after a fairly rainy period, and with any boat approaching the limit, it would be prudent to check the latest situation with the navigation service.

About 1km upstream of Geraardsbergen, control of the navigation passes from the Flemish to the Walloon authorities.

Contact phone for locks from Deux-Acren to Ath Tel 0 75 81 22 18.

Lessines (51km) L bank quay without facilities between upper end of lock and town lift bridge. Water reported available at lock.

Bilhée Lock (61km) has a water point and a rubbish container.

Ath (63km) Attractive town with good range of shops and restaurants. Moor either to substantial quay R bank just below lock 21 (which is the start of the Blaton-Ath Canal) or the R bank quay above lock 20 which has coin in slot electricity, but may suffer from noise being close to the railway lines and station.

Between Ath and Blaton most of the locks are manual, and both locks and bridges will be operated by travelling lock-keepers, with whom you need to agree your departure time on the previous day. Contact phone for locks 21 (Ath) up to 16 (Maffle) Tel 0475 81 22 19.

Lock 17 (Maffle) (66km) Quay with bollards below.
Contact phone for locks 15 (Ladeuze) up to 11 (Beloeil) Tel 0477 38 14 21. Water and rubbish collection at lock 15.

Beloeil (74km) The village and spectacular Château and Gardens of Beloeil can be visited by mooring above lock 11 (Beloeil). There is a small pontoon close to the lift bridge, but the bridge is very clattery, and to moor with spikes to the bank nearer to the lock will be rather quieter.

South of Beloeil there is a 6km summit level, and then the canal descends through 10 locks down to an arm off the Nimy-Blaton-Péronnes canal. There are moorings without facilities in this arm.

Contact phone no. for locks 10 (Stambruges) down to 1 (Blaton) Tel 0475 81 22 20. Water and rubbish collection at lock 4.

If taking this route from south to north, you can advise either the Obourg or Péronnes lock on the Nimy-Blaton-Péronnes canal of your intention, and they will alert the Blaton lock-keeper.

Zeeschelde (Escaut Maritime)

Gent to Rupelmonde	72km 1 lock	tidal water 4.2m air	*Fluviacarte/Navicarte* 23

It is sensible to use the tide and essential for low powered craft. For places upstream of Antwerpen tide time differences relative to Vlissingen may be found in the Dutch ANWB Wateralmanak vol.2. It should be noted that the further upstream one goes the greater the asymmetry between rise and fall, with the rise being faster and for a shorter time than the fall. At the sea lock at Merelbecke (at the southern end of the Gent Ringvaart) there is about 3½ hours of rise and 9 hours of fall. This difference will be increased at times of flood and decreased at times of drought. Tidal range is about 5m at Rupelmonde, reducing to 4m at Gent.

For most pleasure craft going upstream, departure from Rupelmonde any time between LW and LW + 4 hours should enable you to reach Gent before the ebb starts to flow strongly against you.

Travelling downstream, you are bound to face an adverse tide for part of the time, and departure time will be most influenced by destination and required time of arrival.

The flood tide runs most strongly (up to 4 knots) around Dendermonde. Also note that depth in the approach to the sea lock at Merelbecke may be little more than 1m at low water. (When locking down, note that the depth in the downstream exit from the lock is displayed on a large illuminated sign about 500m above the lock entrance.)

Distances below are approximate from Merelbecke sea lock.

Repairs and chandlery (see individual entry for details)
Gent

Zele (29km) Mooring pontoon and café/bar on L bank.

Dendermonde (32km) Junction with R Dendre, a recently reopened route south. Note that the L bank pontoon about 1km downstream of the Dendre entrance dries at LW and is only suitable for small craft.

Baasrode (37km) R bank pontoon moorings

Hamme (52km) L bank moorings at Drie Goten YC with water & electricity. Only small craft on inside of pontoons, and on outside check there will be sufficient depth at low water. Tel 0479 52 93 15

Temse (57km) L bank pontoon moorings.

Steendorp (62km) Pontoon mooring. Uncomfortable due to barge wash.

Rupelmonde (64km) Pontoon moorings. Uncomfortable due to wash, but attractive town, birthplace of Mercator.

Zeeschelde (Escaut Maritime) to Antwerpen

15km 0 locks	deep tidal water no limit air	Fluviacarte/Navicarte 23

Antwerpen (Anvers) There are three main mooring possibilities:
- Jachthaven NIC Marina lies on the Schelde L bank, opposite the main part of the city. Full facilities including fuel. The Royal Yacht Club of Belgium and Liberty Yacht Club based there. City is 10-15 min walk . Waiting pontoon in river close to entrance. Entry and departure possible only + or -1 hour HW.
- In the port of Antwerpen itself, notably at Jachthaven Antwerpen Willemsdok, which can be reached from the Schelde via the R bank Royersluis or from the Albert or Schelde-Rhine canals via the docks. The cost per night is €1.5 per metre plus €2.5 for electricity. All facilities including laundrette and diesel. Details on useful website www.jachthaven-antwerpen.be. which also covers the NIC marina. The website also provides a means of obtaining an FD number (see below) via the internet.
- Other port moorings in Straatsburgdok or in the marina at Nieuw Lobroekdok which is near to the start of the Albertkanaal. The Nieuw Lobroekdok is situated partly under a motorway but is surprisingly quiet. There are two main mooring places - at opposite ends of the dock. At one end is Antwerpse Yacht Club, at the other is Sodipa-watersport. The main part of the city is a 5 min walk + 10 minute tramride away.

Antwerpen is an enormous port. A charge is made for passage into or through the port. Every vessel is allocated an FD number. If you do not already have one, harbour control will give you one after asking for the name of the boat, length, beam, draught, gross tonnage and the owner's name and address. The charge will be sent to that address. For most pleasure craft, the charge is approximately €20 (plus VAT) for a stay of up to 30 days. This is reduced to €7.50 (plus VAT) for a port stay of less than 36 hours. However, passage is free for boats en route to or from the Albertkanaal and which enter the port via one of three locks (Royersluis, Van Cauwelaertsluis or Boudewijnsluis). Pleasure craft should normally use Royersluis to enter from or join the Schelde.

Arrival into and departure from the port must be reported to harbour control on VHF. English is acceptable. Use VHF 2 for arrival from the north via the Rhine-Schelde canal on passing the Noordlandbrug; VHF 20 if arriving via the Albertkanaal; VHF 22 for entry via the Royersluis; VHF 71 for entry via Van Cauwelaertsluis or Boudewijnsluis. If you do not have VHF you must report by telephone on 035 41 00 43 (manned 24hrs a day.)

NORTH EAST BELGIUM

River Rupel and Beneden Nete

| Rupelmonde to Viersel | 39km 2 locks | 2.5m water 4.4m air | Fluviacarte/Navicarte 23 |

For those who want to get from the Brussels area to the smaller and quieter canals of Northern Belgium without passing through Antwerpen, this is an attractive alternative route.
23km are tidal, 16km are in the Netekanaal, from the sea-lock to Viersel at the junction with the Albertkanaal via the pleasant town of Lier. The Kanaal Bocholt-Herentals is a further 10km east along the busy Albertkanaal.

The tidal stretch requires some care, particularly when making the passage with an ebb tide. There are lots of mud flats. The navigable channel tends to be on the outer edges of bends. It offers no possibilities of mooring. There is a moving railway bridge at Boom which may need lifting during the top half of the tidal range. (There are headroom gauges showing the headroom when it is in its usual down position).

Repairs and chandlery (see individual entry for details)
Boom

Boom There is a substantial R bank pontoon, from which the foot ferry plies to and from Klein Willebroek on the opposite bank. The upstream half of the river side of this is reserved for the ferry, but the downstream half, and the landward side are free for use by other craft for up to 24 hours, and have coin in slot electricity points. (Use the landward side if you can since the river side is a popular 'shopping stop' for barges.)

Jachtwerk Vennekens R bank about 1km upstream of the Boom pontoon, a boatyard with large crane and dry dock facilities. Do not arrive without warning – the entrance dries. Tel 038 88 16 53.

Duffel. About 500m above the sea-lock, there is a small inlet, which is being developed by VVW

Nete. Moorings in pleasant surroundings but some distance from shops or restaurants. About 500m further on is a quay with water & electricity.

Lier. VVW Emblem have a small marina with water & electricity. Lier is an attractive town which is famous for its horological clock and it has plenty of shops and restaurants. It is a 20-25 minute walk from the marina but there are reasonably frequent buses.

Kanaal van Bocholt naar Herentals

| Herentals to Bocholt | 58km 10 locks | 2.1m water 4.5m air | Fluviacarte/Navicarte 23 |

There are two parts to this canal. From Herentals at the Albertkanaal junction to the Kanaal Dessel-Turnhout-Schoten junction 27km 7 locks, then to Bocholt 31km 3 locks. The route is mainly through pleasant, often wooded, countryside. Still has a certain amount of commercial traffic.

Repairs and chandlery (see individual entry for details)
Herentals

Herentals About 3km above the lock on R bank is the Jachthaven Herentals, which can take boats up to 15m. Water, electricity and showers.

Geel/Aart VVW Geel lies between locks 8 and 9. Fluviacarte/Navicarte shows this as a port de plaisance - it is more a halte!

Dessel Moorings just below lock 5 on L bank. Pleasant surroundings but no facilities and some distance from shops or restaurants, other than a pancake boat that closes early and a very small shop/pub with a limited range of goods. There are also several places to moor above lock 4, just downstream of the canal 'crossroads' which is the junction between Kanaal Bocholt-Herentals, Kanaal Dessel–Turnhout-Schoten (to the North) and Kanaal Dessel-Kwaadmechelen (to the south) which rejoins the Albertkanaal after 16kms lock-free.

Lommel Fairly new yacht Harbour in basin on north bank.

Neerpelt End on moorings with water & electricity.

Huibrechts-Lille South bank plaisance quay about 4km before the junction with the Zuid-Willemsvaart.

Bocholt. Continue SW for Maastricht. The passantenhaven is on the L bank about 1km after junction with Zuid Willemsvaart.

Zuid-Willemsvaart

Netherlands Border to Maastricht	47km 3 locks	1.9m water 5m air	*Fluviacarte/Navicarte 23*

This is an alternative route to travel to Maastricht or Liège from further north and east in the Netherlands, for those who wish to avoid the very busy Maas. It also provides a more direct route to Maasbracht. Although there is a fair amount of commercial traffic, the vessels are generally slower and smaller than those on the Maas. Two locks are close to Bocholt in the North and there is a Dutch lock shortly before entering the Maas at Maastricht.

To go towards Veert and Maasbracht by way of the Zuid-Willemsvaart, at the junction about 1km north of Bocholt, take the northermost route and descend through the two locks, both of which have recently been equipped with VHF. Sluis Bocholt - VHF 18, Sluis Lozen- VHF 17.

Between the Lozen lock and the Netherlands border, sloping stone banks have collapsed into the channel, especially of the R (south) bank, making crossing with approaching vessels difficult. Pass at dead slow, staying as near to the centre of the channel as approaching traffic will permit.

Fuel can be obtained at a quay on the border between Belgium and The Netherlands about 2km east of Sluis Lozen.

Bocholt. L Bank Passantenhaven with robust finger pontoons, water & electricity and basic shower. Close to town centre, laundrette & shops, including 2 bakers with dispensing machines which sell bread out of hours.

Heading south from Bocholt towards Maasbracht, the distances below are approximate km from Bocholt.

Bree (6km) Long L bank quays.

Tongerlo (8km) R bank restaurant with mooring.

Neeroerteren (15km) R bank entrance to VVW Neeroerteren, best approached from south.

Eisden (24km) Substantial new L bank pontoons, but no sign of water or electricity.

Rekem (32km) L Bank staging near restaurant.

Neerharen (34km) Here the Zuid-Willemsvaart bears east, whilst the straight-on route stays within the Belgian border, and joins the Kanaal Briegden-Neerharen which in turn joins the Albertkanaal.
The Zuid-Willemsvaart crosses the border into the Netherlands at Sneermaas, where there is a long quay alongside the old customs post. Bearing east again takes one to a Dutch lock above which one joins the Maas. It is also possible to reach the marina 't Bassin' (see later note on Maastricht) down a very narrow 'straight-on' arm, but the lock on this route is only worked once per day, (primarily to keep a slight water flow through the 't Bassin') so heading east for the Maas is normally the best option.

Kanaal van Dessel over Turnhout naar Schoten

Dessel to Schoten	63km 10 locks	1.9m water 5m air	*Fluviacarte/Navicarte 23*

This pleasant canal has long tree-lined stretches, particularly in the first 25km.
Past Turnhout, more of industrial Belgium becomes evident, although most still hidden from the canal. It runs from the junction with the Kanaal Bocholt-Herentals (near Dessel) to the junction with the Albertkanaal (near Schoten).

There are 18 moveable bridges, mostly of the tilting variety, several of which are at the ends of locks, others are operated by lock keepers. Some lock keepers are responsible for several locks and/or bridges and travel with you along the tow path by bicycle, moped or small van.
Lifting bridges from Dessel to Turnhout listen on VHF10. Many of the bridges have signal lights on them but often even the red light does not go on until the operator has arrived and starts to lower the road barriers!
Some commercial traffic, but less than found on most of Belgium's waterways.

In addition to the 'official' moorings noted below, it is possible to moor alongside the bank in pleasant countryside in many places. Secure well because there is still a small amount of commercial traffic and barges exert amazing suction!

Retie North of Dessel, shortly before the first tilting bridge, on the L bank, there is a small inlet with basic moorings. The Antwerpse Jachtclub is based there.

Turnhout A large basin with substantial finger pontoons, with water & electricity, run by VVW Taxandria. No clubhouse or other facilities. (The café/bar on the quayside that used to offer showers etc is now closed.) Town centre with pleasant square and shops and restaurants about 15 min walk, but bakery and small supermarket in new development only about 300m.

Brechtse On L bank, between the 9th and 10th lifting bridges (after leaving the basin at Turnhout) and about 4km before Sluis (lock) 2, there is a basin which houses Brechtse Yachtclub; it has pontoons with water & electricity, a clubhouse with showers, washing machine and drier, and there is a restaurant close. Tel 033 13 73 72.

St-Job On L bank, shortly after Sluis 4, there is a basin with the St. Job Yachtclub. Water, electricity and showers. Tel 0495 53 34 16 or 0475 59 09 62.

Schoten On L bank there is a large (and often very full) marina, which is Schoten Yachtclub, with all facilities other than fuel. The pleasant town of Schoten is 5 min walk away. It has a full range of shops and restaurants and a supermarket very close to the marina. Tel 0496 07 42 06.

Kanaal van Dessel naar Kwaadmechelen

| 16km 0 locks | 2.8m water 5.2m air | *Fluviacarte/Navicarte 23* |

Tree-lined, dead straight and rather dull. For the most part the bank depth is about 0.5m, so there are no possibilities of mooring save at the ends.

Kanaal van Beverloo

| 15km 0 locks | 2.1m water 4.1m air | *Fluviacarte/Navicarte 23* |

This is a pleasant and quiet side canal off the Kanaal Herentals-Bocholt just above Sluis Mol. Be aware that large barges turn in front of the entrance to the canal. There is a lifting bridge about 5km from the junction alongside a Union Miniere plant. The bridge will be lifted when convenient to the company and its road traffic, which is particularly busy between 13h00 and 14h30.

Kerkhoven Jachtclub De Blauwe Reige. Water, electricity and close pleasant restaurant.

Leopoldsburg Jachtclub Leopoldsburg. All facilities. Fuel from a service station about 200m from marina.

Schelde Rijnverbinding

| Tholen to Antwerpen | 38km 1 lock | 3m water>6m air | *Fluviacarte/Navicarte 23* |

This is the route from the Netherlands Oosterschelde, down the Schelde Rijnverbinding (Rhine-Schelde) canal. Tholen and Bergen-op-Zoom have the last significant marinas in the Netherlands before crossing the border into Belgium.

Rather dull! the Rhine-Schelde canal is large and passes through flat countryside before reaching Antwerpen.

The Noordlandbrug, at the edge of the port control area, has a notice which reads AANMELDEN KAN 2 (Call port control office on VHF 2). On leaving the port control area one must UITMELDEN (report out). Harbour control will ask for your FD number. (See also Antwerpen).

It will take about 2 hours to pass through Antwerpen docks to either the lock into the River Schelde or to the start of Albertkanaal and the marina at Nieuw Lobroekdok .

Albertkanaal

| Antwerpen (Anvers) to Liège (Luik) | 130km 6 locks | 3.4m water 5.25m air | *Fluviacarte/Navicarte 23* |

There is little to commend the Albertkanaal to pleasure craft unless speed and time are important. It is an extremely busy waterway, capable of taking vessels up to 2,000 tonnes. The 6 locks are very large. Most have three chambers, although all three will not necessarily be operating together. The water tends to be choppy (by inland waterways standards) and there are limited facilities and little attractive scenery. On Sundays and feast-days the locks are closed, save for two that operate for pleasure craft only. The maximum speed is 15km/hr.

Hasselt Marina with all facilities except fuel.

Genk-Kolenhaven Genk Pontoons, water & electricity.

Liège (See Belgian Meuse).

About 17km north of Liège, the écluse de Lanaye gives access to the Dutch Meuse (Maas) and the prospect of a detour to the attractive Dutch town of Maastricht.

Écluse de Lanaye
There are three operational lock chambers, traffic light controlled, so significant delays are unusual. (In May 2009 both the 2 smaller chambers were out of action.) Whilst the fall is considerable (14m), the ascent/descent is usually smooth. Only the large (R bank) chamber has floating bollards, so crew should be prepared to move lines up/down the bollards set in the walls. 2km north, there are possibilities for mooring, or even anchoring, in a lake opening off the R bank. Slightly further north is a yacht harbour set in R bank. In summer 2011 work started on the construction of an even larger 4th lock chamber, and the work may well cause delays to traffic for the next few years.

- **Maastricht** (NL) On L bank upstream there is a new marina, St. Pieter's harbour with visitor's pontoon, showers, laundrette, restaurant. Good security. Small supermarket across the road. 2km from town which is well worth a visit.
- Close to the centre of Maastricht, a training wall in mid stream joins 2 bridges. It is possible to moor to the west side of this wall. No charge, but no facilities except rubbish disposal. Reports of boats being untied so attach further lines at low level.
- L bank downstream of the centre at about Maas pk 13.7, a narrow entrance and a lock provide access to 't Bassin' a re-opened commercial basin, surrounded by old warehouses which have been converted into apartments with bars and restaurants around much of the quayside.

Other waterways in Belgium

Kanaal Leuven- Dijle	31km 5 locks	2.3m water 6m air
Kanaal Roeselare-Leie	17km 1 locks	2.1m water 4.8m air
Boudewijnkanaal	12km 1 lock (plus sea-lock)	4m water 6m air

We would like to include more details of these waterways in future editions. Reports are requested.

Appendix i
Signals

All vessels must carry a copy of the CEVNI rules for Inland Waterways, but it is probably worth noting the following points.

Blue Flagging

A blue flag is used by barges and large vessels to indicate that the vessel is taking advantage of, or staying out of, the current, and may be navigating on the 'wrong' side of the waterway. But it may also be used when approaching a corner, or a landing stage or a mooring. It is usually initiated by the barge travelling upstream, and the downstream boats affected acknowledge it by displaying their blue flags. Small craft are not expected to display a blue flag, but it is sensible to show by change of course or aspect that you understand the intention.

- Especially on rivers, look out for ships or barges with a blue flag or board displayed on the starboard side of the wheelhouse.
- At night or in poor visibility a flashing white light has the same meaning. The flashing white light is usually left operating whenever the blue flag or board is displayed, and is helpful in distinguishing it from washing or house flags.
- A book on the CEVNI rules published by the RYA in 2004, gives the impression that small craft do not necessarily need to respect the Blue Flagging rule. Legalistically this may be true, but realistically a barge skipper seeing you approaching, from perhaps a km away, is hardly in a position to know whether your craft is 20.1metres long and hence must comply, or only 14.9m and therefore need not do this, so provided that you can safely comply (always look astern first) then you should do so.

Another signal which is not uncommon on inland waterways and sometimes misunderstood is the "Diver Down" code flag A. This is a white and blue flag with a fishtail, often in rigid form painted onto a sheet of board. It is used to warn of the presence of an operating diver.

Appendix ii
BIBLIOGRAPHY

Maps and charts
France

- **Inland Waterways of France Map** (1:500,000) giving distances, number of locks, etc. Imray 2001.
- **Fluviacarte/Navicarte Carte-Guides** More than 20 published. English, French and German text and clear maps. No 21 is a good route planning chart. From November 2007, new editions are being published under the name Fluviacarte.
- **Vagnon Carte-Guides** Not as comprehensive a range as Navicartes, although fairly similar and usually thickened up by local advertisements. Again, English, French and German text. (No. 1 is the route planner.) Some have been re-published under the name Chagnon Carte-Guides.
- **Breil's French Waterway Guides** A new series of 15 and growing Guides in A4 format, and again, trilingual. Editions du Breil, Domaine de Fitou, 11400 Castelnaudary.
- **Crown-Blue Line Waterways Guides** Published by the well-known hire firm. Series of about 8 guides giving coverage of hire boat territory. Text in English, French and German.
- **Michelin Road** Maps (1:200,000) Useful to show surrounding countryside and places of interest.
- **Michelin Green Tourist Guides**
- **IGN Maps** are the French equivalent of the UK Ordnance Survey and are generally of high quality and regularly revised. Should you use them, note that the units of latitude & longitude are Grads, which are one hundredth of a right angle, whereas a degree is a ninetieth. Further, the chart datum for longitude runs through Paris not Greenwich.

Belgium

- **Fluviacarte/Navicarte** 23 In the form of a map and is not as detailed as the series covering the French canals. Fluviacarte/Navicarte 9 Includes the Belgian sections of the Meuse and the Sambre.
- **Carte touristique fluviale Région Nord-Pas-de-Calais**, Province de Flandre Occidentale et Province de Hainault – Not a very detailed chart but it has some useful information. Free from tourist offices in area.
- **Tourist Navigation Guide** - West Vlaanderen, Oost Vlaanderen, Vlaams-Brabant, Brussels, Brabant Wallon, Hainault, Nord-Pas-de-Calais. A comprehensive (272 page) and well laid out Carte-Guide, in English and German, published in 2000 by the Provinces of East Flanders and West Flanders. Covers the whole of Belgium and parts of Northern France.
- **ANWB Waterkaart Vlaanderen Wallonië** NWFrankrijk – This chart is not as detailed as the ANWB Waterkaart series for the Dutch waterways.
- **Carte des voies navigables de Belgique** A plastic-coated coloured map of the Belgian waterways on a scale of 1:250,000 (size 80 x 120 cm), which gives the gauges of the waterways and the location and dimensions of locks and bridges can be obtained from Institut Géographique National, 13 Abbaye de la Cambre, B-1050 Bruxelles (Tel: 02-629.82.11)
- **Geocart Map of the Belgian Waterways** – four maps in a folder covering all the Belgian waterways. They contain a lot of detail, but are not drawn to scale and some people may find them difficult to use at first.
- **Guide de navigation de Belgique** L. De Clercq.

Books and pamphlets

- **The Adlard Coles Book of EuroRegs for Inland Waterways** A pleasure boater's guide to CEVNI, Marion Martin, Adlard Coles Nautical 3rd edition 2008. A good summary of the most important CEVNI rules in English, set out in the sequence of the official CEVNI publication..
- **European Waterways Regulations** (the CEVNI Rules explained). Tam Murrell, RYA 2004. A more comprehensive and detailed account.
- **Code Vagnon Fluvial Henri Vagnon**, Les Editions du Plaisancier, 43rdedition, 2009 A full account of the CEVNI rules in French, well illustrated, so a fairly painless way of learning some navigational French. Vagnon Carte de Plaisance is an abbreviated version.
- **The European Waterways** A Manual for first time users. Marian Martin, Adlard Coles Nautical 2nd edition 2003.
- **RYA CEVNI Handbook**. Roy Gibson, RYA 2010. A good general summary.

Guides

- **Small Boat in/to/through ....** A series of about 20 books by Roger Pilkington describing cruises through France, Belgium and other European countries. Published between about 1959 and 1989, they are long out of print but are often available from 2nd hand bookshops. They are of little use for navigation, but they provide a wealth of history, folklore and fable on the areas cruised.
- **Cruising the Canals & Rivers of Europe, Waterways of France EuroCanals Guide** published by Tom Somers, Books and CDs available. www.eurocanals.com.

France

- **Cruising French Waterways** Hugh McKnight. 3nd Edition. Adlard Coles Nautical 1999. Detailed descriptions of navigable waterways. Useful information and bibliography but in need of updating.
- **Inland Waterways of France** David Edwards-May. 8th Edition. Imray 2010. A very comprehensive reference book, with a geographic and historical summary of every navigable French river and canal, together with comprehensive reference data, plans and distances and useful large scale

- plans of ports and junctions. This book was printed with an incomplete index; a full index is available from the author's website www.euromapping.com.
- **River Seine Cruising Guide** Derek Bowskill. Imray 1996. Good for Seine up to Paris.
- **Brittany and Channel Islands Cruising Guide** David Jefferson. 3rd Edition. Adlard Coles Nautical 1991. Useful chapter on the Brittany canals.
- **Paris by Boat** David Jefferson. Adlard Coles Nautical 1997 Good for Seine up to Paris. The Channel to the Med, Derek Bowskill Opus Books 1995.
- **Through the French Canals** David Jefferson 11th edition Adlard Coles Nautical 2006. Useful for route planning.
- **Floating Through France** Brenda Davison. Librario Publishing 2001. An account of her introduction to French Inland Cruising by one of the authors of these notes. (Amazon)
- **Fluvial Magazine** French Inland Waterway Magazine Published 10 times a year (in French). They now also publish the Fluviacartes. Fluvial, 2 Rue des Consuls, C.S. 30031, 34973, Lattes cedex, France. Maps and Guides may be bought from www.librarie.fluvial.com.

At www.fluvialnet.com the magazine also offers a route planning programme on the website, note that they use the official water depth figures published by VNF which do not take into account lloss of depth due to lack of maintenance.

- **Le Guide du Tourisme Fluvial** Published by Nouvelles Editions de l'Université in a series of guide books under the trade mark 'Petite Futé'. Limited information about navigation, but useful summaries of the tourist attractions and the restaurants within easy reach of rivers and canals. 7th edition 2011. This is a useful complement to the well known red Michelin guide.
- **Chômages** Official list of stoppage dates for French rivers and canals. Essential for cruise planning. Published on the VNF website from end of February/March, and available from the VNF offices that sell the Vignette.

Belgium
- **ANWB Wateralmanak Vol. 2** Although primarily designed as a guide to the Dutch waterways, this annual publication has almost 50 pages devoted to the Belgian waterways. Although written in Dutch, it is a mine of useful information, some of which can be deduced after careful study. Published annually in March.
- **La plaisance sur les voies Navigable de Wallonie** Published by the department responsible for the inland waterways in Wallonia. It contains a lot of useful information about each of the canals, including lock operating times, places to moor, speed limits, licences etc. It can be downloaded in English, French or Flemish from www.voies-hydrauliques.wallonie.be. . It was updated in Summer 2007.
- **De pleziervaart op de bevaarbare waterwegen in Vlaanderen** Published by the department responsible for the inland waterways in Flanders. Written in Dutch, it is a concise summary of the regulations for pleasure craft in Flemish waterways. Although it has some useful information on such matters as lock operating times, speed limits and licences, it does not give any details of places to moor or other facilities. It was last updated in December 2006.
- **Inland Waterways of Belgium**, Jacqueline Jones, Imray Laurie Norie & Wilson 1st edition 2005. A welcome new and comprehensive guide in English, with thorough navigational information coupled with readable accounts of what is worth seeing or visiting, plus in some cases, what is worth eating and drinking.
- **Floating Through Holland (and Belgium**) 2008 also by Brenda Davison. Describes route from IJsselmere (Randmeren) through Holland via Maastricht, into Belgium via Namur and on into France at Givet. www.lulu.com.

In practice, the regulations relevant to pleasure craft in both Flemish and Walloon areas can be downloaded from the websites listed in Appendix iv.

Appendix iii
Addresses

Imray, Laurie, Norie and Wilson Ltd,
Wych House,
The Broadway,
St Ives,
Huntingdon,
Cambridgeshire, PE17 4BT.
Tel 01480 462114. Mail order service. Catalogue.
www.imray.com.

Kelvin Hughes Ltd
New North Road
Hainault, Ilford, Essex, IG6 2UR
Tel 020 8502 6887.
(Website:for book and chart sales www.bookharbour.com.).

DBA – The Barge Association,
Cormorant
Spade Oak Road
Cookham
Berkshire SL6 9RQ
www.barges.org.

France
VNF 175 Rue Ludovic Boutleux, B.P.820, 62408 Béthune Cedex.
Tel 03 21 63 24 54. Fax 03 21 63 24 42.

French Government Tourist Office 300 High Holborn, London WC1 7JH. French government publications and information, including chômages list.

Belgium
Federal government Ministère des Communications et de l'Infrastructure, Administration des Affaires Maritimes et de la Navigation, Service Sécurité de la Navigation, Rue d'Arlon 104, 1040 Bruxelles. Tel: 02-233.12.11; Fax: 02-230.19.69; good internet site, with summaries of licensing system and relevant rules, in English, French or Flemish, plus a reasonable downloadable map.
www.mobilit.fgov.be/fr/aqua. provides a link to a short official summary 'Information leaflet for foreigners who would like to use a pleasure boat on the Belgian Waterways' in French & English, and a useful "Vademecum de la navigation de plaisance en Belgique" which was revised in September 2011.

Flanders Ministerie van de Vlaamse Gemeenschap, Administratie Waterwegen en Zeewezen, Graaf de Ferraris-gebouw – 6e verdieping, Emile Jacqmainlaan 156 – bus 5, 1000 Brussel. Tel: 02-553.77.02; Fax: 02-553.77.35

Wallonia Ministère wallon de l'Equipement et des Transports, Direction Générale des Voies hydrauliques (D.G.2), Direction de la Reglementation (D.253), WTC, Tour 3, Boulevard Simon Bolivar 30, B-1000 Bruxelles. Tel: 02-208.35.11; Fax: 02-508.40.55

Brussels Port de Bruxelles, Place des Armateurs 6, 1000 Bruxelles - Haven van Brussel, Redersplein 6, 1000 Brussel. Tel: 02-420.67.00; Fax: 02-420.69.74

Appendix iv
Web Sites

Cruising Association www.cruising.org.uk.
The Barge Association www.barges.org.
Royal Yachting Association www.rya.org.uk

Google Earth can provide a useful supplement to published charts and maps, especially in urban areas where the aerial photographs are often of high enough resolution to be able to distinguish individual boats, pontoons etc. earth.google.com

German Rail website is another excellent source of European Railway information. This works in English, French or German and can handle journeys that cross European boundaries, and even go to places that do not have any direct rail service. http://reiseauskunft.bahn.de/query.exe/e

France

VNF VNF (www.vnf.fr.) The website of the navigation authority, Easiest way to purchase vignette. Weekly updates on problems, closures, floods etc. (Situation hebdomadaire du réseau.) Schedule of planned closures (Chômages), lock opening hours (les Horaires). Key documents available in English, but worth going through the information provided under La Capitainerie.

Official Journal This is a French Government website for publishing Official Information, and in principle the Chômages should be published here rather sooner than on the VNF website, but the sheer volume of information may make them hard to find. www.journal-officiel.gouv.fr.

French Railway Timetables Useful for planning crew changes etc. Because railways tend to follow the routes of canals, a good part of the waterway system is accessible by rail. www.voyages-sncf.com.

www.davisons-afloat.com. A comprehensive website created by one of the editors of this document, giving a wealth of information about cruising the French Inland Waterways.

Canal du Midi General information on Midi canals. www.canal-du-midi.org.

Tourist Information Offices Comprehensive listing including phone numbers and addresses for the whole of France, starting from www.tourisme.fr.

www.LeBoat.com. The website of the merged Crown Blue Line and Connoiseur hire boat companies. Can be used to find useful information about the larger mooring places in the areas where hire boats cruise. Information is varied, but may include major tourist attractions, markets and shopping possibilities, hotels and restaurants, taxi and car hire companies, banks, pharmacies, doctors, dentists vets etc

http://projetbabel.org/fluvial/rica_marne-rhin-canal.htm a useful website for photos and information about all the waterways in France. Also putting 'Histoire & Patrimoine des Rivières & Canaux' into Google produces a wealth of sites about the French canals. It is also worth noting that there is so much information about canals, locks, rivers etc. on the Internet that it is worth just using a key word in Google to find out what information is out there.

www.fluvialnet.com/fluviacap a very useful route planning site

Belgium

Belgian Railway Timetables Belgian rail services are efficient and cheap.
Useful for planning crew changes etc. in English, www.b-rail.be. (See also reference to German Rail website above).

Brussels Royal Yacht Club Multilingual information about club, city & navigation www.belgi.net/bryc/

Cycling Belgium's Waterways, Dan Gamber. Lots of useful information and waterways maps, albeit written from towpath, but has not been updated since September 2010. www.gamber.net/cyclebel.

Navigation Notices – Wallonia Useful and up to date notice on closures etc in French plus downloadable guides, including an English one, from www.voies-hydrauliques.wallonie.be.

Similar and sometimes overlapping information is also available on www.opvn.be.

RTBF The website of the French language television network. Click on Teletexte, and access page 519 of the teletext service which offers up to 10 sub pages of inland waterway news. Page 520 provides tidal information for Oostende and Antwerp. www.rtbf.be.

www.vpf.be. The website of the Vlaamse Pleziervaart Federatie, (the Federation of Flemish cruising clubs) useful links and contact information for a range of their member clubs. The VPF also runs central yacht harbours in Brugge and Gent.

www.waterrecreatie.be. A promotional website to encourage watersports and cruising, switchable between English, Flemish, French & German, with downloadable maps, lock and bridge operating hours and other information.

Index to Place Names

Aa, 93
Aalst, 122
Aart, 125
Abbaye d'Aulne, 110
Abbécourt, 99
Abbeville, 101
Abergement-la-Ronce, 78
Accolay, 32
Adour, 104
Afleidingskanaal, 121
Agde, 67, 70, 71
Agen, 64, 65, 66
Aigues-Mortes, 61, 62
Aiguillon, 72
Aire, 94, 96
Aire, Canal d', 96
Aire-sur-la-Lys, 94
Aisne, 11, 99, 101, 102, 103
Aisne à la Marne, Canal de l', 48, 99
Aisne, Canal lateral à l', 99
Albert, 124
Albertkanaal, 105, 124, 125, 126, 127, 128
Albigny-sur-Saône, 56
Alsace, 81, 82
Alsace, Grand Canal d', 81
Ambés, 63
Amfreville, 22, 23, 25
Amiens, 101
Ampsin Neuville, 107
Ancenis, 77
Ancerville, 49
Ancy-le-Franc, 43
Andance, 59
Andancette, 59
Andelys, Les, 25
Andenne, 107
Andresy, 26
Angers, 77, 78
Anglet Port de Brise-Lames, 104
Angoulême, 104
Anhée, 107
Anizy-le-Château, 99
Anseremme, 107
Antoing, 20, 105, 111
Antwerp, 9, 20, 105, 114, 123, 124, 125, 128, 135
Anvers, 124, 128
Apach, 87, 88
Arcs-les-Gray, 53
Ardennes, 91

Ardennes, Canal des, 101, 102
Argens-Minervois, 69
Arlaix, 39
Arles, 60, 61
Arles à Fos, Canal d', 61
Arleux, 97, 98, 105
Armentières, 94
Arnage, 78
Arques, 94
Arras, 96
Arzal, 74, 76
Arzviller, 84
Asfeld, 103
Asnières, 26, 55
Ath, 122, 123
Atlantic, 13
Attaques, Les, 93
Attigny, 103
Auby, 96
Aude, 71
Aulne, 73, 76
Autigny-le-Grand, 49
Auvelais, 111
Auvers-sur-Oise, 102
Auvignon, 65
Auxerre, 29, 31
Auxerrre, 29
Auxonne, 53
Avaloire, L', 99
Avignon, 60
Avrilly, 39
Avril-sur-Loire, 39
Baasrode, 124
Bac, Le, 102
Bac-St-Maur, 94
Badour, 112
Bailly, 31
Baïse, 13, 65, 71, 72
Balesmes, 50
Balesmes Tunnel, 49
Bar-le-Duc, 86
Bas d'Esnon, 42
Bassée, La, 96
Basse-Ferme, 46
Bassin à Flot, 63
Bassou, 30
Baulay, 52
Baume-les-Dames, 79
Bauvin, 96
Bavans, 80

Bayard, 67
Bayard-sur-Marne, 49
Baye, 31, 33
Bayonne, 104
Béarnais, 67
Beaucaire, 60, 61, 62
Beaujolais, 51
Beaulieu, 36
Beaulon, 39
Beaumont-sur-Oise, 102
Bec d'Ambes, 63
Beernem, 118
Beez, 107
Beffes, 38
Bègles, 64
Belfort, 80
Belgian border, 97, 127
Belgian Meuse, 105
BELGIUM, 4, 5, 8, 9, 12, 13, 14, 15, 19, 20, 21, 94, 96, 97, 101, 103, 105, 108, 109, 110, 113, 124, 125, 126, 127, 128, 131, 132, 133, 135
BELGIUM, NORTH EAST, 125
BELGIUM, WEST, 115
Bellegarde, 62
Belleville, 36, 56
Beloeil, 123
Beneden Nete, 125
Berchem-Kerkhove, 111
Bergen, 112
Bergen-op-Zoom, 128
Berlaimont, 109
Berre, Etang de, 61
Berry-au-Bac, 99, 100
Besançon, 79
Beslé, 75
Béthune, 96
Betton, 74
Beuvry, 96
Beverloo, Kanaal van, 128
Béziers, 67, 70
Bilhée, 123
Biscay, 63, 72, 73
Bissert, 87
Bisseui, 48
Blanzy, 40
Blaton, 112, 122, 123
Blaton-Ath Canal, 112, 122, 123
Blavet, 73, 76
Bocholt, 20, 105, 125, 126
Bocholt-Herentals, Kanaal, 125, 126, 127
Boë, 65
Boel, 75
Bois l'Abbaye, 108

Bollène, 60
Bonnand, 39
Boofzheim, 82
Boom, 114, 125
Bordeaux, 11, 63, 64
Bossuit, 111, 112
Bossuit-Kortrijk, Kanaal, 111
Bouchemaine, 72
Boudewijnkanaal, 118, 129
Boudewijnsluis, 124
Bougival, 26
Bourbonnais, 11
Bourg, 63
Bourg-et-Comin, 99
Bourgogne, Canal de, 9, 12, 30, 41, 54
Bourogne, 80
Boussières-sur-Sambre, 110
Boussois, 110
Boutonne, 104
Bouzigues, 71
Brabant Wallon, 131
Bram, 67, 68
Branges, 55
Bras de la Cité, 27
Bras de la Monnaie, 27
Bras St. Louis, 27
Bray, 29
Brazey-en-Plaine, 45
Brechtse, 127
Bree, 126
Breisach, 82
Brest, 73, 76
Briare, 10, 34, 35, 36
Briare, Canal de, 10, 34
Briegden-Neerharen, Kanaal, 127
Briennon, 40
Brienon-sur-Armançon, 42
Brittany, 5, 6, 7, 8, 11, 13, 72, 74, 75, 132
Bruant, 45
Brugge (Bruges), 116, 117, 118, 135
Brussels, 9, 20, 105, 113, 114, 125, 131, 133, 135
Brusselsepoort, 120
Burgundy, 41
Bussière-sur-Ouche, La, 45
Buzet, 65, 71
Cadillac, 64
Cahors, 72
Calais, 8, 9, 11, 93, 131
Calais, Canal de, 93
Cambrai, 97
Cannes, 29
Capestang, 67, 69

137

Cappy, 101
Carcassonne, 67, 68
Caronte, Canal de, 61
Carvin, 96
Cassine, La, 103
Castanet, 68
Castelmoron, 72
Castelnaudary, 67, 68, 130
Castelsarrazin, 66
Castets-en-Dorthe, 64
Castillon-la-Bataille, 63
Castlesarrasin, 64
Caudebec-en-Caux, 22, 24
Caumont, 65
Celle, La, 28
Cendrecourt, 52
Centre, Canal du, 10, 12, 40, 112, 113
Cépoy, 35
Cercy-la-Tour, 33
Cergy-Pontoise, 102
Cézy, 30
Chagny, 41
Châlons-en-Champagne, 48
Châlons-sur-Marne, 48
Chalon-sur-Saône, 10, 40, 41, 51, 55
Chamouilley, 49
Champagne et Bourgogne, Canal entre, 10, 49
Champagne-sur-Seine, 28
Champigneulles, 85
Champvert, 33
Chapelle-Montlinard, La, 38
Charente, La, 104
Charentenay, 52
Charité-sur-Loire, La, 38
Charleroi, 108, 110, 111, 113
Charleroi à Brussels à Rupel, Canal de, 108
Charleroi-Brussels, Canal, 113
Charleville-Mézières, 91, 92
Charly, 47
Charmes, 90
Charrey, 43
Chartrettes, 28
Château Gontier, 77
Châteaulin, 73, 76
Châteauneuf-du-Faou, 77
Châteauneuf-sur-Sarth, 78
Chateau-Regnault, 92
Château-Thierry, 47
Châtel-Censoir, 32
Châtelet, Le, 54
Châtelier, 73, 74
Châtillon-Coligny, 35
Châtillon-en-Bazois, 12, 33

Châtillon-sur-Loire, 36
Chaumont, 50
Chaumot, 33
Chaumousey, 89
Chauny, 97, 98, 99, 100, 103
Chausée-sur-Marne, La, 48
Chavanay, 59
Cheilly, 41
Chenillé-Changé, 77
Chepy, 48
Chesne, Le, 103
Chevillon, 49
Chevroches, 32
Chitry-les-Mines, 20, 31, 33
Choisey, 78
Clairac, 72
Clamecy, 31, 32
Clerval, 79
Cognac, 104
Collonges-au-Mont-d'Or, 57
Colmar, 81, 82
Colme, Canal de la, 94
Colombier-Châtelot, 80
Colombier-Fontaine, 80
Colombiers, 67, 70
Comines, 20, 95, 105
Commercy, 91
Compiègne, 20, 98, 99, 101, 102, 103, 105
Condé, 115
Condé- sur-Aisne, 99
Condé-sur-Aisne, 99
Condé-sur-Marne, 48, 93, 99, 100
Condom, 71
Conflandey, 52
Conflans-Ste-Honorine, 19, 26, 101
Conflans-sur-Seine, 29
Consenvoye, 91
Corbehem, 96
Corbie, 101
Corny-sur-Moselle, 88
Corre, 51, 89
Côte d'Or, 51
Coudray-sur-Seine, 28
Coulanges, 32, 39
Coupure, 118
Coupure, Canal, 118
Courcelles, 47
Courcelles-lès-Lens, 96
Courchelettes, 96
Cours-les-Barres, 38
Courtaron, 47
Courtrai, 95, 118
Couzon, 57

Cran, 75
Cravant, 32
Crégols, 72
Creil, 102
Crevic, 85
Croix-Rouge, La, 39
Croix-sur-Meuse, La, 91
Cruas, 59
Crugey, 44
Cry, 43
Cubzac-les-Ponts, 63
Cuisery, 55
Cumières, 48
Damazan, 65
Damery, 47
Dannemarie, 80
Daon, 77
Daours, 101
Dax, 104
De Gavers Country Park, 122
Decize, 31, 34, 39
Deluz, 79
Demange, 86
Dender, 122
Denderleeuw, 122
Dendermonde, 112, 122, 123, 124
Dépôt, Le, 40
Dessel, 126, 127
Dessel naar Kwaadmechelen, Kanaal van, 128
Dessel over Turnhout naar Schoten, Kanaal van, 127
Dessel-Kwaadmechelen, Kanaal, 126
Dessel-Turnhout-Schoten, Kanaal, 125, 126
Dettwiller, 84
Deûle, Canal de la, 96, 115
Deûlemont, 94
Deux-Acren, 122
Dienze, 94, 95, 120, 121, 122
Dieue, 91
Dieupentale, 64, 66
Digoin, 10, 36, 39, 40
Dijksmuide, 105
Dijon, 41, 45
Diksmuide, 14, 20, 117
Dinan, 73, 74
Dinant, 105, 107
Dinard, 73
Diou, 39
Dizy, 46
Dole, 78
Dombasle-sur-Meurthe, 85
Dommarien, 50
Dompierre-sur-Besbre, 39

Donjeux, 49
Dordives, 35
Dordogne, 63
Dorignies, 96
Dormans, 47
Douai, 96, 97
Doubs, 54, 78
Drongen, 122
Duclair, 22, 24
Duffel, 125
Dunkerque-Escaut waterway, 93
Dunkirk (Dunkerque), 8, 9, 11, 93, 94, 97, 115, 116
Dun-sur-Meuse, 91
Ecluse du Banet, 45
Einville, 85
Eisden, 126
Elbeuf, 24
ENGLAND, 6, 11, 93
English Channel, 12, 100
Epernay, 10, 46, 48
Épinal, 90
Erdre, 76
Erquelinnes, 109, 110
Erquinghem, 94
Esbly, 46
Escaut, 9, 93, 96, 97, 111, 115
Escaut, Haut, 9
Escommes, 44
Espierres, Canal de l', 111, 115
Est, Canal de l', 51, 89, 90, 102, 103, 105
Est, Canal de l' (Branche Sud), 51, 89, 91
Est, Canal de l', (Branche Nord), 86, 91
Est, Canal de l', (Nancy branch), 85
Estaires, 94
Etang de Thau, 70
Etreux, 108, 109
Etrun, 97
Ettring, 87
Euville, 91
Evergen, 119
Evran, 74
Evry, 28
Fains, 86
Fargniers, 103, 108
Ferté-sous-Jouarre, La, 47
Fessenheim, 81
Feugarolles, 65
Fintele, 117
Fintelsluis, 117
Flanders, 8, 9, 20, 105, 111, 121, 131, 132, 133
Fleurey-sur-Ouche, 45
Fleury, 33

Fleury-sur-Loire, 38
Flogny, 43
Floreffe, 111
Fonsérannes, 70
Fontaines-sur-Saône, 57
Fontenoy-le-Château, 89
Fontet, 65
Fouchécourt, 52
Foug, 86
Foulain, 50
Fourques, 65
Fragnes, 41
FRANCE, 4, 5, 6, 7, 9, 12, 13, 15, 72, 81, 82, 90, 93, 94, 103, 105, 108, 109, 118, 119, 130, 131, 133, 134
FRANCE, EASTERN, 18
FRANCE, NORTH, 93, 131
FRANCE, NORTH-EAST, 78
Fresnes-sur-Escaut, 97
Frette, La, 26
Frise, 101
Froncles, 49
Frontières, 110
Frontignan, 62, 67
Frouard, 85
Fumay, 92
Fumel, 72
Furnes (Veurne), 14, 115, 116, 117
Furnes, Canal de, 9, 115
Gallician, 62
Gand, 117, 118
Gannay-sur-Loire, 36, 39
Gardouch, 68
Garnat-sur-Engièvre, 39
Garonne, 64, 65, 67, 71
Garonne, Canal de, 64
Garonne, Canal Latéral à la, 64, 71
Gavere, 111
Geel, 125
Génélard, 40
Genk-Kolenhaven Genk., 128
Gent, 9, 96, 111, 117, 118, 120, 121, 122, 123, 135
Gent Ringvaart, 118, 119, 120, 121, 123
Gent-Terneuzen, Zeekanaal, 15, 119, 120, 121
Geraardsbergen, 122
Gergy, 55
GERMANY, 6, 82, 87, 88, 90
Germigny, 42
Ghlin, 112
Gigny, 55
Girancourt, 89
Gironde, 63

Gissey, 44
Gissey-sur-Ouche, 45
Giverny, 25
Givet, 91, 93, 105, 132
Givors, 59
Givry, 103
Goariva, 77
Golfe de Fos, 61
Gondrexange, 84, 87
Gosselies, 113
Grand Gabarit, 93, 94, 96, 97, 105
Grande-Motte, La, 62
Granges, Les, 33
Grau d'Orgon,, 61
Grau-d'Agde, Le, 20, 71
Grau-du-Roi, Le, 62
Gravelines, 9, 93
Gravière, La, 30
Gray, 51, 52
Grevenmacher, 88
Grez-Neuville, 77
Grisolles, 64, 66
Gua, 71
Guerlédan, 76
Guétin, Le, 38
Guily-Glaz, 76
Guipry-Messac, 75
Gurgy, 31
Hachette, 109
Hagenbach, 80
Hainault, 131
Halle, 114
Ham, 101
Hamme, 124
Handelsdok, 119
Harelbeke, 95
Hasselt, 128
Hastière, 106
Haut Escaut, 111, 115
Hautmont, 110
Havre, 112
Havre, Le, 8, 11, 22, 23
Haybes, 92
Hédé, 74
Heer, 106
Heming, 84
Hennebont, 76
Hérault, 70, 71
Herentals, 125
Herentals-Bocholt, Kanaal, 128
Hérrines, 111, 115
Herry, 38
Hers, Ecluse de l', 66

Hesse, 83, 84
Heuilley, 10, 49, 53
Heuilley-Cotton, 50
Heuilley-sur-Saone, 53
Heuilley-sur-Saône, 50
Hingene, 114
Hochfelden, 83
Homps, 67, 69
Honfleur, 18, 22, 23
Honnecourt, 97
Houillères de la Saar, Canal des, 87
Houillon, 87
Houlle, River, 93
Houx, 107
Huibrechts-Lille, 126
Huningue, Canal de, 81
Huy, 107
l'Ille-et-Rance, 74
Ieper, 117
Ieper – Ijzer, Kanaal, 117
IJsselmere, 132
IJzer, 117
Île Barbe, 57
Ile de la Cité, 27
Ile St. Louis, 27
Ill, 83
Ille-et-Rance, Canal d', 73, 74
Isbergues, 96
Isle-Adam, L', 102
Isle-St-Aubin, 77
Isle-sur-le-Doubs, 79
Ittre, 114
Ivoz Ramet, 108
Jachtwerk Vennekens, 125
Janville, 100
Jarnac, 104
Jaulgonne, 47
Jaux, 102
Jeumont, 110
Joigny, 29, 30
Joinville, 49
Joinville-le Pont, 46
Jonction, Canal de, 71
Josselin, 76
Jussy, 98
Kembs, 81
Kerkhoven., 128
Ketelvaart, 119, 120
Klein, 114
Klein Willebroek, 125
Knokkebrug, 117
Koblenz, 87
Konz, 87

Kortrijk, 95, 111, 112, 118
Krafft, 82
Kunheim, 82
Kuurne, 95
L'Eveque, 69
La Falotte, 65
Lacourt, 66
Lacourtensourt, 66
Lagarde, 83, 85
Lagny, 46
Lahonce, 104
Laifour, 92
Laissey, 79
Lamarche-sur-Saône, 53
Lanaye, 128, 129
Lanaye, Canal de, 9
Landelies, 110
Landévénnec, 76
Landrecies, 103, 108, 109
Laneuville-devant-Nancy, 85, 90
Langerbrugge, 120
Langres, 50
Laredorte, 69
Laroche Migennes, 29
Laroche-Migennes, 9, 30, 42
Laroche-Saint-Cydroine, 30
Lattes, 62
Laval, 77
Lavardac, 71
Le Peyruque, 68
Le Pont de Pierre, 63
Leernebrug, 122
Leffinge., 117
Leie, 9, 94, 95, 96, 112, 118, 119, 120, 121
Leie, Afleidingskanaal van de (Leie diversion canal), 118
Leie, Afleidingskanaal, Northern Arm, 120
Leie, Afleidingskanaal, Southern Arm, 120
Leopoldsburg, 128
Léré, 37
Lesdins, 97
Lessines, 123
Leuven- Dijle, Kanaal, 129
Leval, 109
Lez, 62
Lézignan-Corbières, 69
Lézinnes, 43
Libourne, 63
Liège, 20, 105, 106, 107, 108, 126, 128
Lier, 125
Ligny-en-Barrois, 86
Lille, 111, 115
Limanton, 33

Limay, 23, 25
Liverdun, 85, 87
Lobbes, 110
Loing, Canal du, 10, 28, 34
Loire, 31, 34, 36, 37, 39, 72, 76, 77
Loire, Canal Latéral à la, 10, 34, 36
Loivre, 100
Lokanaal, 117
Lokeren, 120, 121
Lommel, 126
Long, 101
Longeaux, 86
Longecourt-en-Plaine, 45
Longueil-Annel, 100
Lorient, 73, 76
Lormont, 63
Lot, 65, 71, 72
Louhans, 55
Louviere, La, 113
Lozen, 126
Lucy-sur-Yonne, 32
Luik, 105, 128
Lumes, 92
Lutzelbourg, 83, 84
LUXEMBOURG, 4, 6, 87, 88
Luzech, 72
Lyon, 9, 10, 51, 56, 57, 58
Lys, 9, 94, 118, 121
Maas, 9, 126, 127, 128, 129
Maasbracht, 126
Maastricht, 9, 126, 127, 128, 129, 132
Mâcon, 51, 56
Maffle, 123
Mailleraye, La, 23
Mailly-la-Ville, 32
Mailly-le-Port, 53
Maine, 77
Maisons-Alfort, 46
Malause, 66
Malestroit, 76
Malmy, 103
Mans, Le, 77, 78
Mantes-la-Jolie, 25
Mantoche, 53
Marans, 104
Marchienne au Pont, 110
Marchiennes, 96
Marcilly, 27, 29
Mareuil-sur-Ay, 48
Marigny-le-Cahouët, 44
Marigny-sur-Yonne, 33
Maritime Canal, 62
Markolsheim, 82

Marne, 3, 9, 10, 11, 19, 46, 48, 53, 82, 83, 86, 87, 88, 89, 90, 91, 93, 99, 101
Marne à la Saône, Canal de la, 10, 48, 49, 53, 86
Marne au Rhin, Canal de la, 9, 48, 82, 83, 87, 88, 90, 91
Marne, Canal Latéral à la, 10, 48, 86, 100
Marne, Upper, 18
Maroilles, 109
Marolles, 29
Maron, 90
Marpent, 108
Marquion, 98
Marseillan, 70
Marseille, 61
Marseilles-lès-Aubigny, 36, 38
Marseillette, 69
Martigues, 61
Mary-sur-Marne, 46
Mascaret, Le, 23
Mas-d'Agenais, Le, 65
Mauberge, 108, 110
Mauvages, 86
Maxence, 102
Maxilly, 50
Mayenne, 77
Meaux, 46
Mediterranean, 4, 5, 6, 9, 12, 13, 23, 61, 62, 71, 93
Meilhan, 65
Melay, 40
Méloménil, 89
Melun, 28
Menacourt, 86
Mendonk, 121
Menen, 94, 95
Ménétréol-sous-Sancerre, 38
Merelbecke, 119, 120, 123
Méréville, 90
Méricourt, 23, 25
Merry-sur-Yonne, 32
Merville, 94
Meschers, 63
Messac, 75
Metz, 88
Meulan, 26
Meuse, 9, 86, 91, 101, 103, 105, 108, 131
Meuse Ardennais, La, 91
Meuse Lorraine. La, 91
Meuse, Belgian, 106, 111
Meuse, Dutch, 128
Mèze, 71
Mézy-sur-Seine, 47

Midi, 11, 63
Midi, Canal du, 13, 67, 70, 71, 134
Millery, 88
Minimes, 67
Mittersheim, 87
Moervaart, 120, 121
Moislains, 98
Moissac, 64, 66
Molinet, 39
Monéteau, 31
Mons, 112, 115
Mont St-Père, 47
Montargis, 34, 35
Montauban, 64, 66
Montauban branch canal, 66
Montbard, 43
Montbéliard, 80
Montbelliard, 78
Montbouy, 35
Montceau-les-Mines, 40
Montchanin, 40, 41
Montcresson, 35
Montech, 66
Montélimar, 60
Montereau, 9, 27, 28, 29
Montgiscard, 68
Montgon, 102, 103
Montgon flight, 103
Monthermé, 92
Montmerle, 56
Montpellier, 67
Montreux-Château, 80
Montureux-les-Baulay, 52
Moret-sur-Loing, 34
Mortagne, 63, 96
Mortagne-du-Nord, 97
Morvillars, 80
Moselle, 6, 17, 85, 87, 89, 90
Motte, 41
Mouzon, 92
Moy de l'Aisne, 109
Muide Spoorbrug, 119
Mulhouse, 78, 80, 81
Namen, 105, 107, 111
Namur, 20, 103, 105, 107, 108, 111, 132
Nancy, 85, 90
Nantes, 72, 73, 76, 77
Nantes à Brest Canal, 73, 76
Nantes, Canal de, 76
Nantieul, 47
Narbonne, 67, 69, 71
Neerharen, 127
Neeroerteren, 126

Neerpelt, 126
Négra, Ecluse de, 68
Nemours, 34
Nérac, 71
Néronville, 35
Nete, 125
Netekanaal, 125
NETHERLANDS, 6, 9, 12, 121, 126, 127, 128
Netherlands Border, 126
Neuf Brisach, 81
Neufossé, Canal de, 94
Neuilly-sur-Marne, 46
Neuves-Maisons, 87, 89, 90
Neuville-sur-Saône, 56
Nevers, 38
Nicole, 71, 72
Niderviller, 83, 84
Nieuw Dam bridge, 95
Nieuw Lobroekdok, 124, 128
Nieuwe Damme, 118
Nieuwpoort, 9, 105, 115, 116, 117
Nieuwpoort-Dunkerken, Kanaal, 9, 115
Niffer, 81
Nimy-Blaton-Péronnes, Canal, 9, 109, 112, 122, 123
Ninove, 122
Niort, 104
Nivernais, Canal du, 12, 20, 29, 31, 34, 39
Nogent-l'Artaud, 47
Nogent-sur-Marne, 46
Nogent-sur-Seine, 29
Nomexy, 90
Noordlandbrug, 124, 128
Nord sur Erdre, 76
Nord, Canal du, 11, 97, 98, 101, 105
Nord-Pas-de-Calais, 131
Normandy, 25
Notre Dame, 27
Novillars, 79
Noyon, 98, 99, 101
Obourg, 123
Oise, 11, 26, 93, 101, 105
Oise à l'Aisne, Canal de, 98, 99
Oise, Canal Latéral à l', 98, 100, 103, 108
Oisilly, 50
Oissel, 24
Omicourt, 103
Onglous, Les, 67, 70
Onze Ecluses, Les, 74
Ooigem, 95
Oost Vlaanderen, 131
Oostbuitenhaven, 120
Oostende, 9, 116, 117, 118, 135

143

Oostende to Gent Canal,, 117
Oosterschelde, 128
Oostsluis, 120
Orconte, 49
Origny St. Benoite, 108, 109
Origny Ste Benoîte, 108
Ostend, 119
Ostend canal, 119
Ottmarsheim, 81
Oudenaarde, 111
Oudenburg, 117
Oudon, 77
Ougney-la-Roche, 79
Ourcq, 26
Ouzouer-sur-Trézée, 36
Overleide Brug, 121
Pagny-sur-Meuse, 86
Palavas-les-Flots, 62
Palinges, 40
Panneçot, 33
Paray-le-Monial, 40
Pargny Filain, 99
Pargny-sur-Saulx, 86
Paris, 6, 9, 10, 11, 12, 19, 22, 25, 26, 27, 28, 29, 33, 41, 46, 48, 85, 93, 99, 100, 101, 102, 103, 130, 132
Paris Arsenal, 26
Pauillac, 63
Peigney, 50
Penne d'Agenais, 72
Péronne, 11, 98, 101, 105
Péronnes, 109, 112, 123
Péruwelz, 112
Petit Rhône, 61
Petite France, 83
Petite Seine, La, 29
Peyrehorade, 104
Piépape, 50
Pierrefitte-sur-Loire, 39
Pierre-la-Treiche, 90
Pignicourt, 99
Plagny, 38
Plassendale, 116, 117
Plassendale, Kanaal, 116, 117
Plobsheim, 82
Plombières, 45
Pogney, 48
Poilhès, 69
Poincy, 46
Poissy, 26
Polhuern, 73
Pommeroeul à Condé, Canal de, 115
Pommevic, 66

Pompey, 85, 88
Pont au Change, 27
Pont Battant, 79
Pont d' Aquitaine, 63
Pont d'Arciat, 56
Pont de Bord, 40
Pont de la Concorde, 27
Pont de Loup, 111
Pont l'Evêque, 100
Pont Réan, 75
Pont Sully, 27
Pont Térénez, 76
Pont-à-Bar, 91, 92, 102, 103, 105
Pont-à-Celles, 113
Pontailler, 53
Pont-à-Mousson, 88
Pont-de-Houmée, 104
Pont-de-Ladonne, 65
Pont-de-Pany, 45
Pont-des-Sables, 65
Pont-de-Vaux, 55
Pont-de-Vic, 93
Pont-d'Ouche, 44
Pontivy, 73, 76
Pontoise, 102
Pont-Royal, 44
Pont-sur-Sambre, 109
Pont-sur-Yonne, 30
Port 2, 60
Port Carhaix, 73, 76
Port Cassafières, 70
Port d'Embouchure, 67
Port d'Envaux, 104
Port de Bouc, 61
Port de l' Ardoise, 60
Port de l'Embouchure, 67
Port Fontenoy, 99
Port la Robine, 69
Port Lalande, 72
Port Launay, 76
Port Lauragais, 68
Port Minervois, 69
Port Napoléon, 58
Port Renard, 29
Port Sisley, 26
Port St-Louis, 26
Port St-Sauveur, 67
Port, Le, 59
Port-à-Binson, 47
Port-Arianne, 62
Port-aux-Cerises, 27
Port-Camargue, 62
Portets, 64

Portiragnes, 70
Port-la-Nouvelle, 71
Port-St-Louis, 23
Port-St-Louis-du-Rhône, 57, 61
Port-St--Louis-du-Rhône, 10, 20
Port-sur-Saône, 52
Poses, 25
Pouillenay, 44
Pouilly-en-Auxois, 12, 44
Pouilly-sur-Meuse, 91
Pouilly-sur-Vingeanne, 50
Pousseaux, 32
Pouzin, Le, 59
Puichéric, 69
Quessy, 98
Quilleboeuf, 23, 24
Rade de Brest, 76
Ramonville, 68
Rance, 74
Rance Barrage, 74
Rance Maritime, 73
Ranchot, 78
Randmeren, 132
Ravières, 43
Ray-sur-Saône, 52
Rechicourt, 84
Redon, 72, 73, 76
Reims, 93, 99, 100
Rekem, 126
Remich, 88
Remilly-Aillicourt, 92
Rennes, 72, 73, 74, 75
Rethel, 103
Retie, 127
Rettel, 88
Reuil, 47
Revin, 92
Rhinau, 82
Rhine, 78, 81, 82, 83, 87, 89
Rhône, 9, 10, 11, 15, 19, 51, 57, 58, 60, 61, 62
Rhône à Fos, Canal du, 61
Rhône à Sète, Canal du, 60, 61, 70, 71
Rhône au Rhin, Canal du, 9, 53, 78
Rhône au Rhin, Canal du, Branch Nord, 82
Rhône, Canal du, 81
Riaucourt, 49
Ribemont, 109
Richardménil, 90
Rigny, 52
Riqueval Tunnel, 97
Roanne, 39, 40
Roanne à Digoin, Canal de, 39
Robine Canal de la, 71

Roche, La, 59
Roche-Bernard, La, 75
Roche-de-Glun, La, 59
Rochefort, 104
Rochefort-sur-Nenon, 78
Roches-de-Condrieu, Les, 59
Roesbrugge, 117
Roeselare, 95
Roeselare-Leie, Kanaal, 129
Rogny, 34, 36
Rohan, 76
Rolampont, 50
Rolleboise, 25
Ronquières, 113
Roquemaure, 60
Roubaix, Canal de, 111, 115
Roubia, 69
Rouen, 7, 8, 22, 23, 24
Roux, 113
Roville, 90
Royan, 63
Royersluis, 114, 124
Rueil-Malmaison, 26
Rully, 41
Rupel, 114, 125
Rupelmonde, 114, 123, 124, 125
Saar, 87
Saarbrücken, 87
Sablé, 78
Sablé-sur-Sarthe, 77
Sablonniere, 35
Sailly-Laurette, 101
Sailly-sur-la-Lys, 94
Saint-Christophe, 66
Saintes, 104
Saint-Jory, 66
Sallèles-d'Aude, 71
Sambre, 9, 103, 108, 109, 131
Sambre à l'Oise, Canal de la, 98, 103, 108
Samois, 28
Sampigny, 91
Santenay, 41
Saône, 9, 10, 11, 15, 19, 50, 51, 52, 54, 55, 57, 78, 89
Sardy, 33
Sarreguemines, 87
Sarthe, 77
Sas van Gent, 120
Sauzens, 68
Saverne, 83, 84
Scarpe, 9
Scarpe Inférieure, 96
Scarpe Supérieure, 96

Scey-sur-Saône, 52
Schelde, 9, 111, 112, 114, 119, 120, 121, 122, 124, 128
Schelde Rijnverbinding (Rhine-Schelde) canal, 124, 128
Schengen, 88
Schoten, 127
Schwebsange, 88
Sclayn, 107
Sedan, 92
Ségala, Le, 68
Segre, 77
Seille, 55
Seine, 7, 9, 11, 12, 15, 18, 19, 22, 23, 26, 27, 28, 29, 93, 101, 132
Seine, Upper, 29
Selles, 89
Seneffe, 112, 113
Sens, 30
Sensée, Canal de la, 97, 98
Séraucourt-le-Grand, 98
Sérignac-sur-Garonne, 65
Sermaize-les-Bains, 86
Sète, 11, 61, 62, 63, 67, 71
Seurre, 54
Seveux-Savoyeux, 52
Sèvre Niortaise, 104
Sierck-les-Bains, 88
Sillery, 100
Sint-Baafs-Vijve, 95
Sireuil, 104
Sluis Hingene, 114
Sluis Zwevegem, 112
Sneermaas, 127
Soing, 52
Soissons, 99
Somail, Le, 69
Somme, 7, 9, 11, 100, 101, 105
Somme, Canal de la, 98, 100, 101
Sommerville, 85
Sormont, 100
Souffelweyersheim, 83
Soulanges, 48
Souppes-sur-Loing, 34, 35
SPAIN, 71
Spechbach, 80
Spiere – Helkijn, 115
St Agnetabrug, 119
St Amand-les-Eaux, 96
St Andre, 115
St Bérain-sur-Dheune, 41
St Christ-Briost, 98, 101
St Cyr, 57

St Denis, 26
St Dizier, 49
St Domineuc, 74
St Etienne-des-Sorts, 60
St Florentin, 42
St Fons, 58
St Germain, 74
St Germain-au-Mont-d'Or, 56
St Gilles, 62
St Gilles canal, 62
St Jean les Deux Jumeaux, 47
St Jean-de-Losne, 9, 19, 20, 41, 45, 51, 54
St Job, 127
St Jorissluis, 116, 117
St Julien-sur-Dheune, 41
St Léger-des-Vignes, 33
St Léger-sur-Dheune, 41
St Leu-d'Esserent, 102
St Livrade, 72
St Louis, Canal, 61
St Malo, 72, 73, 74
St Mammès, 10, 27, 28, 34
St Martens-Latem, 122
St Martens-Leerne., 122
St Martin, 26
St Mihiel, 91
St Nazaire, 76
St Omer, 93, 94
St Porquier, 66
St Quentin, 98
St Quentin, Canal de, 11, 97, 98, 101, 108
St Romain-des-Iles, 56
St Saveur, 50
St Savinien, 104
St Seine-sur-Vingeanne, 50
St Simon, 11, 98, 100, 101
St Sylvestre, 72
St Symphorien, 78
St Thibault, 37
St Valéry-sur-Somme, 11, 100
St Vallier, 59
St Venant, 94
St Victor-sur-Ouche, 45
St Vinnemer, 43
St Vit, 79
Stalhille, 117
Stambruges, 123
Ste Sabine, 44
Steendorp, 124
Steinberg, 84
Stenay, 91
St-Gilles, 62
St-Jean-de-Losne, 42

Straatsburgdok, 124
Strasbourg, 81, 82, 83, 85
Strépy-Thieu, 113
St-Symphorien, 78
Sucé-sur-Erdre, 76
Sully, 35
Suresnes/St Cloud, 26
Sury-près-Léré, 37
Tancarville, 22, 24
Tancarville Canal, 22
Tanlay, 43
Tannay, 33
Tarascon, 60, 62
Tarn, 66
Temse, 124
Tergnier, 98, 108
Terneuzen, 9, 120
Thaon-les-Vosges, 90
Thau, Étang de, 63, 70, 71
Thionville, 88
Thoissey, 56
Tholen, 128
Thoraise, 79
Thuin, 110
Tille, 53
Tinténiac, 74
Tongerlo, 126
Tonnay-Charente, 104
Tonnerre, 43
Toul, 83, 85, 86, 87, 89, 90, 91
Toulouse, 64, 66, 67, 68
Tourcoing, 115
Tournai, 111
Tournon, 59
Tournus, 55
Tours, 48
Toutevoie, 102
Trèbes, 67, 69
Trégarvan, 76
Trévoux, 56
Troussey, 86, 91
Truchère, La, 55
Tubize, 114
Tupigny, 109
Turnhout, 127
Uzemain, 89
Vadencourt, 108, 109
Vaires-sur-Marne, 46
Val St. Martin, 25
Valdieu, 80
Valence, 58, 59, 71
Valence d'Agen, 64, 66
Valence Port de l'Epervière, 58, 59

Valence sur Baïse, 71
Valenciennes, 97, 115
Vallabrègues, 60
Valvins, 28
Van Cauwelaertsluis, 124
Vandenesse, 42
Vandenesse-en-Auxois, 44
Vandières, 47
Vanneaux, 39
Varangeville, 85
Variscourt, 99
Veerhaven, 120
Veert, 126
Velars-sur-Ouche, 45
Velet, 53
Venarey-les-Laumes, 43
Vendenheim, 83
Vendhuille, 97
Vendin le Vieil, 96
Ventenac-en-Minervois, 69
Verberie, 102
Verbindingsluis, 118
Verdun, 91
Verdun-sur-le-Doubs, 54
Vermenton, 31, 32
Verneuil-sur-Seine, 26
Vernon, 25
Verrerie, La, 100
Vésines, 55
Veuvey-sur-Ouche, 45
Vicomté-sur Rance, La, 74
Vienne, 59
Viersel, 125
Vieux les Asfeld, 102
Vieux-les-Asfeld, 99
Viéville, 49
Vigneux, 27
Vilaine, 73, 74, 75, 76
Villefranche-sur-Saône, 56
Villeguisen, 50
Villeneuve, 72
Villeneuve St. Georges, 27
Villeneuve-lès-Bézier, 70
Villeneuve-sur-Vingeanne, La, 50
Villeneuve-sur-Yonne, 30
Villers-sur-Marne, 49
Villeton, 65
Villey le Sec, 90
Villiers-sur-Yonne, 33
Vincelles, 32
Vincelottes, 31
Vireux-Wallerand, 92
Visservaart, 120

Vitry-le-François, 10, 48, 49, 83, 86
Viviers, 60
Vlaams-Brabant, 131
Vlissingen, 123
Vogelgrun, 81, 82
Void, 86
Voorhaven, 119
Vosges, Canal des, 89
Vouécourt, 49
Vred, 96
Wachtebeke, 121
Wallonia, 8, 9, 20, 132, 133, 135
Waltenheim, 83
Wanze, 107
Warneton, 95
Wasserbillig, 87, 89
Watten, 93, 94
Waulsort, 106
Wervik, 95
West Vlaanderen, 131
Westhoek, 116
Willebroek, 114
Wintam, 114
Wittring, 87
Wormeldange, 88
Wulpen, 116
Xouxange, 84
Xures, 85
Yonne, 3, 9, 18, 21, 28, 29, 31
Ypres, 14, 117
Yvoir, 107
Zandvoorde, 116
Zeebrugge, 9, 118
Zeeschelde (Escaut Maritime), 123, 124
Zeeschelde (Sea Canal), 114
Zele, 124
Zelzate, 120
Zijzanaal, 120
Zillisheim, 81
Zuid-Willemsvaart, 9, 126, 127

Join the Cruising Association

These are just some of the benefits you can enjoy.

Access to an unrivalled store of online and offline information and advice about cruising in small boats, whether around the next headland, or across the next ocean

A worldwide organisation where you'll always find a friendly face on board a boat flying a CA burgee

Discounts on chandlery and sails from top suppliers. The savings available can pay for CA membership in one go! Ask CA House for details of current discount suppliers

Discounts on many charts and publications, combined with free postage, when ordered through the CA

A 10% discount on boat insurance from Haven Knox-Johnston, for CA members

Local sections around the UK coast organise cruises, lectures, meetings, discussions and social activities throughout the year. Many maintain their own websites and publish regular newsletters

Three major international sections for the Baltic, the Mediterranean and European Inland Waterways, offering support and information for those who cruise – or wish to cruise - those waters

A worldwide network of Honorary Local Representatives (HLRs) to provide assistance, information and often, access to local discounts

Thousands of members-only pages on MyCA website. As well as static data myCA contains dynamic information generated through members' own questions, and the responses to them

A free Crewing Service to match skippers to crew. Detailed lists are posted on an exclusive website or sent by post detailing what crew are looking for, and what skippers are offering. Many members cruise all over the world with contacts made through this facility. Skippers find it particularly useful when cruising shorthanded

An annual yearbook packed with essential information – members listed by name and boat, contact details for HLRs and full details of all our member services

Our house magazine, Cruising, is mailed to members, wherever they live. There's a wealth of technical and non-technical articles. All the articles are exclusive and won't be found in the commercial boating press.

A range of CA-published books and booklets covering specialist cruise areas like harbours of the Baltic States, lay-up yards, and French and Belgian canals. These are reprinted and updated regularly to keep up with changes to regulations and facilities.

A discounted price on the famous Cruisng Almanac. Covering the coasts between Gibraltar and the Faroes. In its 500 or so pages you'll find excellent charts, passage notes and port details contributed by members. Real-time updates are published on MyCA and are mailed out with Cruising.

Our Regulatory and Technical Services Committee (RATS) works for the benefit of small boat cruisers. Widely consulted by government on proposed legislation and matters of safety and concern to cruising sailors, RATS attends public enquiries and meetings on a wide range of subjects that affect our sport.

A range of customised clothing, flags and burgees are available, and the CA holds an Admiralty warrant allowing you to fly the Association's defaced blue ensign.

CA House is just ten minutes from the City of London. There's a marina under our windows, and free car parking for members using HQ facilities. Accommodation is available at very competitive rates for out-of-town members.

CA House holds regular RYA syllabus courses, including first aid and diesel maintenance.

CA House has an extensive lecture and social activity calendar, especially in the autumn, winter and early spring. Members can hire rooms for private functions and bar and catering facilities are provided when activities take place.

With 10,000 volumes the world famous Cruising Association Library (a unique collection), is the finest collection of nautical books in private hands in the world. It is a lending library and such an important collection that publishers of nautical books send us copies of new books. A librarian helps members with its use. There's no need to come to London as loan books are mailed out free.

The library houses our worldwide collection of charts and pilot books. These are used extensively by members for cruise planning.

CRUISING INFORMATION

APPLICATION FOR MEMBERSHIP OF THE CRUISING ASSOCIATION

CA CRUISING ASSOCIATION

CA House
1 Northey Street
Limehouse Basin
London E14 8BT

Tel: +44 (0)20 7537 2828
Fax: +44 (0)20 7537 2266
Email: office@cruising.org.uk
www.cruising.org.uk

Please use this form to apply for membership. Note that data marked # (or *) will be published in the Year book unless you opt otherwise. **Data marked * is required.**

I hereby apply to become a member of the Cruising Association and agree, if elected by Council, to abide by the rules, regulations & code of the Association.

Membership Category applied for:

Title:*   Surname:*   Honours/Qualifications

Forenames:*

Address:*

Postcode:*   Country:#

Occupation/Profession:

Skills and expertise I could offer the CA:

Telephone: Home:#   Work:

Mobile: Email:*

Boat Name:#   Class/Type   Rig: LOA:

Boat Location: Sailing/Cruising Area:

I give my permission for my details to be published to other members Yes / No

Where did you hear about the Cruising Association?

At a Boatshow	❑	From a friend/other boater	❑
From a news article	❑	Via the Crewing Service	❑
On the Internet	❑	The CA Website	❑
At a yacht/boat club	❑	Other	❑

Cruising Association Membership Rates

Type	Cheque	Debit or Credit Card	Direct Debit
Ordinary Member	£126.00 ❑	❑	£118.00 ❑
Partner Member	£31.50 ❑	❑	£28.50 ❑
Overseas Member[†]	£61.00 ❑	❑	
Partner Overseas[†] Member	£19.50 ❑	❑	
Young Member (under 25)[††]	£27.00 ❑	❑	£24.00 ❑
Entrance Fee	£10.00 ❑	❑	

[†] Resident Overseas for the full membership year.
[††] Please provide your date of birth: Day: Month: Year:

I hereby apply to become a member of the Cruising Association and agree, if elected by the Council, to abide by the Memorandum and Articles of Association and Regulations.

PLEASE TICK AS APPROPRIATE

❑ Direct Debit Mandate (& entrance fee of £10.00). If you wish to pay by Direct Debit, you will be sent a Direct Debit form to complete. You will be given the option to pay for your first year's subscription by debit or credit card. This may be particularly useful for those who wish to confirm their membership quickly.

❑ £   as payment for one year's subscription & entrance fee.

Signed: Date:

Please return the completed from to:
Membership Secretary, The Cruising Association, CA House, 1, Northey Street, Limehouse Basin, London, E14 8BT
Tel: 0207 537 2828 Fax: 0207 537 2266 email: membership@cruising.org.uk www.cruising.org.uk

Please photocopy this form if you do not want to tear this page.

You can also apply online at www.cruising.org.uk. Click on 'Join the CA'

REPORT CHANGES FORM

Thanks to members submitting Cruising Information, the provision of up-to-date information is a major strength of the CA, and this is particularly valuable when cruising inland, since the commercially published charts/guides are usually only revised very infrequently.

All members cruising inland are asked to assist by submitting cruising reports whenever they discover something that may be helpful to other members. Please use the blank sheet provided on the next page.

It need not be something strictly related to moorings – we are also keen to learn about **Chandlery**, **Service & Repairs**, **Lifting-out**, **Overwintering**, **WiFi, laundry** etcetera.

Refuelling is also important – the ban on using red diesel has led to difficulties in some areas where waterside suppliers do not feel that the costs of maintaining a second tanks and pumps for the limited and seasonal demand from pleasure craft is justified compared with their 'bread and butter' business of supplying commercial shipping. Therefore it is helpful to indicate where there are filling stations within trundling distance of a mooring, as well as keeping us updated on waterside refuelling points.

Basic information that is needed:-

Your Name and Name of Boat

Date of Information

Water and Air Draught of Boat

Country

Waterway

Position – preferably by name of place, kilometre marking (pk on French Charts) or any other identifier e.g. 'L bank 3.5km above lock 27'.

A note of the **chart guide** you are using is helpful e.g 'Fluviacarte No. 24 – Picardie'

For **Moorings** size - e.g. 'space for 5 boats' (assume a 10 to 12m boat) or '60m long quay', and if you can estimate it, the water depth. Also what facilities are offered, a contact telephone number, and in these days of a weak pound, approximate cost.

In a large town, there is probably little point in providing information about shops and restaurants, but in smaller places, and especially when their locations are not obvious from the mooring, it can be very helpful e.g. 'baker 500m up path to north of road bridge'.

Other information that may be helpful includes proximity of ATMs (cash machines), Internet access, and WiFi points, as well as web addresses and telephone numbers of marinas etc.

Please help us to provide current information. Do not assume that someone else will have reported your findings. Even if they have, confirmation that it is still existing is useful. Send by post or by email, to the CA Library or to The Editors, Cruising the Inland Waterways of France and Belgium, CA House, 1 Northey St, Limehouse Basin, London E14 8BT.

Changes Report Form for Editors of Cruising the Inland Waterways of France and Belgium, CA House, 1 Northey St. Limehouse Basin, London W14 8BT.

Please use this page to report your changes, or send by email to european_inland_waterways@cruiising.org.uk. Or via an app. to the CA website.